The Unseen World and Other Essays

By

John Fiske

The Unseen World
and Other Essays

Preface

To
James Sime.

My Dear Sime:

Life has now and then some supreme moments of pure happiness, which in reminiscence give to single days the value of months or years. Two or three such moments it has been my good fortune to enjoy with you, in talking over the mysteries which forever fascinate while they forever baffle us. It was our midnight talks in Great Russell Street and the Addison Road, and our bright May holiday on the Thames, that led me to write this scanty essay on the "Unseen World," and to whom could I so heartily dedicate it as to you? I only wish it were more worthy of its origin. As for the dozen papers which I have appended to it, by way of clearing out my workshop, I hope you will read them indulgently, and believe me

Ever faithfully yours,
John
Fiske.

HARVARD UNIVERSITY, February 3, 1876.

I. THE UNSEEN WORLD.

PART FIRST.

"What are you, where did you come from, and whither are you bound?"—the question which from Homer's days has been put to the wayfarer in strange lands—is likewise the all-absorbing question which man is ever asking of the universe of which he is himself so tiny yet so wondrous a part. From the earliest times the ultimate purpose of all scientific research has been to elicit fragmentary or partial responses to this question, and philosophy has ever busied itself in piecing together these several bits of information according to the best methods at its disposal, in order to make up something like a satisfactory answer. In old times the best methods which philosophy had at its disposal for this purpose were such as now seem very crude, and accordingly ancient philosophers bungled considerably in their task, though now and then they came surprisingly near what would to-day be called the truth. It was natural that their methods should be crude, for scientific inquiry had as yet supplied but scanty materials for them to work with, and it was only after a very long course of speculation and criticism that men could find out what ways of going to work are likely to prove successful and what are not. The earliest thinkers, indeed, were further hindered from accomplishing much by the imperfections of the language by the aid of which their thinking was done; for science and philosophy have had to make a serviceable terminology by dint of long and arduous trial and practice, and linguistic processes fit for expressing general or abstract notions accurately grew up only through numberless failures and at the expense of much inaccurate thinking and loose talking. As in most of nature's processes, there was a great waste of energy before a good result could be secured. Accordingly primitive men were very wide of the mark in their views of nature. To them the world was a sort of enchanted ground, peopled with sprites and goblins; the quaint notions with which we now amuse our children in fairy tales represent a style of thinking which once was current among grown men and women, and which is still current wherever men remain in a savage condition. The theories of the world wrought out by early priest-philosophers were in great part made up of such grotesque notions; and having become variously implicated with ethical opinions as to the nature and consequences of right and wrong behaviour, they acquired a kind of sanctity, so that any thinker who in the light of a wider experience ventured to alter or amend the primitive theory was likely to be vituperated as an irreligious man or atheist. This sort of inference has not yet been wholly abandoned, even in civilized communities. Even to-day books are written about "the conflict between religion and science," and other books are written with intent to reconcile the two presumed antagonists. But when we look beneath the surface of things, we see that in reality there has never been any conflict between religion and science, nor is any reconciliation called for where harmony has always existed. The real historical conflict, which has been thus curiously misnamed, has been the conflict between the more-crude opinions belonging to the science of an earlier age and the less-crude opinions belonging to the science of a later age. In the course of this contest the more-crude opinions have usually been defended in the name of religion, and the less-crude opinions have invariably won the victory; but religion itself, which is not concerned with opinion, but with the aspiration which leads us to strive after a purer and holier life, has seldom or never been attacked. On the contrary, the scientific men who have conducted the battle on behalf of the less-crude opinions have generally been influenced by this religious aspiration quite as strongly as the apologists of the more-crude opinions, and so far from religious feeling having been weakened by their perennial series of victories, it has apparently been growing deeper and stronger all the time. The religious sense is as yet too feebly developed in most of us; but certainly in no preceding age have men taken up the work of life with more earnestness or with more real faith in the unseen than at the present day, when so much of what was once deemed all-important knowledge has been consigned to the limbo of mythology.

The more-crude theories of early times are to be chiefly distinguished from the less-crude theories of to-day as being largely the products of random guesswork. Hypothesis, or guesswork, indeed, lies at the foundation of all scientific knowledge. The riddle of the universe, like less important riddles, is unravelled only by approximative trials, and the most brilliant discoverers have usually been the bravest guessers. Kepler's laws were the result of indefatigable guessing, and so, in a somewhat different sense, was the wave-theory of light. But the guesswork of scientific inquirers is very different now from what it was in older times. In the first place, we have slowly learned that a guess must be verified before it can be accepted as a sound theory; and, secondly, so many truths have been established beyond contravention, that the latitude for hypothesis is much less than it once was. Nine tenths of the guesses which might have occurred to a mediaeval philosopher would now be ruled out as inadmissible, because they would not harmonize with the knowledge which has been acquired since the Middle Ages. There is one direction especially in which this continuous limitation of guesswork by ever-accumulating experience has manifested itself. From first to last, all our speculative successes and failures have agreed in teaching us that the most general principles of action which prevail to-day, and in our own corner of the universe, have always prevailed throughout as much of the universe as is accessible to our research. They have taught us that for the deciphering of the past and the predicting of the future, no hypotheses are admissible which are not based upon the actual behaviour of things in the present. Once there was unlimited facility for guessing as to how the solar system might have come into existence; now the origin of the sun and planets is adequately explained when we have unfolded all that is implied in the processes which are still going on in the solar system. Formerly appeals were made to all manner of violent agencies to account for the changes which the earth's surface has undergone since our planet began its independent career; now it is seen that the same slow working of rain and tide, of wind and wave and frost, of secular contraction and of earthquake pulse, which is visible to-day, will account for the whole. It is not long since it was supposed that a species of animals or plants could be swept away only by some unusual catastrophe, while for the origination of new species something called an act of "special creation" was necessary; and as to the nature of such extraordinary events there was endless room for guesswork; but the discovery of natural selection was the discovery of a process, going on perpetually under our very eyes, which must inevitably of itself extinguish some species and bring new ones into being. In these and countless other ways we have learned that all the rich variety of nature is pervaded by unity of action, such as we might expect to find if nature is the manifestation of an infinite God who is without variableness or shadow of turning, but quite incompatible with the fitful behaviour of the anthropomorphic deities of the old mythologies. By thus abstaining from all appeal to agencies that are extra-cosmic, or not involved in the orderly system of events that we see occurring around us, we have at last succeeded in eliminating from philosophic speculation the character of random guesswork which at first of necessity belonged to it. Modern scientific hypothesis is so far from being a haphazard mental proceeding that it is perhaps hardly fair to classify it with guesses. It is lifted out of the plane of guesswork, in so far as it has acquired the character of inevitable inference from that which now is to that which has been or will be. Instead of the innumerable particular assumptions which were once admitted into cosmic philosophy, we are now reduced to the one universal assumption which has been variously described as the "principle of continuity," the "uniformity of nature," the "persistence of force," or the "law of causation," and which has been variously explained as a necessary datum for scientific thinking or as a net result of all induction. I am not unwilling, however, to adopt the language of a book which has furnished the occasion for the present discussion, and say that this grand assumption is a supreme act of faith, the definite expression of a trust that the infinite Sustainer of the universe "will not put us to permanent intellectual confusion." For in this mode of statement the harmony between the scientific and the religious points of view is well brought out. It is as affording the only outlet from permanent intellectual confusion that inquirers have been driven to appeal to the principle of continuity; and it is by unswerving reliance upon this principle that we have obtained such insight into the past, present, and future of the world as we now possess.

The work just mentioned[1] is especially interesting as an attempt to bring the probable destiny of the human soul into connection with the modern

---

[1] The Unseen Universe; or, Physical Speculations on a Future State. [Attributed to Professors TAIT and BALFOUR STEWART.] New York: Macmillan & Co. 1875. 8vo. pp. 212.

theories which explain the past and future career of the physical universe in accordance with the principle of continuity. Its authorship is as yet unknown, but it is believed to be the joint production of two of the most eminent physicists in Great Britain, and certainly the accurate knowledge and the ingenuity and subtlety of thought displayed in it are such as to lend great probability to this conjecture. Some account of the argument it contains may well precede the suggestions presently to be set forth concerning the Unseen World; and we shall find it most convenient to begin, like our authors, with a brief statement of what the principle of continuity teaches as to the proximate beginning and end of the visible universe. I shall in the main set down only results, having elsewhere[2] given a simple exposition of the arguments upon which these results are founded.

The first great cosmological speculation which has been raised quite above the plane of guesswork by making no other assumption than that of the uniformity of nature, is the well-known Nebular Hypothesis. Every astronomer knows that the earth, like all other cosmical bodies which are flattened at the poles, was formerly a mass of fluid, and consequently filled a much larger space than at present. It is further agreed, on all hands, that the sun is a contracting body, since there is no other possible way of accounting for the enormous quantity of heat which he generates. The so-called primeval nebula follows as a necessary inference from these facts. There was once a time when the earth was distended on all sides away out to the moon and beyond it, so that the matter now contained in the moon was then a part of our equatorial zone. And at a still remoter date in the past, the mass of the sun was diffused in every direction beyond the orbit of Neptune, and no planet had an individual existence, for all were indistinguishable parts of the solar mass. When the great mass of the sun, increased by the relatively small mass of all the planets put together, was spread out in this way, it was a rare vapour or gas. At the period where the question is taken up in Laplace's treatment of the nebular theory, the shape of this mass is regarded as spheroidal; but at an earlier period its shape may well have been as irregular as that of any of the nebulae which we now see in distant parts of the heavens, for, whatever its primitive shape, the equalization of its rotation would in time make it spheroidal. That the QUANTITY of rotation was the same then as now is unquestionable; for no system of particles, great or small, can acquire or lose rotation by any action going on within itself, any more than a man could pick himself up by his waistband and lift himself over a stone wale So that the primitive rotating spheroidal solar nebula is not a matter of assumption, but is just what must once have existed, provided there has been no breach of continuity in nature's operations. Now proceeding to reason back from the past to the present, it has been shown that the abandonment of successive equatorial belts by the

---

[2] Outlines of Cosmic Philosophy, based on the Doctrine of Evolution. Boston: J. R. Osgood & Co. 1875. 2 vols. 8vo.

contracting solar mass must have ensued in accordance with known mechanical laws; and in similar wise, under ordinary circumstances. each belt must have parted into fragments, and the fragments chasing each other around the same orbit, must have at last coalesced into a spheroidal planet. Not only this, but it has also been shown that as the result of such a process the relative sizes of the planets would be likely to take the order which they now follow; that the ring immediately succeeding that of Jupiter would be likely to abort and produce a great number of tiny planets instead of one good-sized one; that the outer planets would be likely to have many moons, and that Saturn, besides having the greatest number of moons, would be likely to retain some of his inner rings unbroken; that the earth would be likely to have a long day and Jupiter a short one; that the extreme outer planets would be not unlikely to rotate in a retrograde direction; and so on, through a long list of interesting and striking details. Not only, therefore, are we driven to the inference that our solar system was once a vaporous nebula, but we find that the mere contraction of such a nebula, under the influence of the enormous mutual gravitation of its particles, carries with it the explanation of both the more general and the more particular features of the present system. So that we may fairly regard this stupendous process as veritable matter of history, while we proceed to study it under some further aspects and to consider what consequences are likely to follow.

Our attention should first be directed to the enormous waste of energy which has accompanied this contraction of the solar nebula. The first result of such a contraction is the generation of a great quantity of heat, and when the heat thus generated has been lost by radiation into surrounding space it becomes possible for the contraction to continue. Thus, as concentration goes on, heat is incessantly generated and incessantly dissipated. How long this process is to endure depends chiefly on the size of the contracting mass, as small bodies radiate heat much faster than large ones. The moon seems to be already thoroughly refrigerated, while Jupiter and Saturn are very much hotter than the earth, as is shown by the tremendous atmospheric phenomena which occur on their surfaces. The sun, again, generates heat so rapidly, owing to his great energy of contraction, and loses it so slowly, owing to his great size, that his surface is always kept in a state of incandescence. His surface-temperature is estimated at some three million degrees of Fahrenheit, and a diminution of his diameter far too small to be detected by the finest existing instruments would suffice to maintain the present supply of heat for more than fifty centuries. These facts point to a very long future during which the sun will continue to warm the earth and its companion planets, but at the same time they carry on their face the story of inevitable ultimate doom. If things continue to go on as they have all along gone on, the sun must by and by grow black and cold, and all life whatever throughout the solar system must come to an end. Long before this consummation, however, life will probably have become extinct through the refrigeration of each of the planets into a state like the present state of the moon, in which the atmosphere and oceans have disappeared from the surface.

No doubt the sun will continue to give out heat a long time after heat has ceased to be needed for the support of living organisms. For the final refrigeration of the sun will long be postponed by the fate of the planets themselves. The separation of the planets from their parent solar mass seems to be after all but a temporary separation. So nicely balanced are they now in their orbits that they may well seem capable of rolling on in their present courses forever. But this is not the case. Two sets of circumstances are all the while striving, the one to drive the planets farther away from the sun, the other to draw them all into it. On the one hand, every body in our system which contains fluid matter has tides raised upon its surface by the attraction of neighbouring bodies. All the planets raise tides upon the surface of the sun and the periodicity of sun-spots (or solar cyclones) depends upon this fact. These tidal waves act as a drag or brake upon the rotation of the sun, somewhat diminishing its rapidity. But, in conformity with a principle of mechanics well known to astronomers, though not familiar to the general reader, all the motion of rotation thus lost by the sun is added to the planets in the shape of annual motion of revolution, and thus their orbits all tend to enlarge,—they all tend to recede somewhat from the sun. But this state of things, though long-enduring enough, is after all only temporary, and will at any rate come to an end when the sun and planets have become solid. Meanwhile another set of circumstances is all the time tending to bring the planets nearer to the sun, and in the long run must gain the mastery. The space through which the planets move is filled with a kind of matter which serves as a medium for the transmission of heat and light, and this kind of matter, though different in some respects from ordinary ponderable matter, is yet like it in exerting friction. This friction is almost infinitely little, yet it has a wellnigh infinite length of time to work in, and during all this wellnigh infinite length of time it is slowly eating up the momentum of the planets and diminishing their ability to maintain their distances from the sun. Hence in course of time the planets will all fall into the sun, one after another, so that the solar system will end, as it began, by consisting of a single mass of matter.

But this is by no means the end of the story. When two bodies rush together, each parts with some of its energy of motion, and this lost energy of motion reappears as heat. In the concussion of two cosmical bodies, like the sun and the earth, an enormous quantity of motion is thus converted into heat. Now heat, when not allowed to radiate, or when generated faster than it can be radiated, is transformed into motion of expansion. Hence the shock of sun and planet would at once result in the vaporization of both bodies; and there can be no doubt that by the time the sun has absorbed the outermost of his attendant planets, he will have resumed something like his original nebulous condition. He will have been dilated into a huge mass of vapour, and will have become fit for a new process of contraction and for a new production of life-bearing planets.

We are now, however, confronted by an interesting but difficult question. Throughout all this grand past and future career of the solar system which we have just briefly traced, we have been witnessing a most prodigal dissipation of energy in the shape of radiant heat. At the outset we had an enormous quantity of what is called "energy of position," that is, the outer parts of our primitive nebula had a very long distance through which to travel towards one another in the slow process of concentration; and this distance was the measure of the quantity of work possible to our system. As the particles of our nebula drew nearer and nearer together, the energy of position continually lost reappeared continually as heat, of which the greater part was radiated off, but of which a certain amount was retained. All the gigantic amount of work achieved in the geologic development of our earth and its companion planets, and in the development of life wherever life may exist in our system, has been the product of this retained heat. At the present day the same wasteful process is going on. Each moment the sun's particles are losing energy of position as they draw closer and closer together, and the heat into which this lost energy is metamorphosed is poured out most prodigally in every direction. Let us consider for a moment how little of it gets used in our system. The earth's orbit is a nearly circular figure more than five hundred million miles in circumference, while only eight thousand miles of this path are at any one time occupied by the earth's mass. Through these eight thousand miles the sun's radiated energy is doing work, but through the remainder of the five hundred million it is idle and wasted. But the case is far more striking when we reflect that it is not in the plane of the earth's orbit only that the sun's radiance is being poured out. It is not an affair of a circle, but of a sphere. In order to utilize all the solar rays, we should need to have an immense number of earths arranged so as to touch each other, forming a hollow sphere around the sun, with the present radius of the earth's orbit. We may well believe Professor Tyndall, therefore, when he tells us that all the solar radiance we receive is less than a two-billionth part of what is sent flying through the desert regions of space. Some of the immense residue of course hits other planets stationed in the way of it, and is utilized upon their surfaces; but the planets, all put together, stop so little of the total quantity that our startling illustration is not materially altered by taking them into the account. Now this two-billionth part of the solar radiance poured out from moment to moment suffices to blow every wind, to raise every cloud, to drive every engine, to build up the tissue of every plant, to sustain the activity of every animal, including man, upon the surface of our vast and stately globe. Considering the wondrous richness and variety of the terrestrial life wrought out by the few sunbeams which we catch in our career through space, we may well pause overwhelmed and stupefied at the thought of the incalculable possibilities of existence which are thrown away with the potent actinism that darts unceasingly into the unfathomed abysms of immensity. Where it goes to or what becomes of it, no one of us can surmise.

Now when, in the remote future, our sun is reduced to vapour by the impact of the several planets upon his surface, the resulting nebulous mass must be a very insignificant affair compared with the nebulous mass with which we started. In order to make a second nebula equal in size and potential energy to the first one, all the energy of position at first existing should have been retained in some form or other. But nearly all of it has been lost, and only an insignificant fraction remains with which to endow a new system. In order to reproduce, in future ages, anything like that cosmical development which is now going on in the solar system, aid must be sought from without. We must endeavour to frame some valid hypothesis as to the relation of our solar system to other systems.

Thus far our view has been confined to the career of a single star,—our sun,—with the tiny, easily-cooling balls which it has cast off in the course of its development. Thus far, too, our inferences have been very secure, for we have been dealing with a circumscribed group of phenomena, the beginning and end of which have been brought pretty well within the compass of our imagination. It is quite another thing to deal with the actual or probable career of the stars in general, inasmuch as we do not even know how many stars there are, which form parts of a common system, or what are their precise dynamic relations to one another. Nevertheless we have knowledge of a few facts which may support some cautious inferences. All the stars which we can see are undoubtedly bound together by relations of gravitation. No doubt our sun attracts all the other stars within our ken, and is reciprocally attracted by them. The stars, too, lie mostly in or around one great plane, as is the case with the members of the solar system. Moreover, the stars are shown by the spectroscope to consist of chemical elements identical with those which are found in the solar system. Such facts as these make it probable that the career of other stars, when adequately inquired into, would be found to be like that of our own sun. Observation daily enhances this probability, for our study of the sidereal universe is continually showing us stars in all stages of development. We find irregular nebulae, for example; we find spiral and spheroidal nebulae; we find stars which have got beyond the nebulous stage, but are still at a whiter heat than our sun; and we also find many stars which yield the same sort of spectrum as our sun. The inference seems forced upon us that the same process of concentration which has gone on in the case of our solar nebula has been going on in the case of other nebulae. The history of the sun is but a type of the history of stars in general. And when we consider that all other visible stars and nebulae are cooling and contracting bodies, like our sun, to what other conclusion could we very well come? When we look at Sirius, for instance, we do not see him surrounded by planets, for at such a distance no planet could be visible, even Sirius himself, though fourteen times larger than our sun, appearing only as a "twinkling little star." But a comparative survey of the heavens assures us that Sirius can hardly have arrived at his present stage of concentration without detaching, planet-forming rings, for there is no reason for supposing that mechanical laws out there are at all different from what they are in our own system. And the same kind of inference must apply to all the matured stars which we see in the heavens.

When we duly take all these things into the account, the case of our solar system will appear as only one of a thousand cases of evolution and dissolution with which the heavens furnish us. Other stars, like our sun, have undoubtedly started as vaporous masses, and have thrown off planets in contracting. The inference may seem a bold one, but it after all involves no other assumption than that of the continuity of natural phenomena. It is not likely, therefore, that the solar system will forever be left to itself. Stars which strongly gravitate toward each other, while moving through a perennially resisting medium, must in time be drawn together. The collision of our extinct sun with one of the Pleiades, after this manner, would very likely suffice to generate even a grander nebula than the one with which we started. Possibly the entire galactic system may, in an inconceivably remote future, remodel itself in this way; and possibly the nebula from which our own group of planets has been formed may have owed its origin to the disintegration of systems which had accomplished their career in the depths of the bygone eternity.

When the problem is extended to these huge dimensions, the prospect of an ultimate cessation of cosmical work is indefinitely postponed, but at the same time it becomes impossible for us to deal very securely with the questions we have raised. The magnitudes and periods we have introduced are so nearly infinite as to baffle speculation itself: One point, however, we seem dimly to discern. Supposing the stellar universe not to be absolutely infinite in extent, we may hold that the day of doom, so often postponed, must come at last. The concentration of matter and dissipation of energy, so often checked, must in the end prevail, so that, as the final outcome of things, the entire universe will be reduced to a single enormous ball, dead and frozen, solid and black, its potential energy of motion having been all transformed into heat and radiated away. Such a conclusion has been suggested by Sir William Thomson, and it is quite forcibly stated by the authors of "The Unseen Universe." They remind us that "if there be any one form of energy less readily or less completely transformable than the others, and if transformations constantly go on, more and more of the whole energy of the universe will inevitably sink into this lower grade as time advances." Now radiant heat, as we have seen, is such a lower grade of energy. "At each transformation of heat-energy into work, a large portion is degraded, while only a small portion is transformed into work. So that while it is very easy to change all of our mechanical or useful energy into heat, it is only possible to transform a portion of this heat-energy back again into work. After each change, too, the heat becomes more and more dissipated or degraded, and less and less available for any future transformation. In other words," our authors continue, "the tendency of heat is towards equalization; heat is par excellence the communist of our universe, and it will no doubt ultimately bring the system to an end. .... It is absolutely certain that life, so far as it is physical, depends essentially upon transformations of energy; it is also absolutely certain that age after age the possibility of such transformations is becoming less and less; and, so far as we yet know, the final state of the present universe must be an aggregation (into one mass) of all the matter it contains, i. e. the potential energy gone, and a practically useless state of kinetic energy, i. e. uniform temperature throughout that mass." Thus our authors conclude that the visible universe began in time and will in time come to an end; and they add that under the physical conditions of such a universe "immortality is impossible."

Concerning the latter inference we shall by and by have something to say. Meanwhile this whole speculation as to the final cessation of cosmical work seems to me—as it does to my friend, Professor Clifford [3]—by no means trustworthy. The conditions of the problem so far transcend our grasp that any such speculation must remain an unverifiable guess. I do not go with Professor Clifford in doubting whether the laws of mechanics are absolutely the same throughout eternity; I cannot quite reconcile such a doubt with faith in the principle of continuity. But it does seem to me needful, before we conclude that radiated energy is absolutely and forever wasted, that we should find out what becomes of it. What we call radiant heat is simply transverse wave-motion, propagated with enormous velocity through an ocean of subtle ethereal matter which bathes the atoms of all visible or palpable bodies and fills the whole of space, extending beyond the remotest star which the telescope can reach. Whether there are any bounds at all to this ethereal ocean, or whether it is as infinite as space itself, we cannot surmise. If it be limited, the possible dispersion of radiant energy is limited by its extent. Heat and light cannot travel through emptiness. If the ether is bounded by surrounding emptiness, then a ray of heat, on arriving at this limiting emptiness, would be reflected back as surely as a ball is sent back when thrown against a solid wall. If this be the case, it will not affect our conclusions concerning such a tiny region of space as is occupied by the solar system, but it will seriously modify Sir William Thomson's suggestion as to the fate of the universe as a whole. The radiance thrown away by the sun is indeed lost so far as the future of our system is concerned, but not a single unit of it is lost from the universe. Sooner or later, reflected back in all directions, it must do work in one quarter or another, so that ultimate stagnation be comes impossible. It is true that no such return of radiant energy has been detected in our corner of the world; but we have not yet so far disentangled all the force-relations of the universe that we are entitled to regard such a return as impossible. This is one way of escape from the consummation of things depicted by our authors. Another way of escape is equally available, if we suppose that while the ether is without bounds the stellar universe also extends to infinity. For in this case the reproduction of nebulous masses fit for generating new systems of worlds must go on through

---

[3] Fortnightly Review, April, 1875.

space that is endless, and consequently the process can never come to an end and can never have had a beginning. We have, therefore, three alternatives: either the visible universe is finite, while the ether is infinite; or both are finite; or both are infinite. Only on the first supposition, I think, do we get a universe which began in time and must end in time. Between such stupendous alternatives we have no grounds for choosing. But it would seem that the third, whether strictly true or not, best represents the state of the case relatively to our feeble capacity of comprehension. Whether absolutely infinite or not, the dimensions of the universe must be taken as practically infinite, so far as human thought is concerned. They immeasurably transcend the capabilities of any gauge we can bring to bear on them. Accordingly all that we are really entitled to hold, as the outcome of sound speculation, is the conception of innumerable systems of worlds concentrating out of nebulous masses, and then rushing together and dissolving into similar masses, as bubbles unite and break up—now here, now there—in their play on the surface of a pool, and to this tremendous series of events we can assign neither a beginning nor an end.

We must now make some more explicit mention of the ether which carries through space the rays of heat and light. In closest connection with the visible stellar universe, the vicissitudes of which we have briefly traced, the all-pervading ether constitutes a sort of unseen world remarkable enough from any point of view, but to which the theory of our authors ascribes capacities hitherto unsuspected by science. The very existence of an ocean of ether enveloping the molecules of material bodies has been doubted or denied by many eminent physicists, though of course none have called in question the necessity for some interstellar medium for the transmission of thermal and luminous vibrations. This scepticism has been, I think, partially justified by the many difficulties encompassing the conception, into which, however, we need not here enter. That light and heat cannot be conveyed by any of the ordinary sensible forms of matter is unquestionable. None of the forms of sensible matter can be imagined sufficiently elastic to propagate wave-motion at the rate of one hundred and eighty-eight thousand miles per second. Yet a ray of light is a series of waves, and implies some substance in which the waves occur. The substance required is one which seems to possess strangely contradictory properties. It is commonly regarded as an "ether" or infinitely rare substance; but, as Professor Jevons observes, we might as well regard it as an infinitely solid "adamant." "Sir John Herschel has calculated the amount of force which may be supposed, according to the undulatory theory of light, to be exerted at each point in space, and finds it to be 1,148,000,000,000 times the elastic force of ordinary air at the earth's surface, so that the pressure of the ether upon a square inch of surface must be about 17,000,000,000,000, or seventeen billions of pounds."[4] Yet at the same time the resistance offered by

---

[4] Jevons's Principles of Science, Vol. II. p. 145. The figures, which in the English system of numeration read as seventeen billions, would in the American system read as seventeen trillions.

the ether to the planetary motions is too minute to be appreciable. "All our ordinary notions," says Professor Jevons, "must be laid aside in contemplating such an hypothesis; yet [it is] no more than the observed phenomena of light and heat force us to accept. We cannot deny even the strange suggestion of Dr. Young, that there may be independent worlds, some possibly existing in different parts of space, but others perhaps pervading each other, unseen and unknown, in the same space. For if we are bound to admit the conception of this adamantine firmament, it is equally easy to admit a plurality of such."

The ether, therefore, is unlike any of the forms of matter which we can weigh and measure. In some respects it resembles a fluid, in some respects a solid. It is both hard and elastic to an almost inconceivable degree. It fills all material bodies like a sea in which the atoms of the material bodies are as islands, and it occupies the whole of what we call empty space. It is so sensitive that a disturbance in any part of it causes a "tremour which is felt on the surface of countless worlds." Our old experiences of matter give us no account of any substance like this; yet the undulatory theory of light obliges us to admit such a substance, and that theory is as well established as the theory of gravitation. Obviously we have here an enlargement of our experience of matter. The analysis of the phenomena of light and radiant heat has brought us into mental relations with matter in a different state from any in which we previously knew it. For the supposition that the ether may be something essentially different from matter is contradicted by all the terms we have used in describing it. Strange and contradictory as its properties may seem, are they any more strange than the properties of a gas would seem if we were for the first time to discover a gas after heretofore knowing nothing but solids and liquids? I think not; and the conclusion implied by our authors seems to me eminently probable, that in the so-called ether we have simply a state of matter more primitive than what we know as the gaseous state. Indeed, the conceptions of matter now current, and inherited from barbarous ages, are likely enough to be crude in the extreme. It is not strange that the study of such subtle agencies as heat and light should oblige us to modify them; and it will not be strange if the study of electricity should entail still further revision of our ideas.

We are now brought to one of the profoundest speculations of modern times, the vortex-atom theory of Helmholtz and Thomson, in which the evolution of ordinary matter from ether is plainly indicated. The reader first needs to know what vortex-motion is; and this has been so beautifully explained by Professor Clifford, that I quote his description entire: "Imagine a ring of india-rubber, made by joining together the ends of a cylindrical piece (like a lead-pencil before it is cut), to be put upon a round stick which it will just fit with a little stretching. Let the stick be now pulled through the ring while the latter is kept in its place by being pulled the other way on the outside. The india-rubber has then what is called vortex-motion. Before the ends were joined together, while it was straight, it might have been made to turn around without changing position, by rolling it between the hands. Just the same motion of rotation it has on the stick, only that the ends are now joined together. All the inside surface of the ring is going one way, namely, the way the stick is pulled; and all the outside is going the other way. Such a vortex-ring is made by the smoker who purses his lips into a round hole and sends out a puff of smoke. The outside of the ring is kept back by the friction of his lips while the inside is going forwards; thus a rotation is set up all round the smoke-ring as it travels out into the air." In these cases, and in others as we commonly find it, vortex-motion owes its origin to friction and is after a while brought to an end by friction. But in 1858 the equations of motion of an incompressible frictionless fluid were first successfully solved by Helmholtz, and among other things he proved that, though vortex-motion could not be originated in such a fluid, yet supposing it once to exist, it would exist to all eternity and could not be diminished by any mechanical action whatever. A vortex-ring, for example, in such a fluid, would forever preserve its own rotation, and would thus forever retain its peculiar individuality, being, as it were, marked off from its neighbour vortex-rings. Upon this mechanical truth Sir William Thomson based his wonderfully suggestive theory of the constitution of matter. That which is permanent or indestructible in matter is the ultimate homogeneous atom; and this is probably all that is permanent, since chemists now almost unanimously hold that so-called elementary molecules are not really simple, but owe their sensible differences to the various groupings of an ultimate atom which is alike for all. Relatively to our powers of comprehension the atom endures eternally; that is, it retains forever unalterable its definite mass and its definite rate of vibration. Now this is just what a vortex-ring would do in an incompressible frictionless fluid. Thus the startling question is suggested, Why may not the ultimate atoms of matter be vortex-rings forever existing in such a frictionless fluid filling the whole of space? Such a hypothesis is not less brilliant than Huyghens's conjectural identification of light with undulatory motion; and it is moreover a legitimate hypothesis, since it can be brought to the test of verification. Sir William Thomson has shown that it explains a great many of the physical properties of matter: it remains to be seen whether it can explain them all.

Of course the ether which conveys thermal and luminous undulations is not the frictionless fluid postulated by Sir William Thomson. The most conspicuous property of the ether is its enormous elasticity, a property which we should not find in a frictionless fluid. "To account for such elasticity," says Professor Clifford (whose exposition of the subject is still more lucid than that of our authors), "it has to be supposed that even where there are no material molecules the universal fluid is full of vortex-motion, but that the vortices are smaller and more closely packed than those of [ordinary] matter, forming altogether a more finely grained structure. So that the difference between matter and ether is reduced to a mere difference in the size and arrangement of the component vortex-rings. Now, whatever may turn out to be the ultimate nature of the ether and of molecules, we know that to some extent at least they obey the same dynamic laws, and that they act upon one another in accordance with these laws. Until, therefore, it is absolutely disproved, it must remain the simplest and most probable assumption that they are finally made of the same stuff, that the material molecule is some kind of knot or coagulation of ether."[5]

Another interesting consequence of Sir William Thomson's pregnant hypothesis is that the absolute hardness which has been attributed to material atoms from the time of Lucretius downward may be dispensed with. Somewhat in the same way that a loosely suspended chain becomes rigid with rapid rotation, the hardness and elasticity of the vortex-atom are explained as due to the swift rotary motion of a soft and yielding fluid. So that the vortex-atom is really indivisible, not by reason of its hardness or solidity, but by reason of the indestructibleness of its motion.

Supposing, now, that we adopt provisionally the vortex theory,—the great power of which is well shown by the consideration just mentioned,—we must not forget that it is absolutely essential to the indestructibleness of the material atom that the universal fluid in which it has an existence as a vortex-ring should be entirely destitute of friction. Once admit even the most infinitesimal amount of friction, while retaining the conception of vortex-motion in a universal fluid, and the whole case is so far altered that the material atom can no longer be regarded as absolutely indestructible, but only as indefinitely enduring. It may have been generated, in bygone eternity, by a natural process of evolution, and in future eternity may come to an end. Relatively to our powers of comprehension the practical difference is perhaps not great. Scientifically speaking, Helmholtz and Thomson are as well entitled to reason upon the assumption of a perfectly frictionless fluid as geometers in general are entitled to assume perfect lines without breadth and perfect surfaces without thickness. Perfect lines and surfaces do not exist within the region of our experience; yet the conclusions of geometry are none the less true ideally, though in any particular concrete instance they are only approximately realized. Just so with the conception of a frictionless fluid. So far as experience goes, such a thing has no more real existence than a line without breadth; and hence an atomic theory based upon such an assumption may be as true ideally as any of the theorems of Euclid, but it can give only an approximatively true account of the actual universe. These considerations do not at all affect the scientific value of the theory; but they will modify the tenour of such transcendental inferences as may be drawn from it regarding, the probable origin and destiny of the universe.

The conclusions reached in the first part of this paper, while we were dealing only with gross visible matter, may have seemed bold enough; but they are far surpassed by the inference which our authors draw from the vortex theory as they interpret it. Our authors exhibit various reasons, more or less

---

[5] Fortnightly Review, June, 1875, p. 784.

sound, for attributing to the primordial fluid some slight amount of friction; and in support of this view they adduce Le Sage's explanation of gravitation as a differential result of pressure, and Struve's theory of the partial absorption of light-rays by the ether,—questions with which our present purpose does not require us to meddle. Apart from such questions it is every way probable that the primary assumption of Helmholtz and Thomson is only an approximation to the truth. But if we accredit the primordial fluid with even an infinitesimal amount of friction, then we are required to conceive of the visible universe as developed from the invisible and as destined to return into the invisible. The vortex-atom, produced by infinitesimal friction operating through wellnigh infinite time, is to be ultimately abolished by the agency which produced it. In the words of our authors, "If the visible universe be developed from an invisible which is not a perfect fluid, then the argument deduced by Sir William Thomson in favour of the eternity of ordinary matter disappears, since this eternity depends upon the perfect fluidity of the invisible. In fine, if we suppose the material universe to be composed of a series of vortex-rings developed from an invisible universe which is not a perfect fluid, it will be ephemeral, just as the smoke-ring which we develop from air, or that which we develop from water, is ephemeral, the only difference being in duration, these lasting only for a few seconds, and the others it may be for billions of years." Thus, as our authors suppose that "the available energy of the visible universe will ultimately be appropriated by the invisible," they go on to imagine, "at least as a possibility, that the separate existence of the visible universe will share the same fate, so that we shall have no huge, useless, inert mass existing in after ages to remind the passer-by of a form of energy and a species of matter that is long since out of date and functionally effete. Why should not the universe bury its dead out of sight?"

In one respect perhaps no more stupendous subject of contemplation than this has ever been offered to the mind of man. In comparison with the length of time thus required to efface the tiny individual atom, the entire cosmical career of our solar system, or even that of the whole starry galaxy, shrinks into utter nothingness. Whether we shall adopt the conclusion suggested must depend on the extent of our speculative audacity. We have seen wherein its probability consists, but in reasoning upon such a scale we may fitly be cautious and modest in accepting inferences, and our authors, we may be sure, would be the first to recommend such modesty and caution. Even at the dimensions to which our theorizing has here grown, we may for instance discern the possible alternative of a simultaneous or rhythmically successive generation and destruction of vortex-atoms which would go far to modify the conclusion just suggested. But here we must pause for a moment, reserving for a second paper the weightier thoughts as to futurity which our authors have sought to enwrap in these sublime physical speculations.

PART SECOND.

UP to this point, however remote from ordinary every-day thoughts may be the region of speculation which we have been called upon to traverse, we have still kept within the limits of legitimate scientific hypothesis. Though we have ventured for a goodly distance into the unknown, we have not yet been required to abandon our base of operations in the known. Of the views presented in the preceding paper, some are wellnigh certainly established, some are probable, some have a sort of plausibility, others—to which we have refrained from giving assent—may possibly be true; but none are irretrievably beyond the jurisdiction of scientific tests. No suggestion has so far been broached which a very little further increase of our scientific knowledge may not show to be either eminently probable or eminently improbable. We have kept pretty clear of mere subjective guesses, such as men may wrangle about forever without coming to any conclusion. The theory of the nebular origin of our planetary system has come to command the assent of all persons qualified to appreciate the evidence on which it is based; and the more immediate conclusions which we have drawn from that theory are only such as are commonly drawn by astronomers and physicists. The doctrine of an intermolecular and interstellar ether is wrapped up in the well-established undulatory theory of light. Such is by no means the case with Sir William Thomson's vortex-atom theory, which to-day is in somewhat the same condition as the undulatory theory of Huyghens two centuries ago. This, however, is none the less a hypothesis truly scientific in conception, and in the speculations to which it leads us we are still sure of dealing with views that admit at least of definite expression and treatment. In other words, though our study of the visible universe has led us to the recognition of a kind of unseen world underlying the world of things that are seen, yet concerning the economy of this unseen world we have not been led to entertain any hypothesis that has not its possible justification in our experiences of visible phenomena.

We are now called upon, following in the wake of our esteemed authors, to venture on a different sort of exploration, in which we must cut loose altogether from our moorings in the world of which we have definite experience. We are invited to entertain suggestions concerning the peculiar economy of the invisible portion of the universe which we have no means of subjecting to any sort of test of probability, either experimental or deductive. These suggestions are, therefore, not to be regarded as properly scientific; but, with this word of caution, we may proceed to show what they are.

Compared with the life and death of cosmical systems which we have heretofore contemplated, the life and death of individuals of the human race may perhaps seem a small matter; yet because we are ourselves the men who live and die, the small event is of vastly greater interest to us than the grand series of events of which it is part and parcel. It is natural that we should be more interested in the ultimate fate of humanity than in the fate of a world which is of no account to us save as our present dwelling-place. Whether the human soul is to come to an end or not is to us a more important question than whether the visible universe, with its matter and energy, is to be absorbed in an invisible ether. It is indeed only because we are interested in the former question that we are so curious about the latter. If we could dissociate ourselves from the material universe, our habitat, we should probably speculate much less about its past and future. We care very little what becomes of the black ball of the earth, after all life has vanished from its surface; or, if we care at all about it, it is only because our thoughts about the career of the earth are necessarily mixed up with our thoughts about life. Hence in considering the probable ultimate destiny of the physical universe, our innermost purpose must be to know what is to become of all this rich and wonderful life of which the physical universe is the theatre. Has it all been developed, apparently at almost infinite waste of effort, only to be abolished again before it has attained to completeness, or does it contain or shelter some indestructible element which having drawn sustenance for a while from the senseless turmoil of physical phenomena shall still survive their final decay? This question is closely connected with the time-honoured question of the meaning, purpose, or tendency of the world. In the career of the world is life an end, or a means toward an end, or only an incidental phenomenon in which we can discover no meaning? Contemporary theologians seem generally to believe that one necessary result of modern scientific inquiry must be the destruction of the belief in immortal life, since against every thoroughgoing expounder of scientific knowledge they seek to hurl the charge of "materialism." Their doubts, however, are not shared by our authors, thorough men of science as they are, though their mode of dealing with the question may not be such as we can well adopt. While upholding the doctrine of evolution, and all the so-called "materialistic" views of modern science, they not only regard the hypothesis of a future life as admissible, but they even go so far as to propound a physical theory as to the nature of existence after death. Let us see what this physical theory is.

As far as the visible universe is concerned, we do not find in it any evidence of immortality or of permanence of any sort, unless it be in the sum of potential and kinetic energies on the persistency of which depends our principle of continuity. In ordinary language "the stars in their courses" serve as symbols of permanence, yet we have found reason to regard them as but temporary phenomena. So, in the language of our authors, "if we take the individual man, we find that he lives his short tale of years, and that then the visible machinery which connects him with the past, as well as that which enables him to act in the present, falls into ruin and is brought to an end. If any germ or potentiality remains, it is certainly not connected with the visible order of things." In like manner our race is pretty sure to come to an end long before the destruction of the planet from which it now gets its sustenance. And in our authors opinion even the universe will by and by become "old and effete, no less truly than the individual: it is a glorious garment this visible universe, but not an immortal one; we must look elsewhere if we are to be clothed with immortality as with a garment."

It is at this point that our authors call attention to "the apparently wasteful character of the arrangements of the visible universe." The fact is one which we have already sufficiently described, but we shall do well to quote the words in which our authors recur to it: "All but a very small portion of the sun's heat goes day by day into what we call empty space, and it is only this very small remainder that is made use of by the various planets for purposes of their own. Can anything be more perplexing than this seemingly frightful expenditure of the very life and essence of the system? That this vast store of high-class energy should be doing nothing but travelling outwards in space at the rate of 188,000 miles per second is hardly conceivable, especially when the result of it is the inevitable destruction of the visible universe."

Pursuing this teleological argument, it is suggested that perhaps this apparent waste of energy is "only an arrangement in virtue of which our universe keeps up a memory of the past at the expense of the present, inasmuch as all memory consists in an investiture of present resources in order to keep a hold upon the past." Recourse is had to the ingenious argument in which Mr. Babbage showed that "if we had power to follow and detect the minutest effects of any disturbance, each particle of existing matter must be a register of all that has happened. The track of every canoe, of every vessel that has yet disturbed the surface of the ocean, whether impelled by manual force or elemental power, remains forever registered in the future movement of all succeeding particles which may occupy its place. The furrow which is left is, indeed, instantly filled up by the closing waters; but they draw after them other and larger portions of the surrounding element, and these again, once moved, communicate motion to others in endless succession." In like manner, "the air itself is one vast library, on whose pages are forever written all that man has ever said or even whispered. There in their mutable but unerring characters, mixed with the earliest as well as the latest sighs of mortality, stand forever recorded vows unredeemed, promises unfulfilled, perpetuating in the united movements of each particle the testimony of man's changeful will."[6] In some such way as this, records of every movement that takes place in the world are each moment transmitted, with the speed of light, through the invisible ocean of ether with which the world is surrounded. Even the molecular displacements which occur in our brains when we feel and think are thus propagated in their effects into the unseen world. The world of ether is thus regarded by our authors as in some sort the obverse or complement of the world of sensible matter, so that whatever energy is dissipated in the one is by the same act accumulated in the other. It is like the negative plate in photography, where light answers to shadow and shadow to light. Or, still better, it is like the case

---

[6] Babbage, Ninth Bridgewater Treatise, p. 115; Jevons, Principles of Science, Vol. II. p. 455.

of an equation in which whatever quantity you take from one side is added to the other with a contrary sign, while the relation of equality remains undisturbed. Thus, it will be noticed, from the ingenious and subtle, but quite defensible suggestion of Mr. Babbage, a leap is made to an assumption which cannot be defended scientifically, but only teleologically. It is one thing to say that every movement in the visible world transmits a record of itself to the surrounding ether, in such a way that from the undulation of the ether a sufficiently powerful intelligence might infer the character of the generating movement in the visible world. It is quite another thing to say that the ether is organized in such a complex and delicate way as to be like a negative image or counterpart of the world of sensible matter. The latter view is no doubt ingenious, but it is gratuitous. It is sustained not by scientific analogy, but by the desire to find some assignable use for the energy which is constantly escaping from visible matter into invisible ether. The moment we ask how do we know that this energy is not really wasted, or that it is not put to some use wholly undiscoverable by human intelligence, this assumption of an organized ether is at once seen to be groundless. It belongs not to the region of science, but to that of pure mythology.

In justice to our authors, however, it should be remembered that this assumption is put forth not as something scientifically probable, but as something which for aught we know to the contrary may possibly be true. This, to be sure, we need not deny; nor if we once allow this prodigious leap of inference, shall we find much difficulty in reaching the famous conclusion that "thought conceived to affect the matter of another universe simultaneously with this may explain a future state." This proposition, quaintly couched in an anagram, like the discoveries of old astronomers, was published last year in "Nature," as containing the gist of the forthcoming book. On the negative-image hypothesis it is not hard to see how thought is conceived to affect the seen and the unseen worlds simultaneously. Every act of consciousness is accompanied by molecular displacements in the brain, and these are of course responded to by movements in the ethereal world. Thus as a series of conscious states build up a continuous memory in strict accordance with physical laws of motion,[7] so a correlative memory is simultaneously built up in the ethereal world out of the ethereal correlatives of the molecular displacements which go on in our brains. And as there is a continual transfer of energy from the visible world to the ether, the extinction of vital energy which we call death must coincide in some way with the awakening of vital energy in the correlative world; so that the darkening of consciousness here is coincident with its dawning there. In this way death is for the individual but a transfer from one physical state of existence to another; and so, on the largest scale, the death or final loss of energy by the whole visible universe has its counterpart in the acquirement of a maximum of life by the correlative unseen world.

---

[7] See my Outlines of Cosmic Philosophy, Vol. II. pp. 142-148.

There seems to be a certain sort of rigorous logical consistency in this daring speculation; but really the propositions of which it consists are so far from answering to anything within the domain of human experience that we are unable to tell whether any one of them logically follows from its predecessor or not. It is evident that we are quite out of the region of scientific tests, and to whatever view our authors may urge we can only languidly assent that it is out of our power to disprove it.

The essential weakness of such a theory as this lies in the fact that it is thoroughly materialistic in character. It is currently assumed that the doctrine of a life after death cannot be defended on materialistic grounds, but this is altogether too hasty an assumption. Our authors, indeed, are not philosophical materialists, like Dr. Priestley,—who nevertheless believed in a future life,— but one of the primary doctrines of materialism lies at the bottom of their argument. Materialism holds for one thing that consciousness is a product of a peculiar organization of matter, and for another thing that consciousness cannot survive the disorganization of the material body with which it is associated. As held by philosophical materialists, like Buchner and Moleschott, these two opinions are strictly consistent with each other; nay, the latter seems to be the inevitable inference from the former, though Priestley did not so regard it. Now our authors very properly refuse to commit themselves to the opinion that mind is the product of matter, but their argument nevertheless implies that some sort of material vehicle is necessary for the continuance of mind in a future state of existence. This material vehicle they seek to supply in the theory which connects by invisible bonds of transmitted energy the perishable material body with its counterpart in the world of ether. The materialism of the argument is indeed partly veiled by the terminology in which this counterpart is called a "spiritual body," but in this novel use or abuse of scriptural language there seems to me to be a strange confusion of ideas. Bear in mind that the "invisible universe" into which energy is constantly passing is simply the luminiferous ether, which our authors, to suit the requirements of their hypothesis, have gratuitously endowed with a complexity and variety of structure analogous to that of the visible world of matter. Their language is not always quite so precise as one could desire, for while they sometimes speak of the ether itself as the "unseen universe," they sometimes allude to a primordial medium yet subtler in constitution and presumably more immaterial. Herein lies the confusion. Why should the luminiferous ether, or any primordial medium in which it may have been generated, be regarded as in any way "spiritual"? Great physicists, like less trained thinkers, are sometimes liable to be unconsciously influenced by old associations of ideas which, ostensibly repudiated, still lurk under cover of the words we use. I fear that the old associations which led the ancients to describe the soul as a breath or a shadow, and which account for the etymologies of such words as "ghost" and "spirit," have had something to do with this spiritualization of the interstellar ether. Some share may also have been contributed by the Platonic notion of the "grossness" or "bruteness" of tangible matter,—a notion which has survived in Christian theology, and which educated men of the present day have by no means universally outgrown. Save for some such old associations as these, why should it be supposed that matter becomes "spriritualized" as it diminishes in apparent substantiality? Why should matter be pronounced respectable in the inverse ratio of its density or ponderability? Why is a diamond any more chargeable with "grossness" than a cubic centimetre of hydrogen? Obviously such fancies are purely of mythologic parentage. Now the luminiferous ether, upon which our authors make such extensive demands, may be physically "ethereal" enough, in spite of the enormous elasticity which leads Professor Jevons to characterize it as "adamantine"; but most assuredly we have not the slightest reason for speaking of it as "immaterial" or "spiritual." Though we are unable to weigh it in the balance, we at least know it as a transmitter of undulatory movements, the size and shape of which we can accurately measure. Its force-relations with ponderable matter are not only universally and incessantly maintained, but they have that precisely quantitative character which implies an essential identity between the innermost natures of the two substances. We have seen reason for thinking it probable that ether and ordinary matter are alike composed of vortex-rings in a quasi-frictionless fluid; but whatever be the fate of this subtle hypothesis, we may be sure that no theory will ever be entertained in which the analysis of ether shall require different symbols from that of ordinary matter. In our authors' theory, therefore, the putting on of immortality is in no wise the passage from a material to a spiritual state. It is the passage from one kind of materially conditioned state to another. The theory thus appeals directly to our experiences of the behaviour of matter; and in deriving so little support as it does from these experiences, it remains an essentially weak speculation, whatever we may think of its ingenuity. For so long as we are asked to accept conclusions drawn from our experiences of the material world, we are justified in demanding something more than mere unconditioned possibility. We require some positive evidence, be it ever so little in amount; and no theory which cannot furnish such positive evidence is likely to carry to our minds much practical conviction.

This is what I meant by saying that the great weakness of the hypothesis here criticized lies in its materialistic character. In contrast with this we shall presently see that the assertion of a future life which is not materially conditioned, though unsupported by any item of experience whatever, may nevertheless be an impregnable assertion. But first I would conclude the foregoing criticism by ruling out altogether the sense in which our authors use the expression "Unseen Universe." Scientific inference, however remote, is connected by such insensible gradations with ordinary perception, that one may well question the propriety of applying the term "unseen" to that which is presented to "the mind's eye" as inevitable matter of inference. It is true that we cannot see the ocean of ether in which visible matter floats; but there are many other invisible things which yet we do not regard as part of the "unseen world." I do not see the air which I am now breathing within the four walls of my study, yet its existence is sufficiently a matter of sense-perception as it fills my lungs and fans my cheek. The atoms which compose a drop of water are not only invisible, but cannot in any way be made the objects of sense-perception; yet by proper inferences from their behaviour we can single them out for measurement, so that Sir William Thomson can tell us that if the drop of water were magnified to the size of the earth, the constituent atoms would be larger than peas, but not so large as billiard-balls. If we do not see such atoms with our eyes, we have one adequate reason in their tiny dimensions, though there are further reasons than this. It would be hard to say why the luminiferous ether should be relegated to the "unseen world" any more than the material atom. Whatever we know as possessing resistance and extension, whatever we can subject to mathematical processes of measurement, we also conceive as existing in such shape that, with appropriate eyes and under proper visual conditions, we MIGHT see it, and we are not entitled to draw any line of demarcation between such an object of inference and others which may be made objects of sense-perception. To set apart the ether as constituting an "unseen universe" is therefore illegitimate and confusing. It introduces a distinction where there is none, and obscures the fact that both invisible ether and visible matter form but one grand universe in which the sum of energy remains constant, though the order of its distribution endlessly varies.

Very different would be the logical position of a theory which should assume the existence of an "Unseen World" entirely spiritual in constitution, and in which material conditions like those of the visible world should have neither place nor meaning. Such a world would not consist of ethers or gases or ghosts, but of purely psychical relations akin to such as constitute thoughts and feelings when our minds are least solicited by sense-perceptions. In thus marking off the "Unseen World" from the objective universe of which we have knowledge, our line of demarcation would at least be drawn in the right place. The distinction between psychical and material phenomena is a distinction of a different order from all other distinctions known to philosophy, and it immeasurably transcends all others. The progress of modern discovery has in no respect weakened the force of Descartes's remark, that between that of which the differential attribute is Thought and that of which the differential attribute is Extension, there can be no similarity, no community of nature whatever. By no scientific cunning of experiment or deduction can Thought be weighed or measured or in any way assimilated to such things as may be made the actual or possible objects of sense-perception. Modern discovery, so far from bridging over the chasm between Mind and Matter, tends rather to exhibit the distinction between them as absolute. It has, indeed, been rendered highly probable that every act of consciousness is accompanied by a molecular motion in the cells and fibres of the brain; and materialists have found great comfort in this fact, while theologians and persons of little faith have been very much frightened by it. But since no one ever pretended that thought can go on, under the conditions of the present life, without a brain, one finds it rather hard to sympathize either with the self-congratulations of Dr. Buchner's disciples [8] or with the terrors of their opponents. But what has been less commonly remarked is the fact that when the thought and the molecular movement thus occur simultaneously, in no scientific sense is the thought the product of the molecular movement. The sun-derived energy of motion latent in the food we eat is variously transformed within the organism, until some of it appears as the motion of the molecules of a little globule of nerve-matter in the brain. In a rough way we might thus say that the chemical energy of the food indirectly produces the motion of these little nerve-molecules. But does this motion of nerve-molecules now produce a thought or state of consciousness? By no means. It simply produces some other motion of nerve-molecules, and this in turn produces motion of contraction or expansion in some muscle, or becomes transformed into the chemical energy of some secreting gland. At no point in the whole circuit does a unit of motion disappear as motion to reappear as a unit of consciousness. The physical process is complete in itself, and the thought does not enter into it. All that we can say is, that the occurrence of the thought is simultaneous with that part of the physical process which consists of a molecular movement in the brain.[9] To be sure, the thought is always there when summoned, but it stands outside the dynamic circuit, as something utterly alien from and incomparable with the events which summon it. No doubt, as Professor Tyndall observes, if we knew exhaustively the physical state of the brain, "the corresponding thought or feeling might be inferred; or, given the thought or feeling, the corresponding state of the brain might be inferred. But how inferred? It would be at bottom not a case of logical inference at all, but of empirical association. You may reply that many of the inferences of science are of this character; the inference, for example, that an electric current of a given direction will deflect a magnetic needle in a definite way; but the cases differ in this, that the passage from the current to the needle, if not demonstrable, is thinkable, and that we entertain no doubt as to the final mechanical solution of the problem. But the passage from the physics of the brain to the corresponding facts of consciousness is unthinkable. Granted that a definite thought and a definite molecular action in the brain occur simultaneously; we do not possess the intellectual organ, nor apparently any rudiment of the organ, which would enable us to pass by a process of reasoning from the one to the other. They appear together, but we do not know why."[10]

---

[8] The Nation once wittily described these people as "people who believe that they are going to die like the beasts, and who congratulate themselves that they are going to die like the beasts."
[9] For a fuller exposition of this point, see my Outlines of Cosmic Philosophy, Vol. II. pp. 436-445.
[10] Fragments of Science, p. 119.

An unseen world consisting of purely psychical or spiritual phenomena would accordingly be demarcated by an absolute gulf from what we call the material universe, but would not necessarily be discontinuous with the psychical phenomena which we find manifested in connection with the world of matter. The transfer of matter, or physical energy, or anything else that is quantitatively measurable, into such an unseen world, may be set down as impossible, by reason of the very definition of such a world. Any hypothesis which should assume such a transfer would involve a contradiction in terms. But the hypothesis of a survival of present psychical phenomena in such a world, after being denuded of material conditions, is not in itself absurd or self-contradictory, though it may be impossible to support it by any arguments drawn from the domain of human experience. Such is the shape which it seems to me that, in the present state of philosophy, the hypothesis of a future life must assume. We have nothing to say to gross materialistic notions of ghosts and bogies, and spirits that upset tables and whisper to ignorant vulgar women the wonderful information that you once had an aunt Susan. The unseen world imagined in our hypothesis is not connected with the present material universe by any such "invisible bonds" as would allow Bacon and Addison to come to Boston and write the silliest twaddle in the most ungrammatical English before a roomful of people who have never learned how to test what they are pleased to call the "evidence of their senses." Our hypothesis is expressly framed so as to exclude all intercourse whatever between the unseen world of spirit unconditioned by matter and the present world of spirit conditioned by matter in which all our experiences have been gathered. The hypothesis being framed in such a way, the question is, What has philosophy to say to it? Can we, by searching our experiences, find any reason for adopting such an hypothesis? Or, on the other hand, supposing we can find no such reason, would the total failure of experimental evidence justify us in rejecting it?

The question is so important that I will restate it. I have imagined a world made up of psychical phenomena, freed from the material conditions under which alone we know such phenomena. Can we adduce any proof of the possibility of such a world? Or if we cannot, does our failure raise the slightest presumption that such a world is impossible?

The reply to the first clause of the question is sufficiently obvious. We have no experience whatever of psychical phenomena save as manifested in connection with material phenomena. We know of Mind only as a group of activities which are never exhibited to us except through the medium of motions of matter. In all our experience we have never encountered such activities save in connection with certain very complicated groupings of highly mobile material particles into aggregates which we call living organisms. And we have never found them manifested to a very conspicuous extent save in connection with some of those specially organized aggregates which have vertebrate skeletons and mammary glands. Nay, more, when we survey the net results of our experience up to the present time, we find indisputable evidence that in the past history of the visible universe psychical phenomena have only begun to be manifested in connection with certain complex aggregates of material phenomena. As these material aggregates have age by age become more complex in structure, more complex psychical phenomena have been exhibited. The development of Mind has from the outset been associated with the development of Matter. And to-day, though none of us has any knowledge of the end of psychical phenomena in his own case, yet from all the marks by which we recognize such phenomena in our fellow-creatures, whether brute or human, we are taught that when certain material processes have been gradually or suddenly brought to an end, psychical phenomena are no longer manifested. From first to last, therefore, our appeal to experience gets but one response. We have not the faintest shadow of evidence wherewith to make it seem probable that Mind can exist except in connection with a material body. Viewed from this standpoint of terrestrial experience, there is no more reason for supposing that consciousness survives the dissolution of the brain than for supposing that the pungent flavour of table-salt survives its decomposition into metallic sodium and gaseous chlorine.

Our answer from this side is thus unequivocal enough. Indeed, so uniform has been the teaching of experience in this respect that even in their attempts to depict a life after death, men have always found themselves obliged to have recourse to materialistic symbols. To the mind of a savage the future world is a mere reproduction of the present, with its everlasting huntings and fightings. The early Christians looked forward to a renovation of the earth and the bodily resurrection from Sheol of the righteous. The pictures of hell and purgatory, and even of paradise, in Dante's great poem, are so intensely materialistic as to seem grotesque in this more spiritual age. But even to-day the popular conceptions of heaven are by no means freed from the notion of matter; and persons of high culture, who realize the inadequacy of these popular conceptions, are wont to avoid the difficulty by refraining from putting their hopes and beliefs into any definite or describable form. Not unfrequently one sees a smile raised at the assumption of knowledge or insight by preachers who describe in eloquent terms the joys of a future state; yet the smile does not necessarily imply any scepticism as to the abstract probability of the soul's survival. The scepticism is aimed at the character of the description rather than at the reality of the thing described. It implies a tacit agreement, among cultivated people, that the unseen world must be purely spiritual in constitution. The agreement is not habitually expressed in definite formulas, for the reason that no mental image of a purely spiritual world can be formed. Much stress is commonly laid upon the recognition of friends in a future life; and however deep a meaning may be given to the phrase "the love of God," one does not easily realize that a heavenly existence could be worth the longing that is felt for it, if it were to afford no further scope for the pure and tender household affections which give to the present life its powerful though indefinable charm. Yet the recognition of friends in a purely spiritual world is something of which we can frame no conception whatever. We may look with unspeakable reverence on the features of wife or child, less because of their physical beauty than because of the beauty of soul to which they give expression, but to imagine the perception of soul by soul apart from the material structure and activities in which soul is manifested, is something utterly beyond our power. Nay, even when we try to represent to ourselves the psychical activity of any single soul by itself as continuing without the aid of the physical machinery of sensation, we get into unmanageable difficulties. A great part of the contents of our minds consists of sensuous (chiefly visual) images, and though we may imagine reflection to go on without further images supplied by vision or hearing, touch or taste or smell, yet we cannot well see how fresh experiences could be gained in such a state. The reader, if he require further illustrations, can easily follow out this line of thought. Enough has no doubt been said to convince him that our hypothesis of the survival of conscious activity apart from material conditions is not only utterly unsupported by any evidence that can be gathered from the world of which we have experience, but is utterly and hopelessly inconceivable.

It is inconceivable BECAUSE it is entirely without foundation in experience. Our powers of conception are closely determined by the limits of our experience. When a proposition, or combination of ideas, is suggested, for which there has never been any precedent in human experience, we find it to be UNTHINKABLE,—the ideas will not combine. The proposition remains one which we may utter and defend, and perhaps vituperate our neighbours for not accepting, but it remains none the less an unthinkable proposition. It takes terms which severally have meanings and puts them together into a phrase which has no meaning.[11] Now when we try to combine the idea of the continuance of conscious activity with the idea of the entire cessation of material conditions, and thereby to assert the existence of a purely spiritual world, we find that we have made an unthinkable proposition. We may defend our hypothesis as passionately as we like, but when we strive coolly to realize it in thought we find ourselves baulked at every step.

But now we have to ask, How much does this inconceivability signify? In most cases, when we say that a statement is inconceivable, we practically declare it to be untrue; when we say that a statement is without warrant in experience, we plainly indicate that we consider it unworthy of our acceptance. This is legitimate in the majority of cases with which we have to deal in the course of life, because experience, and the capacities of thought called out and limited by experience, are our only guides in the conduct of life. But every one will admit that our experience is not infinite, and that our capacity of conception is not coextensive with the possibilities of existence. It is not only possible, but in the very highest degree probable, that there are many things in heaven, if not on earth, which are undreamed of in our philosophy. Since our ability to conceive

---

[11] See my Outlines of Cosmic Philosophy, Vol. I. pp. 64-67.

anything is limited by the extent of our experience, and since human experience is very far from being infinite, it follows that there may be, and in all probability is, an immense region of existence in every way as real as the region which we know, yet concerning which we cannot form the faintest rudiment of a conception. Any hypothesis relating to such a region of existence is not only not disproved by the total failure of evidence in its favour, but the total failure of evidence does not raise even the slightest prima facie presumption against its validity.

These considerations apply with great force to the hypothesis of an unseen world in which psychical phenomena persist in the absence of material conditions. It is true, on the one hand, that we can bring up no scientific evidence in support of such an hypothesis. But on the other hand it is equally true that in the very nature of things no such evidence could be expected to be forthcoming: even were there such evidence in abundance, it could not be accessible to us. The existence of a single soul, or congeries of psychical phenomena, unaccompanied by a material body, would be evidence sufficient to demonstrate the hypothesis. But in the nature of things, even were there a million such souls round about us, we could not become aware of the existence of one of them, for we have no organ or faculty for the perception of soul apart from the material structure and activities in which it has been manifested throughout the whole course of our experience. Even our own self-consciousness involves the consciousness of ourselves as partly material bodies. These considerations show that our hypothesis is very different from the ordinary hypotheses with which science deals. The entire absence of testimony does not raise a negative presumption except in cases where testimony is accessible. In the hypotheses with which scientific men are occupied, testimony is always accessible; and if we do not find any, the presumption is raised that there is none. When Dr. Bastian tells us that he has found living organisms to be generated in sealed flasks from which all living germs had been excluded, we demand the evidence for his assertion. The testimony of facts is in this case hard to elicit, and only skilful reasoners can properly estimate its worth. But still it is all accessible. With more or less labour it can be got at; and if we find that Dr. Bastian has produced no evidence save such as may equally well receive a different interpretation from that which he has given it, we rightly feel that a strong presumption has been raised against his hypothesis. It is a case in which we are entitled to expect to find the favouring facts if there are any, and so long as we do not find such, we are justified in doubting their existence. So when our authors propound the hypothesis of an unseen universe consisting of phenomena which occur in the interstellar ether, or even in some primordial fluid with which the ether has physical relations, we are entitled to demand their proofs. It is not enough to tell us that we cannot disprove such a theory. The burden of proof lies with them. The interstellar ether is something concerning the physical properties of which we have some knowledge; and surely, if all the things are going on which they suppose in a medium so closely related to ordinary matter, there ought to be some traceable indications of the fact. At least, until the contrary can be shown, we must refuse to believe that all the testimony in a case like this is utterly inaccessible; and accordingly, so long as none is found, especially so long as none is even alleged, we feel that a presumption is raised against their theory.

These illustrations will show, by sheer contrast, how different it is with the hypothesis of an unseen world that is purely spiritual. The testimony in such a case must, under the conditions of the present life, be forever inaccessible. It lies wholly outside the range of experience. However abundant it may be, we cannot expect to meet with it. And accordingly our failure to produce it does not raise even the slightest presumption against our theory. When conceived in this way, the belief in a future life is without scientific support; but at the same time it is placed beyond the need of scientific support and beyond the range of scientific criticism. It is a belief which no imaginable future advance in physical discovery can in any way impugn. It is a belief which is in no sense irrational, and which may be logically entertained without in the least affecting our scientific habit of mind or influencing our scientific conclusions.

To take a brief illustration: we have alluded to the fact that in the history of our present world the development of mental phenomena has gone on hand in hand with the development of organic life, while at the same time we have found it impossible to explain mental phenomena as in any sense the product of material phenomena. Now there is another side to all this. The great lesson which Berkeley taught mankind was that what we call material phenomena are really the products of consciousness co-operating with some Unknown Power (not material) existing beyond consciousness. We do very well to speak of "matter" in common parlance, but all that the word really means is a group of qualities which have no existence apart from our minds. Modern philosophers have quite generally accepted this conclusion, and every attempt to overturn Berkeley's reasoning has hitherto resulted in complete and disastrous failure. In admitting this, we do not admit the conclusion of Absolute Idealism, that nothing exists outside of consciousness. What we admit as existing independently of our own consciousness is the Power that causes in us those conscious states which we call the perception of material qualities. We have no reason for regarding this Power as in itself material: indeed, we cannot do so, since by the theory material qualities have no existence apart from our minds. I have elsewhere sought to show that less difficulty is involved in regarding this Power outside of us as quasi-psychical, or in some measure similar to the mental part of ourselves; and I have gone on to conclude that this Power may be identical with what men have, in all times and by the aid of various imperfect symbols, endeavoured to apprehend as Deity.[12] We are thus led to a view of things not very unlike the views entertained by Spinoza and Berkeley.

---

[12] See my Outlines of Cosmic Philosophy, Part I. Chap. IV.; Part III. Chaps. III., IV.

We are led to the inference that what we call the material universe is but the manifestation of infinite Deity to our finite minds. Obviously, on this view, Matter—the only thing to which materialists concede real existence—is simply an orderly phantasmagoria; and God and the Soul—which materialists regard as mere fictions of the imagination—are the only conceptions that answer to real existences.

In the foregoing paragraph I have been setting down opinions with which I am prepared to agree, and which are not in conflict with anything that our study of the development of the objective world has taught us. In so far as that study may be supposed to bear on the question of a future life, two conclusions are open to us. First we may say that since the phenomena of mind appear and run their course along with certain specialized groups of material phenomena, so, too, they must disappear when these specialized groups are broken up. Or, in other words, we may say that every living person is an organized whole; consciousness is something which pertains to this organized whole, as music belongs to the harp that is entire; but when the harp is broken it is silent, and when the organized whole of personality falls to pieces consciousness ceases forever. To many well-disciplined minds this conclusion seems irresistible; and doubtless it would be a sound one—a good Baconian conclusion—if we were to admit, with the materialists, that the possibilities of existence are limited by our tiny and ephemeral experience.

But now, supposing some Platonic speculator were to come along and insist upon our leaving room for an alternative conclusion; suppose he were to urge upon us that all this process of material development, with the discovery of which our patient study has been rewarded, may be but the temporary manifestation of relations otherwise unknown between ourselves and the infinite Deity; suppose he were to argue that psychical qualities may be inherent in a spiritual substance which under certain conditions becomes incarnated in matter, to wear it as a perishable garment for a brief season, but presently to cast it off and enter upon the freedom of a larger existence;—what reply should we be bound to make, bearing in mind that the possibilities of existence are in no wise limited by our experience? Obviously we should be bound to admit that in sound philosophy this conclusion is just as likely to be true as the other. We should, indeed, warn him not to call on us to help him to establish it by scientific arguments; and we should remind him that he must not make illicit use of his extra-experiential hypotheses by bringing them into the treatment of scientific questions that lie within the range of experience. In science, for example, we make no use of the conception of a "spiritual substance" (or of a "material substance" either), because we can get along sufficiently well by dealing solely with qualities. But with this general understanding we should feel bound to concede the impregnableness of his main position.

I have supposed this theory only as an illustration, not as a theory which I am prepared to adopt. My present purpose is not to treat as an advocate the question of a future life, but to endeavour to point out what conditions should be observed in treating the question philosophically. It seems to me that a great deal is gained when we have distinctly set before us what are the peculiar conditions of proof in the case of such transcendental questions. We have gained a great deal when we have learned how thoroughly impotent, how truly irrelevant, is physical investigation in the presence of such a question. If we get not much positive satisfaction for our unquiet yearnings, we occupy at any rate a sounder philosophic position when we recognize the limits within which our conclusions, whether positive or negative, are valid.

It seems not improbable that Mr. Mill may have had in mind something like the foregoing considerations when he suggested that there is no reason why one should not entertain the belief in a future life if the belief be necessary to one's spiritual comfort. Perhaps no suggestion in Mr. Mill's richly suggestive posthumous work has been more generally condemned as unphilosophical, on the ground that in matters of belief we must be guided, not by our likes and dislikes, but by the evidence that is accessible. The objection is certainly a sound one so far as it relates to scientific questions where evidence is accessible. To hesitate to adopt a well-supported theory because of some vague preference for a different view is in scientific matters the one unpardonable sin,—a sin which has been only too often committed. Even in matters which lie beyond the range of experience, where evidence is inaccessible, desire is not to be regarded as by itself an adequate basis for belief. But it seems to me that Mr. Mill showed a deeper knowledge of the limitations of scientific method than his critics, when he thus hinted at the possibility of entertaining a belief not amenable to scientific tests. The hypothesis of a purely spiritual unseen world, as above described, is entirely removed from the jurisdiction of physical inquiry, and can only be judged on general considerations of what has been called "moral probability"; and considerations of this sort are likely, in the future as in the past, to possess different values for different minds. He who, on such considerations, entertains a belief in a future life may not demand that his sceptical neighbour shall be convinced by the same considerations; but his neighbour is at the same time estopped from stigmatizing his belief as unphilosophical.

The consideration which must influence most minds in their attitude toward this question, is the craving, almost universally felt, for some teleological solution to the problem of existence. Why we are here now is a question of even profounder interest than whether we are to live hereafter. Unfortunately its solution carries us no less completely beyond the range of experience! The belief that all things are working together for some good end is the most essential expression of religious faith: of all intellectual propositions it is the one most closely related to that emotional yearning for a higher and better life which is the sum and substance of religion. Yet all the treatises on natural theology that have ever been written have barely succeeded in establishing a low degree of scientific probability for this belief. In spite of the eight Bridgewater Treatises, and the "Ninth" beside, dysteleology still holds full half the field as against teleology. Most of this difficulty, however, results from the crude anthropomorphic views which theologians have held concerning God. Once admitting that the Divine attributes may be (as they must be) incommensurably greater than human attributes, our faith that all things are working together for good may remain unimpugned.

To many minds such a faith will seem incompatible with belief in the ultimate destruction of sentiency amid the general doom of the material universe. A good end can have no meaning to us save in relation to consciousness that distinguishes and knows the good from the evil. There could be no better illustration of how we are hemmed in than the very inadequacy of the words with which we try to discuss this subject. Such words have all gained their meanings from human experience, and hence of necessity carry anthropomorphic implications. But we cannot help this. We must think with the symbols with which experience has furnished us; and when we so think, there does seem to be little that is even intellectually satisfying in the awful picture which science shows us, of giant worlds concentrating out of nebulous vapour, developing with prodigious waste of energy into theatres of all that is grand and sacred in spiritual endeavour, clashing and exploding again into dead vapour-balls, only to renew the same toilful process without end,—a senseless bubble-play of Titan forces, with life, love, and aspiration brought forth only to be extinguished. The human mind, however "scientific" its training, must often recoil from the conclusion that this is all; and there are moments when one passionately feels that this cannot be all. On warm June mornings in green country lanes, with sweet pine-odours wafted in the breeze which sighs through the branches, and cloud-shadows flitting over far-off blue mountains, while little birds sing their love-songs, and golden-haired children weave garlands of wild roses; or when in the solemn twilight we listen to wondrous harmonies of Beethoven and Chopin that stir the heart like voices from an unseen world; at such times one feels that the profoundest answer which science can give to our questionings is but a superficial answer after all. At these moments, when the world seems fullest of beauty, one feels most strongly that it is but the harbinger of something else,—that the ceaseless play of phenomena is no mere sport of Titans, but an orderly scene, with its reason for existing, its

"One divine far-off event
To which the whole creation moves."Difficult as it is to disentangle the elements of reasoning that enter into these complex groups of feeling, one may still see, I think, that it is speculative interest in the world, rather than anxious interest in self, that predominates. The desire for immortality in its lowest phase is merely the outcome of the repugnance we feel toward thinking of the final cessation of vigorous vital activity. Such a feeling is naturally strong with healthy people. But in the mood which I have above tried to depict, this feeling, or any other which is merely self-regarding, is lost sight of in the

feeling which associates a future life with some solution of the burdensome problem of existence. Had we but faith enough to lighten the burden of this problem, the inferior question would perhaps be less absorbing. Could we but know that our present lives are working together toward some good end, even an end in no wise anthropomorphic, it would be of less consequence whether we were individually to endure. To the dog under the knife of the experimenter, the world is a world of pure evil; yet could the poor beast but understand the alleviation of human suffering to which he is contributing, he would be forced to own that this is not quite true; and if he were also a heroic or Christian dog, the thought would perhaps take away from death its sting. The analogy may be a crude one; but the reasonableness of the universe is at least as far above our comprehension as the purposes of man surpass the understanding of the dog. Believing, however, though as a simple act of trust, that the end will crown the work, we may rise superior to the question which has here concerned us, and exclaim, in the supreme language of faith, "Though He slay me, yet will I trust in Him!"

July, 1875.

II.

"THE TO-MORROW OF DEATH."

Few of those who find pleasure in frequenting bookstores can have failed to come across one or more of the profusely illustrated volumes in which M. Louis Figuier has sought to render dry science entertaining to the multitude. And of those who may have casually turned over their pages, there are probably none, competent to form an opinion, who have not speedily perceived that these pretentious books belong to the class of pests and unmitigated nuisances in literature. Antiquated views, utter lack of comprehension of the subjects treated, and shameless unscrupulousness as to accuracy of statement, are faults but ill atoned for by sensational pictures of the "dragons of the prime that tare each other in their slime," or of the Newton-like brow and silken curls of that primitive man in contrast with whom the said dragons have been likened to "mellow music."

Nevertheless, the sort of scientific reputation which these discreditable performances have gained for M. Figuier among an uncritical public is such as to justify us in devoting a few paragraphs to a book[13] which, on its own merits, is unworthy of any notice whatever. "The To-morrow of Death"—if one were to put his trust in the translator's prefatory note—discusses a grave question upon "purely scientific methods." We are glad to see this remark, because it shows what notions may be entertained by persons of average intelligence with reference to "scientific methods." Those—and they are many—who vaguely think that science is something different from common-sense, and that any book is scientific which talks about perihelia and asymptotes and cetacea, will find their vague notions here well corroborated. Quite different will be the impression made upon those—and they are yet too few—who have learned that the method of science is the common-sense method of cautiously weighing evidence and withholding judgment where evidence is not forthcoming. If talking about remote and difficult subjects suffice to make one scientific, then is M. Figuier scientific to a quite terrible degree. He writes about the starry heavens as if he had been present at the hour of creation, or had at least accompanied the Arabian prophet on his famous night-journey. Nor is his knowledge of physiology and other abstruse sciences at all less remarkable. But these things will cease to surprise us when we learn the sources, hitherto suspected only in mythology, from which favoured mortals can obtain a knowledge of what is going on outside of our planet.

The four inner planets being nearly alike in size (?) and in length of day, M. Figuier infers, by strictly scientific methods, that whatever is true of one of

---

[13] The To-morrow of Death; or, The Future Life according to Science. By Louis Figuier. Translated from the French by S. R. Crocker. Boston: Roberts Brothers. 1872.

them, as our earth, will be true of the others (p. 34). Hence, they are all inhabited by human beings. It is true that human beings must find Venus rather warm, and are not unlikely to be seriously incommoded by the tropical climate of Mercury. But we must remember that "the men of Venus and Mercury are made by nature to resist heat, as those of Jupiter and Saturn are made to endure cold, and those of the Earth and Mars to live in a mean temperature: OTHERWISE THEY COULD NOT EXIST" (p. 72). In view of this charming specimen of a truly scientific inference, it is almost too bad to call attention to the fact that M. Figuier is quite behind the age in his statement of facts. So far from Jupiter and Saturn being cold, observation plainly indicates that they are prodigiously hot, if not even incandescent and partly self-luminous; the explanation being that, by reason of their huge bulk, they still retain much of the primitive heat which smaller planets have more quickly radiated away. As for M. Figuier's statement, that polar snows have been witnessed on these planets, it is simply untrue; no such thing has ever been seen there. Mars, on the other hand, has been observed to resemble in many important respects its near neighbour, the Earth; whence our author declares that if an aeronaut were to shoot clear of terrestrial gravitation and land upon Mars, he would unquestionably suppose himself to be still upon the earth. For aerolites, it seems, are somehow fired down upon our planet both from Mars and from Venus; and aerolites sometimes contain vegetable matter (?). Therefore, Mars has a vegetation, and very likely its red colour is caused by its luxuriant autumnal foliage! (p. 47.) To return to Jupiter: this planet, indeed, has inconveniently short days. "In his 'Picture of the Heavens,' the German astronomer, Littrow (these Germans think of nothing but gormandizing), asks how the people of Jupiter order their meals in the short interval of five hours." Nevertheless, says our author, the great planet is compensated for this inconvenience by its equable and delicious climate.

In view, however, of our author's more striking and original disclosures, one would suppose that all this discussion of the physical conditions of existence on the various planets might have been passed over without detriment to the argument. After these efforts at proving (for M. Figuier presumably regards this rigmarole as proof) that all the members of our solar system are habitable, the interplanetary ether is forthwith peopled thickly with "souls," without any resort to argument. This, we suppose, is one of those scientific truths which as M. Figuier tells us, precede and underlie demonstration. Upon this impregnable basis is reared the scientific theory of a future life. When we die our soul passes into some other terrestrial body, unless we have been very good, in which case we at once soar aloft and join the noble fraternity of the ether-folk. Bad men and young children, on dying, must undergo renewed probation here below, but ultimately all pass away into the interplanetary ether. The dweller in ether is chiefly distinguished from the mundane mortal by his acute senses and his ability to subsist without food. He can see as if through a telescope and microscope combined. His intelligence is so great that in comparison an Aristotle would seem idiotic. It should not be forgotten, too, that he possesses eighty-five per cent of soul to fifteen per cent of body, whereas in terrestrial man the two elements are mixed in equal proportions. There is no sex among the ether-folk, their numbers being kept up by the influx of souls from the various planets. "Alimentation, that necessity which tyrannizes over men and animals, is not imposed upon the inhabitants of ether. Their bodies must be repaired and sustained by the simple respiration of the fluid in which they are immersed, that is, of ether." Most likely, continues our scientific author, the physiological functions of the ether-folk are confined to respiration, and that it is possible to breathe "without numerous organs is proved by the fact that in all of a whole class of animals—the batrachians—the mere bare skin constitutes the whole machinery of respiration" (p. 95). Allowing for the unfortunate slip of the pen by which "batrachians" are substituted for "fresh-water polyps," how can we fail to admire the severity of the scientific method employed in reaching these interesting conclusions?

But the King of Serendib must die, nor will the relentless scythe of Time spare our Etherians, with all their exalted attributes. They will die repeatedly; and after having through sundry periods of probation attained spiritual perfection, they will all pour into the sun. Since it is the sun which originates life and feeling and thought upon the surface of our earth, "why may we not declare that the rays transmitted by the sun to the earth and the other planets are nothing more nor less than the emanations of these souls?" And now we may begin to form an adequate conception, of the rigorously scientific character of our author's method. There have been many hypotheses by which to account for the supply of solar radiance. One of the most ingenious and probable of these hypotheses is that of Helmholtz, according to which the solar radiance is due to the arrested motion of the sun's constituent particles toward their common centre of gravity. But this is too fanciful to satisfy M. Figuier. The speculations of Helmholtz "have the disadvantage of resting on the idea of the sun's nebulosity,—an hypothesis which would need to be more closely examined before serving as a basis for so important a deduction." Accordingly, M. Figuier propounds an explanation which possesses the signal advantage that there is nothing hypothetical in it. "In our opinion, the solar radiation is sustained by the continual influx of souls into the sun." This, as the reader will perceive, is the well-known theory of Mayer, that the solar heat is due to a perennial bombardment of the sun by meteors, save that, in place of gross materialistic meteors, M. Figuier puts ethereal souls. The ether-folk are daily raining into the solar orb in untold millions, and to the unceasing concussion is due the radiation which maintains life in the planets, and thus the circle is complete.

In spite of their exalted position, the ether-folk do not disdain to mingle with the affairs of terrestrial mortals. They give us counsel in dreams, and it is from this source, we presume, that our author has derived his rigid notions as to scientific method. In evidence of this dream-theory we have the usual array of cases, "a celebrated journalist, M. R———," "M. L———, a lawyer," etc., etc., as in most books of this kind.

M. Figuier is not a Darwinian: the derivation of our bodies from the bodies of apes is a conception too grossly materialistic for him. Our souls, however, he is quite willing to derive from the souls of lower animals. Obviously we have pre-existed; how are we to account for Mozart's precocity save by supposing his pre-existence? He brought with him the musical skill acquired in a previous life. In general, the souls of musical children come from nightingales, while the souls of great architects have passed into them from beavers (p. 247). We do not remember these past existences, it is true; but when we become ether-folk, we shall be able to look back in recollection over the whole series.

Amid these sublime inquiries, M. Figuier is sometimes notably oblivious of humbler truths, as might indeed be expected. Thus he repeatedly alludes to Locke as the author of the doctrine of innate ideas (!!),[14] and he informs us that Kepler never quitted Protestant England (p. 336), though we believe that the nearest Kepler ever came to living in England was the refusing of Sir Henry Wotton's request that he should move thither.

And lastly, we are treated to a real dialogue, with quite a dramatic mise en scene. The author's imaginary friend, Theophilus, enters, "seats himself in a comfortable chair, places an ottoman under his feet, a book under his elbow to support it, and a cigarette of Turkish tobacco between his lips, and sets himself to the task of listening with a grave air of collectedness, relieved by a certain touch of suspicious severity, as becomes the arbiter in a literary and philosophic matter." "And so," begins our author, "you wish to know, my dear Theophilus, WHERE I LOCATE GOD? I locate him in the centre of the universe, or, in better phrase, at the central focus, which must exist somewhere, of all the stars that make the universe, and which, borne onward in a common movement, gravitate together around this focus."

Much more, of an equally scientific character, follows; but in fairness to the reader, who is already blaming us for wasting the precious moments over such sorry trash, we may as well conclude our sketch of this new line of speculation.

May, 1872.

---

[14] Pages 251, 252, 287. So in the twenty-first century some avatar of M. Figuier will perhaps describe the late professor Agassiz as the author of the Darwinian theory.

III.

THE JESUS OF HISTORY.[15]

Vie de Jesus, par Ernest Renan. Paris, 1867. (Thirteenth edition, revised and partly rewritten.) In republishing this and the following article on "The Christ of Dogma," I am aware that they do but scanty justice to their very interesting subjects. So much ground is covered that it would be impossible to treat it satisfactorily in a pair of review-articles; and in particular the views adopted with regard to the New Testament literature are rather indicated than justified. These defects I hope to remedy in a future work on "Jesus of Nazareth, and the Founding of Christianity," for which the present articles must be regarded as furnishing only a few introductory hints. This work has been for several years on my mind, but as it may still be long before I can find the leisure needful for writing it out, it seemed best to republish these preliminary sketches which have been some time out of print. The projected work, however, while covering all the points here treated, will have a much wider scope, dealing on the one hand with the natural genesis of the complex aggregate of beliefs and aspirations known as Christianity, and on the other hand with the metamorphoses which are being wrought in this aggregate by modern knowledge and modern theories of the world.

The views adopted in the present essay as to the date of the Synoptic Gospels may seem over-conservative to those who accept the ably-argued conclusions of "Supernatural Religion." Quite possibly in a more detailed discussion these briefly-indicated data may require revision; but for the present it seems best to let the article stand as it was written. The author of "Supernatural Religion" would no doubt admit that, even if the synoptic gospels had not assumed their present form before the end of the second century, nevertheless the body of tradition contained in them had been committed to writing very early in that century. So much appears to be proved by the very variations of text upon which his argument relies. And if this be granted, the value of the synoptics as HISTORICAL evidence is not materially altered. With their value as testimony to so-called SUPERNATURAL events, the present essay is in no way concerned.

Of all the great founders of religions, Jesus is at once the best known and the least known to the modern scholar. From the dogmatic point of view he is the best known, from the historic point of view he is the least known. The Christ of dogma is in every lineament familiar to us from early childhood; but concerning the Jesus of history we possess but few facts resting upon trustworthy evidence, and in order to form a picture of him at once consistent, probable, and distinct in its outlines, it is necessary to enter upon a long and

---

[15] The Jesus of History. Anonymous. 8vo. pp. 426. London: Williams & Norgate, 1869.

difficult investigation, in the course of which some of the most delicate apparatus of modern criticism is required. This circumstance is sufficiently singular to require especial explanation. The case of Sakyamuni, the founder of Buddhism, which may perhaps be cited as parallel, is in reality wholly different. Not only did Sakyamuni live five centuries earlier than Jesus, among a people that have at no time possessed the art of insuring authenticity in their records of events, and at an era which is at best but dimly discerned through the mists of fable and legend, but the work which he achieved lies wholly out of the course of European history, and it is only in recent times that his career has presented itself to us as a problem needing to be solved. Jesus, on the other hand, appeared in an age which is familiarly and in many respects minutely known to us, and among a people whose fortunes we can trace with historic certainty for at least seven centuries previous to his birth; while his life and achievements have probably had a larger share in directing the entire subsequent intellectual and moral development of Europe than those of any other man who has ever lived. Nevertheless, the details of his personal career are shrouded in an obscurity almost as dense as that which envelops the life of the remote founder of Buddhism.

This phenomenon, however, appears less strange and paradoxical when we come to examine it more closely. A little reflection will disclose to us several good reasons why the historical records of the life of Jesus should be so scanty as they are. In the first place, the activity of Jesus was private rather than public. Confined within exceedingly narrow limits, both of space and of duration, it made no impression whatever upon the politics or the literature of the time. His name does not occur in the pages of any contemporary writer, Roman, Greek, or Jewish. Doubtless the case would have been wholly different, had he, like Mohammed, lived to a ripe age, and had the exigencies of his peculiar position as the Messiah of the Jewish people brought him into relations with the Empire; though whether, in such case, the success of his grand undertaking would have been as complete as it has actually been, may well be doubted.

Secondly, Jesus did not, like Mohammed and Paul, leave behind him authentic writings which might serve to throw light upon his mental development as well as upon the external facts of his career. Without the Koran and the four genuine Epistles of Paul, we should be nearly as much in the dark concerning these great men as we now are concerning the historical Jesus. We should be compelled to rely, in the one case, upon the untrustworthy gossip of Mussulman chroniclers, and in the other case upon the garbled statements of the "Acts of the Apostles," a book written with a distinct dogmatic purpose, sixty or seventy years after the occurrence of the events which it professes to record.

It is true, many of the words of Jesus, preserved by hearsay tradition through the generation immediately succeeding his death, have come down to us, probably with little alteration, in the pages of the three earlier evangelists.

These are priceless data, since, as we shall see, they are almost the only materials at our command for forming even a partial conception of the character of Jesus' work. Nevertheless, even here the cautious inquirer has only too often to pause in face of the difficulty of distinguishing the authentic utterances of the great teacher from the later interpolations suggested by the dogmatic necessities of the narrators. Bitterly must the historian regret that Jesus had no philosophic disciple, like Xenophon, to record his Memorabilia. Of the various writings included in the New Testament, the Apocalypse alone (and possibly the Epistle of Jude) is from the pen of a personal acquaintance of Jesus; and besides this, the four epistles of Paul, to the Galatians, Corinthians, and Romans, make up the sum of the writings from which we may expect contemporary testimony. Yet from these we obtain absolutely nothing of that for which we are seeking. The brief writings of Paul are occupied exclusively with the internal significance of Jesus' work. The epistle of Jude—if it be really written by Jesus' brother of that name, which is doubtful—is solely a polemic directed against the innovations of Paul. And the Apocalypse, the work of the fiery and imaginative disciple John, is confined to a prophetic description of the Messiah's anticipated return, and tells us nothing concerning the deeds of that Messiah while on the earth.

Here we touch upon our third consideration,—the consideration which best enables us to see why the historic notices of Jesus are so meagre. Rightly considered, the statement with which we opened this article is its own explanation. The Jesus of history is so little known just because the Christ of dogma is so well known.[16] Other teachers—Paul, Mohammed, Sakyamuni—have come merely as preachers of righteousness, speaking in the name of general principles with which their own personalities were not directly implicated. But Jesus, as we shall see, before the close of his life, proclaimed himself to be something more than a preacher of righteousness. He announced himself—and justly, from his own point of view—as the long-expected Messiah sent by Jehovah to liberate the Jewish race. Thus the success of his religious teachings became at once implicated with the question of his personal nature and character. After the sudden and violent termination of his career, it immediately became all-important with his followers to prove that he was really the Messiah, and to insist upon the certainty of his speedy return to the earth. Thus the first generation of disciples dogmatized about him, instead of narrating his life,—a task which to them would have seemed of little profit. For them the all-absorbing object of contemplation was the immediate future rather than the immediate past. As all the earlier Christian literature informs us, for nearly a century after the death of Jesus, his followers lived in daily anticipation of his triumphant return to the earth. The end of all things being so near at hand, no attempt was made to insure accurate and complete memoirs

---

[16] "Wer einmal vergottert worden ist, der hat seine Mensetheit unwiederbringlich eingebusst."—Strauss, Der alte und der neue Glaube, p. 76.

for the use of a posterity which was destined, in Christian imagination, never to arrive. The first Christians wrote but little; even Papias, at the end of a century, preferring second-hand or third-hand oral tradition to the written gospels which were then beginning to come into circulation.[17] Memoirs of the life and teachings of Jesus were called forth by the necessity of having a written standard of doctrine to which to appeal amid the growing differences of opinion which disturbed the Church. Thus the earlier gospels exhibit, though in different degrees, the indications of a modifying, sometimes of an overruling dogmatic purpose. There is, indeed, no conscious violation of historic truth, but from the varied mass of material supplied by tradition, such incidents are selected as are fit to support the views of the writers concerning the personality of Jesus. Accordingly, while the early gospels throw a strong light upon the state of Christian opinion at the dates when they were successively composed, the information which they give concerning Jesus himself is, for that very reason, often vague, uncritical, and contradictory. Still more is this true of the fourth gospel, written late in the second century, in which historic tradition is moulded in the interests of dogma until it becomes no longer recognizable, and in the place of the human Messiah of the earlier accounts, we have a semi-divine Logos or Aeon, detached from God, and incarnate for a brief season in the likeness of man.

Not only was history subordinated to dogma by the writers of the gospel-narratives, but in the minds of the Fathers of the Church who assisted in determining what writings should be considered canonical, dogmatic prepossession went very much further than critical acumen. Nor is this strange when we reflect that critical discrimination in questions of literary authenticity is one of the latest acquisitions of the cultivated human mind. In the early ages of the Church the evidence of the genuineness of any literary production was never weighed critically; writings containing doctrines acceptable to the majority of Christians were quoted as authoritative while writings which supplied no dogmatic want were overlooked, or perhaps condemned as apocryphal. A striking instance of this is furnished by the fortunes of the Apocalypse. Although perhaps the best authenticated work in the New Testament collection, its millenarian doctrines caused it to become unpopular as the Church gradually ceased to look for the speedy return of the Messiah, and, accordingly, as the canon assumed a definite shape, it was placed among the "Antilegomena," or doubtful books, and continued to hold a precarious position until after the time of the Protestant Reformation. On the other hand, the fourth gospel, which was quite unknown and probably did not exist at the time of the Quartodeciman controversy (A. D. 168), was accepted with little

---

[17] "Roger was the attendant of Thomas [Becket] during his sojourn at Pontigny. We might have expected him to be very full on that part of his history; but, writing doubtless mainly for the monks of Pontigny, he says that HE WILL NOT ENLARGE UPON WHAT EVERY ONE KNOWS, and cuts that part very short."—Freeman, Historical Essays, 1st series, p. 90.

hesitation, and at the beginning of the third century is mentioned by Irenaeus, Clement, and Tertullian, as the work of the Apostle John. To this uncritical spirit, leading to the neglect of such books as failed to answer the dogmatic requirements of the Church, may probably be attributed the loss of so many of the earlier gospels. It is doubtless for this reason that we do not possess the Aramaean original of the "Logia" of Matthew, or the "Memorabilia" of Mark, the companion of Peter,—two works to which Papias (A. D. 120) alludes as containing authentic reports of the utterances of Jesus.

These considerations will, we believe, sufficiently explain the curious circumstance that, while we know the Christ of dogma so intimately, we know the Jesus of history so slightly. The literature of early Christianity enables us to trace with tolerable completeness the progress of opinion concerning the nature of Jesus, from the time of Paul's early missions to the time of the Nicene Council; but upon the actual words and deeds of Jesus it throws a very unsteady light. The dogmatic purpose everywhere obscures the historic basis.

This same dogmatic prepossession which has rendered the data for a biography of Jesus so scanty and untrustworthy, has also until comparatively recent times prevented any unbiassed critical examination of such data as we actually possess. Previous to the eighteenth century any attempt to deal with the life of Jesus upon purely historical methods would have been not only contemned as irrational, but stigmatized as impious. And even in the eighteenth century, those writers who had become wholly emancipated from ecclesiastic tradition were so destitute of all historic sympathy and so unskilled in scientific methods of criticism, that they utterly failed to comprehend the requirements of the problem. Their aims were in the main polemic, not historical. They thought more of overthrowing current dogmas than of impartially examining the earliest Christian literature with a view of eliciting its historic contents; and, accordingly, they accomplished but little. Two brilliant exceptions must, however, be noticed. Spinoza, in the seventeenth century, and Lessing, in the eighteenth, were men far in advance of their age. They are the fathers of modern historical criticism; and to Lessing in particular, with his enormous erudition and incomparable sagacity, belongs the honour of initiating that method of inquiry which, in the hands of the so-called Tubingen School, has led to such striking and valuable conclusions concerning, the age and character of all the New Testament literature. But it was long before any one could be found fit to bend the bow which Lessing and Spinoza had wielded. A succession of able scholars—Semler, Eichhorn, Paulus, Schleiermacher Bretschneider, and De Wette—were required to examine, with German patience and accuracy, the details of the subject, and to propound various untenable hypotheses, before such a work could be performed as that of Strauss. The "Life of Jesus," published by Strauss when only twenty-six years of age, is one of the monumental works of the nineteenth century, worthy to rank, as a historical effort, along with such books as Niebuhr's "History of Rome," Wolf's "Prolegomena," or Bentley's "Dissertations on Phalaris." It instantly superseded and rendered antiquated everything which had preceded it; nor has any work on early Christianity been written in Germany for the past thirty years which has not been dominated by the recollection of that marvellous book. Nevertheless, the labours of another generation of scholars have carried our knowledge of the New Testament literature far beyond the point which it had reached when Strauss first wrote. At that time the dates of but few of the New Testament writings had been fixed with any approach to certainty; the age and character of the fourth gospel, the genuineness of the Pauline epistles, even the mutual relations of the three synoptics, were still undetermined; and, as a natural result of this uncertainty, the progress of dogma during the first century was ill understood. At the present day it is impossible to read the early work of Strauss without being impressed with the necessity of obtaining positive data as to the origin and dogmatic character of the New Testament writings, before attempting to reach any conclusions as to the probable career of Jesus. These positive data we owe to the genius and diligence of the Tubingen School, and, above all, to its founder, Ferdinand Christian Baur. Beginning with the epistles of Paul, of which he distinguished four as genuine, Baur gradually worked his way through the entire New Testament collection, detecting—with that inspired insight which only unflinching diligence can impart to original genius—the age at which each book was written, and the circumstances which called it forth. To give any account of Baur's detailed conclusions, or of the method by which he reached them, would require a volume. They are very scantily presented in Mr. Mackay's work on the "Tubingen School and its Antecedents," to which we may refer the reader desirous of further information. We can here merely say that twenty years of energetic controversy have only served to establish most of Baur's leading conclusions more firmly than ever. The priority of the so-called gospel of Matthew, the Pauline purpose of "Luke," the second in date of our gospels, the derivative and second-hand character of "Mark," and the unapostolic origin of the fourth gospel, are points which may for the future be regarded as wellnigh established by circumstantial evidence. So with respect to the pseudo-Pauline epistles, Baur's work was done so thoroughly that the only question still left open for much discussion is that concerning the date and authorship of the first and second "Thessalonians,"—a point of quite inferior importance, so far as our present subject is concerned. Seldom have such vast results been achieved by the labour of a single scholar. Seldom has any historical critic possessed such a combination of analytic and of co-ordinating powers as Baur. His keen criticism and his wonderful flashes of insight exercise upon the reader a truly poetic effect like that which is felt in contemplating the marvels of physical discovery.

  The comprehensive labours of Baur were followed up by Zeller's able work on the "Acts of the Apostles," in which that book was shown to have been partly founded upon documents written by Luke, or some other companion of Paul, and expanded and modified by a much later writer with the purpose of covering up the traces of the early schism between the Pauline and the Petrine sections of the Church. Along with this, Schwegler's work on the "Post-Apostolic Times" deserves mention as clearing up many obscure points relating to the early development of dogma. Finally, the "New Life of Jesus," by Strauss, adopting and utilizing the principal discoveries of Baur and his followers, and combining all into one grand historical picture, worthily completes the task which the earlier work of the same author had inaugurated.

The reader will have noticed that, with the exception of Spinoza, every one of the names above cited in connection with the literary analysis and criticism of the New Testament is the name of a German. Until within the last decade, Germany has indeed possessed almost an absolute monopoly of the science of Biblical criticism; other countries having remained not only unfamiliar with its methods, but even grossly ignorant of its conspicuous results, save when some German treatise of more than ordinary popularity has now and then been translated. But during the past ten years France has entered the lists; and the writings of Reville, Reuss, Nicolas, D'Eichthal, Scherer, and Colani testify to the rapidity with which the German seed has fructified upon her soil.[18]

None of these books, however, has achieved such wide-spread celebrity, or done so much toward interesting the general public in this class of historical inquiries, as the "Life of Jesus," by Renan. This pre-eminence of fame is partly, but not wholly, deserved. From a purely literary point of view, Renan's work doubtless merits all the celebrity it has gained. Its author writes a style such as is perhaps surpassed by that of no other living Frenchman. It is by far the most readable book which has ever been written concerning the life of Jesus. And no doubt some of its popularity is due to its very faults, which, from a critical point of view, are neither few nor small. For Renan is certainly very faulty, as a historical critic, when he practically ignores the extreme meagreness of our positive knowledge of the career of Jesus, and describes scene after scene in his life as minutely and with as much confidence as if he had himself been present to witness it all. Again and again the critical reader feels prompted to ask, How do you know all this? or why, out of two or three conflicting accounts, do you quietly adopt some particular one, as if its superior authority were self-evident? But in the eye of the uncritical reader, these defects are excellences; for it is unpleasant to be kept in ignorance when we are seeking after definite knowledge, and it is disheartening to read page after page of an elaborate discussion which ends in convincing us that definite knowledge cannot be gained.

In the thirteenth edition of the "Vie de Jesus," Renan has corrected some of the most striking errors of the original work, and in particular has, with praiseworthy candour, abandoned his untenable position with regard to the age

---

[18] But now, in annexing Alsace, Germany has "annexed" pretty much the whole of this department of French scholarship,—a curious incidental consequence of the late war.

and character of the fourth gospel. As is well known, Renan, in his earlier editions, ascribed to this gospel a historical value superior to that of the synoptics, believing it to have been written by an eyewitness of the events which it relates; and from this source, accordingly, he drew the larger share of his materials. Now, if there is any one conclusion concerning the New Testament literature which must be regarded as incontrovertibly established by the labours of a whole generation of scholars, it is this, that the fourth gospel was utterly unknown until about A. D. 170, that it was written by some one who possessed very little direct knowledge of Palestine, that its purpose was rather to expound a dogma than to give an accurate record of events, and that as a guide to the comprehension of the career of Jesus it is of far less value than the three synoptic gospels. It is impossible, in a brief review like the present, to epitomize the evidence upon which this conclusion rests, which may more profitably be sought in the Rev. J. J. Tayler's work on "The Fourth Gospel," or in Davidson's "Introduction to the New Testament." It must suffice to mention that this gospel is not cited by Papias; that Justin, Marcion, and Valentinus make no allusion to it, though, since it furnishes so much that is germane to their views, they would gladly have appealed to it, had it been in existence, when those views were as yet under discussion; and that, finally, in the great Quartodeciman controversy, A. D. 168, the gospel is not only not mentioned, but the authority of John is cited by Polycarp in flat contradiction of the view afterwards taken by this evangelist. Still more, the assumption of Renan led at once into complicated difficulties with reference to the Apocalypse. The fourth gospel, if it does not unmistakably announce itself as the work of John, at least professes to be Johannine; and it cannot for a moment be supposed that such a book, making such claims, could have gained currency during John's lifetime without calling forth his indignant protest. For, in reality, no book in the New Testament collection would so completely have shocked the prejudices of the Johannine party. John's own views are well known to us from the Apocalypse. John was the most enthusiastic of millenarians and the most narrow and rigid of Judaizers. In his antagonism to the Pauline innovations he went farther than Peter himself. Intense hatred of Paul and his followers appears in several passages of the Apocalypse, where they are stigmatized as "Nicolaitans," "deceivers of the people," "those who say they are apostles and are not," "eaters of meat offered to idols," "fornicators," "pretended Jews," "liars," "synagogue of Satan," etc. (Chap. II.). On the other hand, the fourth gospel contains nothing millenarian or Judaical; it carries Pauline universalism to a far greater extent than Paul himself ventured to carry it, even condemning the Jews as children of darkness, and by implication contrasting them unfavourably with the Gentiles; and it contains a theory of the nature of Jesus which the Ebionitish Christians, to whom John belonged, rejected to the last.

In his present edition Renan admits the insuperable force of these objections, and abandons his theory of the apostolic origin of the fourth gospel.

And as this has necessitated the omission or alteration of all such passages as rested upon the authority of that gospel, the book is to a considerable extent rewritten, and the changes are such as greatly to increase its value as a history of Jesus. Nevertheless, the author has so long been in the habit of shaping his conceptions of the career of Jesus by the aid of the fourth gospel, that it has become very difficult for him to pass freely to another point of view. He still clings to the hypothesis that there is an element of historic tradition contained in the book, drawn from memorial writings which had perhaps been handed down from John, and which were inaccessible to the synoptists. In a very interesting appendix, he collects the evidence in favour of this hypothesis, which indeed is not without plausibility, since there is every reason for supposing that the gospel was written at Ephesus, which a century before had been John's place of residence. But even granting most of Renan's assumptions, it must still follow that the authority of this gospel is far inferior to that of the synoptics, and can in no case be very confidently appealed to. The question is one of the first importance to the historian of early Christianity. In inquiring into the life of Jesus, the very first thing to do is to establish firmly in the mind the true relations of the fourth gospel to the first three. Until this has been done, no one is competent to write on the subject; and it is because he has done this so imperfectly, that Renan's work is, from a critical point of view, so imperfectly successful.

The anonymous work entitled "The Jesus of History," which we have placed at the head of this article, is in every respect noteworthy as the first systematic attempt made in England to follow in the footsteps of German criticism in writing a life of Jesus. We know of no good reason why the book should be published anonymously; for as a historical essay it possesses extraordinary merit, and does great credit not only to its author, but to English scholarship and acumen.[19] It is not, indeed, a book calculated to captivate the imagination of the reading public. Though written in a clear, forcible, and often elegant style, it possesses no such wonderful rhetorical charm as the work of Renan; and it will probably never find half a dozen readers where the "Vie de Jesus" has found a hundred. But the success of a book of this sort is not to be measured by its rhetorical excellence, or by its adaptation to the literary tastes of an uncritical and uninstructed public, but rather by the amount of critical sagacity which it brings to bear upon the elucidation of the many difficult and disputed points in the subject of which it treats. Measured by this standard, "The Jesus of History" must rank very high indeed. To say that it throws more light upon the career of Jesus than any work which has ever before been written in English would be very inadequate praise, since the English language has been singularly deficient in this branch of historical literature. We shall convey a more just idea of its merits if we say that it will

---

[19] "The Jesus of History" is now known to have been written by Sir Richard Hanson, Chief Justice of South Australia.

bear comparison with anything which even Germany has produced, save only the works of Strauss, Baur, and Zeller.

The fitness of our author for the task which he has undertaken is shown at the outset by his choice of materials. In basing his conclusions almost exclusively upon the statements contained in the first gospel, he is upheld by every sound principle of criticism. The times and places at which our three synoptic gospels were written have been, through the labours of the Tubingen critics, determined almost to a certainty. Of the three, "Mark" is unquestionably the latest; with the exception of about twenty verses, it is entirely made up from "Matthew" and "Luke," the diverse Petrine and Pauline tendencies of which it strives to neutralize in conformity to the conciliatory disposition of the Church at Rome, at the epoch at which this gospel was written, about A. D. 130. The third gospel was also written at Rome, some fifteen years earlier. In the preface, its author describes it as a compilation from previously existing written materials. Among these materials was certainly the first gospel, several passages of which are adopted word for word by the author of "Luke." Yet the narrative varies materially from that of the first gospel in many essential points. The arrangement of events is less natural, and, as in the "Acts of the Apostles," by the same author, there is apparent throughout the design of suppressing the old discord between Paul and the Judaizing disciples, and of representing Christianity as essentially Pauline from the outset. How far Paul was correct in his interpretation of the teachings of Jesus, it is difficult to decide. It is, no doubt, possible that the first gospel may have lent to the words of Jesus an Ebionite colouring in some instances, and that now and then the third gospel may present us with a truer account. To this supremely important point we shall by and by return. For the present it must suffice to observe that the evidences of an overruling dogmatic purpose are generally much more conspicuous in the third synoptist than in the first; and that the very loose manner in which this writer has handled his materials in the "Acts" is not calculated to inspire us with confidence in the historical accuracy of his gospel. The writer who, in spite of the direct testimony of Paul himself could represent the apostle to the Gentiles as acting under the direction of the disciples at Jerusalem, and who puts Pauline sentiments into the mouth of Peter, would certainly have been capable of unwarrantably giving a Pauline turn to the teachings of Jesus himself. We are therefore, as a last resort, brought back to the first gospel, which we find to possess, as a historical narrative, far stronger claims upon our attention than the second and third. In all probability it had assumed nearly its present shape before A. D. 100, its origin is unmistakably Palestinian; it betrays comparatively few indications of dogmatic purpose; and there are strong reasons for believing that the speeches of Jesus recorded in it are in substance taken from the genuine "Logia" of Matthew mentioned by Papias, which must have been written as early as A. D. 60-70, before the destruction of Jerusalem. Indeed, we are inclined to agree with our author that the gospel, even in its present shape (save only a few interpolated passages), may have existed as early as A. D. 80, since it places the time of Jesus' second coming immediately after the destruction of Jerusalem; whereas the third evangelist, who wrote forty-five years after that event, is careful to tell us, "The end is NOT immediately." Moreover, it must have been written while the Paulo-Petrine controversy was still raging, as is shown by the parable of the "enemy who sowed the tares," which manifestly refers to Paul, and also by the allusions to "false prophets" (vii. 15), to those who say "Lord, Lord," and who "cast out demons in the name of the Lord" (vii. 21-23), teaching men to break the commandments (v. 17-20). There is, therefore, good reason for believing that we have here a narrative written not much more than fifty years after the death of Jesus, based partly upon the written memorials of an apostle, and in the main trustworthy, save where it relates occurrences of a marvellous and legendary character. Such is our author's conclusion, and in describing the career of the Jesus of history, he relies almost exclusively upon the statements contained in the first gospel. Let us now after this long but inadequate introduction, give a brief sketch of the life of Jesus, as it is to be found in our author.

Concerning the time and place of the birth of Jesus, we know next to nothing. According to uniform tradition, based upon a statement of the third gospel, he was about thirty years of age at the time when he began teaching. The same gospel states, with elaborate precision, that the public career of John the Baptist began in the fifteenth year of Tiberius, or A. D. 28. In the winter of A. D. 35-36, Pontius Pilate was recalled from Judaea, so that the crucifixion could not have taken place later than in the spring of 35. Thus we have a period of about six years during which the ministry of Jesus must have begun and ended; and if the tradition with respect to his age be trustworthy, we shall not be far out of the way in supposing him to have been born somewhere between B. C. 5 and A. D. 5. He is everywhere alluded to in the gospels as Jesus of Nazareth in Galilee, where lived also his father, mother brothers and sisters, and where very likely he was born. His parents' names are said to have been Joseph and Mary. His own name is a Hellenized form of Joshua, a name very common among the Jews. According to the first gospel (xiii. 55), he had four brothers,—Joseph and Simon; James, who was afterwards one of the heads of the church at Jerusalem, and the most formidable enemy of Paul; and Judas or Jude, who is perhaps the author of the anti-Pauline epistle commonly ascribed to him.

Of the early youth of Jesus, and of the circumstances which guided his intellectual development, we know absolutely nothing, nor have we the data requisite for forming any plausible hypothesis. He first appears in history about A. D. 29 or 30, in connection with a very remarkable person whom the third evangelist describes as his cousin, and who seems, from his mode of life, to have been in some way connected with or influenced by the Hellenizing sect of Essenes. Here we obtain our first clew to guide us in forming a consecutive theory of the development of Jesus' opinions. The sect of Essenes took its rise in the time of the Maccabees, about B. C. 170. Upon the fundamental doctrines of Judaism it had engrafted many Pythagorean notions, and was doubtless in the time of Jesus instrumental in spreading Greek ideas among the people of Galilee, where Judaism was far from being so narrow and rigid as at Jerusalem. The Essenes attached but little importance to the Messianic expectations of the Pharisees, and mingled scarcely at all in national politics. They lived for the most part a strictly ascetic life, being indeed the legitimate predecessors of the early Christian hermits and monks. But while pre-eminent for sanctity of life, they heaped ridicule upon the entire sacrificial service of the Temple, despised the Pharisees as hypocrites, and insisted upon charity toward all men instead of the old Jewish exclusiveness.

It was once a favourite theory that both John the Baptist and Jesus were members of the Essenian brotherhood; but that theory is now generally abandoned. Whatever may have been the case with John, who is said to have lived like an anchorite in the desert, there seems to have been but little practical Essenism in Jesus, who is almost uniformly represented as cheerful and social in demeanour, and against whom it was expressly urged that he came eating and drinking, making no presence of puritanical holiness. He was neither a puritan, like the Essenes, nor a ritualist, like the Pharisees. Besides which, both John and Jesus seem to have begun their careers by preaching the un-Essene doctrine of the speedy advent of the "kingdom of heaven," by which is meant the reign of the Messiah upon the earth. Nevertheless, though we cannot regard Jesus as actually a member of the Essenian community or sect, we can hardly avoid the conclusion that he, as well as John the Baptist, had been at some time strongly influenced by Essenian doctrines. The spiritualized conception of the "kingdom of heaven" proclaimed by him was just what would naturally and logically arise from a remodelling of the Messianic theories of the Pharisees in conformity to advanced Essenian notions. It seems highly probable that some such refined conception of the functions of the Messiah was reached by John, who, stigmatizing the Pharisees and Sadducees as a "generation of vipers," called aloud to the people to repent of their sins, in view of the speedy advent of the Messiah, and to testify to their repentance by submitting to the Essenian rite of baptism. There is no positive evidence that Jesus was ever a disciple of John; yet the account of the baptism, in spite of the legendary character of its details, seems to rest upon a historical basis; and perhaps the most plausible hypothesis which can be framed is, that Jesus received baptism at John's hands, became for a while his disciple, and acquired from him a knowledge of Essenian doctrines.

The career of John seems to have been very brief. His stern puritanism brought him soon into disgrace with the government of Galilee. He was seized by Herod, thrown into prison, and beheaded. After the brief hints given as to the intercourse between Jesus and John, we next hear of Jesus alone in the desert, where, like Sakyamuni and Mohammed, he may have brooded in solitude over his great project. Yet we do not find that he had as yet formed any distinct conception of his own Messiahship. The total neglect of chronology by our authorities[20] renders it impossible to trace the development of his thoughts step by step; but for some time after John's catastrophe we find him calling upon the people to repent, in view of the speedy approach of the Messiah, speaking with great and commanding personal authority, but using no language which would indicate that he was striving to do more than worthily fill the place and add to the good work of his late master. The Sermon on the Mount, which the first gospel inserts in this place, was perhaps never spoken as a continuous discourse; but it no doubt for the most part contains the very words of Jesus, and represents the general spirit of his teaching during this earlier portion of his career. In this is contained nearly all that has made Christianity so powerful in the domain of ethics. If all the rest of the gospel were taken away, or destroyed in the night of some future barbarian invasion, we should still here possess the secret of the wonderful impression which Jesus made upon those who heard him speak. Added to the Essenian scorn of Pharisaic formalism, and the spiritualized conception of the Messianic kingdom, which Jesus may probably have shared with John the Baptist, we have here for the first time the distinctively Christian conception of the fatherhood of God and the brotherhood of men, which ultimately insured the success of the new religion. The special point of originality in Jesus was his conception of Deity. As Strauss well says, "He conceived of God, in a moral point of view, as being identical in character with himself in the most exalted moments of his religious life, and strengthened in turn his own religious life by this ideal. But the most exalted religious tendency in his own consciousness was exactly that comprehensive love, overpowering the evil only by the good, which he therefore transferred to God as the fundamental tendency of His nature." From this conception of God, observes Zeller, flowed naturally all the moral teaching of Jesus, the insistence upon spiritual righteousness instead of the mere mechanical observance of Mosaic precepts, the call to be perfect even as the Father is perfect, the principle of the spiritual equality of men before God, and the equal duties of all men toward each other.

How far, in addition to these vitally important lessons, Jesus may have taught doctrines of an ephemeral or visionary character, it is very difficult to decide. We are inclined to regard the third gospel as of some importance in settling this point. The author of that gospel represents Jesus as decidedly hostile to the rich. Where Matthew has "Blessed are the poor in spirit," Luke has "Blessed are ye poor." In the first gospel we read, "Blessed are they who hunger and thirst after righteousness, for they will be filled"; but in the third

---

[20] "The biographers [of Becket] are commonly rather careless as to the order of time. Each .... recorded what struck him most or what he best knew, one set down one event and another; and none of them paid much regard to the order of details."—Freeman, Historical Essays, 1st series, p. 94.

gospel we find, "Blessed are ye that hunger now, for ye will be filled"; and this assurance is immediately followed by the denunciation, "Woe to you that are rich, for ye have received your consolation! Woe to you that are full now, for ye will hunger." The parable of Dives and Lazarus illustrates concretely this view of the case, which is still further corroborated by the account, given in both the first and the third gospels, of the young man who came to seek everlasting life. Jesus here maintains that righteousness is insufficient unless voluntary poverty be superadded. Though the young man has strictly fulfilled the greatest of the commandments,—to love his neighbour as himself,—he is required, as a needful proof of his sincerity, to distribute all his vast possessions among the poor. And when he naturally manifests a reluctance to perform so superfluous a sacrifice, Jesus observes that it will be easier for a camel to go through the eye of a needle than for a rich man to share in the glories of the anticipated Messianic kingdom. It is difficult to escape the conclusion that we have here a very primitive and probably authentic tradition; and when we remember the importance which, according to the "Acts," the earliest disciples attached to the principle of communism, as illustrated in the legend of Ananias and Sapphira, we must admit strong reasons for believing that Jesus himself held views which tended toward the abolition of private property. On this point, the testimony of the third evangelist singly is of considerable weight; since at the time when he wrote, the communistic theories of the first generation of Christians had been generally abandoned, and in the absence of any dogmatic motives, he could only have inserted these particular traditions because he believed them to possess historical value. But we are not dependent on the third gospel alone. The story just cited is attested by both our authorities, and is in perfect keeping with the general views of Jesus as reported by the first evangelist. Thus his disciples are enjoined to leave all, and follow him; to take no thought for the morrow; to think no more of laying up treasures on the earth, for in the Messianic kingdom they shall have treasures in abundance, which can neither be wasted nor stolen. On making their journeys, they are to provide neither money, nor clothes, nor food, but are to live at the expense of those whom they visit; and if any town refuse to harbour them, the Messiah, on his arrival, will deal with that town more severely than Jehovah dealt with the cities of the plain. Indeed, since the end of the world was to come before the end of the generation then living (Matt. xxiv. 34; 1 Cor. xv. 51-56, vii. 29), there could be no need for acquiring property or making arrangements for the future; even marriage became unnecessary. These teachings of Jesus have a marked Essenian character, as well as his declaration that in the Messianic kingdom there was to be no more marriage, perhaps no distinction of sex (Matt. xxii. 30). The sect of Ebionites, who represented the earliest doctrine and practice of Christianity before it had been modified by Paul, differed from the Essenes in no essential respect save in the acknowledgment of Jesus as the Messiah, and the expectation of his speedy return to the earth.

How long, or with what success, Jesus continued to preach the coming of the Messiah in Galilee, it is impossible to conjecture. His fellow-townsmen of Nazareth appear to have ridiculed him in his prophetical capacity; or, if we may trust the third evangelist, to have arisen against him with indignation, and made an attempt upon his life. To them he was but a carpenter, the son of a carpenter (Matt. xiii. 55; Mark vi. 3), who told them disagreeable truths. Our author represents his teaching in Galilee to have produced but little result, but the gospel narratives afford no definite data for deciding this point. We believe the most probable conclusion to be that Jesus did attract many followers, and became famous throughout Galilee; for Herod is said to have regarded him as John the Baptist risen from the grave. To escape the malice of Herod, Jesus then retired to Syro-Phoenicia, and during this eventful journey the consciousness of his own Messiahship seems for the first time to have distinctly dawned upon him (Matt. xiv. 1, 13; xv. 21; xvi. 13-20). Already, it appears, speculations were rife as to the character of this wonderful preacher. Some thought he was John the Baptist, or perhaps one of the prophets of the Assyrian period returned to the earth. Some, in accordance with a generally-received tradition, supposed him to be Elijah, who had never seen death, and had now at last returned from the regions above the firmament to announce the coming of the Messiah in the clouds. It was generally admitted, among enthusiastic hearers, that he who spake as never man spake before must have some divine commission to execute. These speculations, coming to the ears of Jesus during his preaching in Galilee, could not fail to excite in him a train of self-conscious reflections. To him also must have been presented the query as to his own proper character and functions; and, as our author acutely demonstrates, his only choice lay between a profitless life of exile in Syro-Phoenicia, and a bold return to Jewish territory in some pronounced character. The problem being thus propounded, there could hardly be a doubt as to what that character should be. Jesus knew well that he was not John the Baptist; nor, however completely he may have been dominated by his sublime enthusiasm, was it likely that he could mistake himself for an ancient prophet arisen from the lower world of shades, or for Elijah descended from the sky. But the Messiah himself he might well be. Such indeed was the almost inevitable corollary from his own conception of Messiahship. We have seen that he had, probably from the very outset, discarded the traditional notion of a political Messiah, and recognized the truth that the happiness of a people lies not so much in political autonomy as in the love of God and the sincere practice of righteousness. The people were to be freed from the bondage of sin, of meaningless formalism, of consecrated hypocrisy,—a bondage more degrading than the payment of tribute to the emperor. The true business of the Messiah, then, was to deliver his people from the former bondage; it might be left to Jehovah, in his own good time, to deliver them from the latter. Holding these views, it was hardly possible that it should not sooner or later occur to Jesus that he himself was the person destined to discharge this glorious function, to liberate his countrymen from the thraldom of Pharisaic ritualism, and to inaugurate the real Messianic kingdom of spiritual righteousness. Had he not already preached the advent of this spiritual kingdom, and been instrumental in raising many to loftier conceptions of duty, and to a higher and purer life? And might he not now, by a grand attack upon Pharisaism in its central stronghold, destroy its prestige in the eyes of the people, and cause Israel to adopt a nobler religious and ethical doctrine? The temerity of such a purpose detracts nothing from its sublimity. And if that purpose should be accomplished, Jesus would really have performed the legitimate work of the Messiah. Thus, from his own point of view, Jesus was thoroughly consistent and rational in announcing himself as the expected Deliverer; and in the eyes of the impartial historian his course is fully justified.

"From that time," says the first evangelist, "Jesus began to show to his disciples that he must go to Jerusalem, and suffer many things from the elders and chief priests and scribes, and be put to death, and rise again on the third day." Here we have, obviously, the knowledge of the writer, after the event, reflected back and attributed to Jesus. It is of course impossible that Jesus should have predicted with such definiteness his approaching death; nor is it very likely that he entertained any hope of being raised from the grave "on the third day." To a man in that age and country, the conception of a return from the lower world of shades was not a difficult one to frame; and it may well be that Jesus' sense of his own exalted position was sufficiently great to inspire him with the confidence that, even in case of temporary failure, Jehovah would rescue him from the grave and send him back with larger powers to carry out the purpose of his mission. But the difficulty of distinguishing between his own words and the interpretation put upon them by his disciples becomes here insuperable; and there will always be room for the hypothesis that Jesus had in view no posthumous career of his own, but only expressed his unshaken confidence in the success of his enterprise, even after and in spite of his death.

At all events, the possibility of his death must now have been often in his mind. He was undertaking a wellnigh desperate task,—to overthrow the Pharisees in Jerusalem itself. No other alternative was left him. And here we believe Mr. F. W. Newman to be singularly at fault in pronouncing this attempt of Jesus upon Jerusalem a foolhardy attempt. According to Mr. Newman, no man has any business to rush upon certain death, and it is only a crazy fanatic who will do so.[21] But such "glittering generalizations" will here help us but little. The historic data show that to go to Jerusalem, even at the risk of death, was absolutely necessary to the realization of Jesus' Messianic project. Mr. Newman certainly would not have had him drag out an inglorious and baffled existence in Syro-Phoenicia. If the Messianic kingdom was to be fairly inaugurated, there was work to be done in Jerusalem, and Jesus must go there as one in authority, cost what it might. We believe him to have gone

---

[21] Phases of Faith, pp. 158-164.

there in a spirit of grand and careless bravery, yet seriously and soberly, and under the influence of no fanatical delusion. He knew the risks, but deliberately chose to incur them, that the will of Jehovah might be accomplished.

We next hear of Jesus travelling down to Jerusalem by way of Jericho, and entering the sacred city in his character of Messiah, attended by a great multitude. It was near the time of the Passover, when people from all parts of Galilee and Judaea were sure to be at Jerusalem, and the nature of his reception seems to indicate that he had already secured a considerable number of followers upon whose assistance he might hope to rely, though it nowhere appears that he intended to use other than purely moral weapons to insure a favourable reception. We must remember that for half a century many of the Jewish people had been constantly looking for the arrival of the Messiah, and there can be little doubt that the entry of Jesus riding upon an ass in literal fulfilment of prophecy must have wrought powerfully upon the imagination of the multitude. That the believers in him were very numerous must be inferred from the cautious, not to say timid, behaviour of the rulers at Jerusalem, who are represented as desiring to arrest him, but as deterred from taking active steps through fear of the people. We are led to the same conclusion by his driving the money-changers out of the Temple; an act upon which he could hardly have ventured, had not the popular enthusiasm in his favour been for the moment overwhelming. But the enthusiasm of a mob is short-lived, and needs to be fed upon the excitement of brilliant and dramatically arranged events. The calm preacher of righteousness, or even the fiery denouncer of the scribes and Pharisees, could not hope to retain undiminished authority save by the display of extraordinary powers to which, so far as we know, Jesus (like Mohammed) made no presence (Matt. xvi. 1-4). The ignorant and materialistic populace could not understand the exalted conception of Messiahship which had been formed by Jesus, and as day after day elapsed without the appearance of any marvellous sign from Jehovah, their enthusiasm must naturally have cooled down. Then the Pharisees appear cautiously endeavouring to entrap him into admissions which might render him obnoxious to the Roman governor. He saw through their design, however, and foiled them by the magnificent repartee, "Render unto Caesar the things that are Caesar's, and unto God the things that are God's." Nothing could more forcibly illustrate the completely non-political character of his Messianic doctrines. Nevertheless, we are told that, failing in this attempt, the chief priests suborned false witnesses to testify against him: this Sabbath-breaker, this derider of Mosaic formalism, who with his Messianic pretensions excited the people against their hereditary teachers, must at all events be put out of the way. Jesus must suffer the fate which society has too often had in store for the reformer; the fate which Sokrates and Savonarola, Vanini and Bruno, have suffered for being wiser than their own generation. Messianic adventurers had already given much trouble to the Roman authorities, who were not likely to scrutinize critically the peculiar claims of Jesus. And when the chief priests accused him before Pilate of professing to be "King of the Jews," this claim could in Roman apprehension bear but one interpretation. The offence was treason, punishable, save in the case of Roman citizens, by crucifixion.

Such in its main outlines is the historic career of Jesus, as constructed by our author from data furnished chiefly by the first gospel. Connected with the narrative there are many interesting topics of discussion, of which our rapidly diminishing space will allow us to select only one for comment. That one is perhaps the most important of all, namely, the question as to how far Jesus anticipated the views of Paul in admitting Gentiles to share in the privileges of the Messianic kingdom. Our author argues, with much force, that the designs of Jesus were entirely confined to the Jewish people, and that it was Paul who first, by admitting Gentiles to the Christian fold without requiring them to live like Jews, gave to Christianity the character of a universal religion. Our author reminds us that the third gospel is not to be depended upon in determining this point, since it manifestly puts Pauline sentiments into the mouth of Jesus, and in particular attributes to Jesus an acquaintance with heretical Samaria which the first gospel disclaims. He argues that the apostles were in every respect Jews, save in their belief that Jesus was the Messiah; and he pertinently asks, if James, who was the brother of Jesus, and Peter and John, who were his nearest friends, unanimously opposed Paul and stigmatized him as a liar and heretic, is it at all likely that Jesus had ever distinctly sanctioned such views as Paul maintained?

In the course of many years' reflection upon this point, we have several times been inclined to accept the narrow interpretation of Jesus' teaching here indicated; yet, on the whole, we do not believe it can ever be conclusively established. In the first place it must be remembered that if the third gospel throws a Pauline colouring over the events which it describes, the first gospel also shows a decidedly anti-Pauline bias, and the one party was as likely as the other to attribute its own views to Jesus himself. One striking instance of this tendency has been pointed out by Strauss, who has shown that the verses Matt. v. 17-20 are an interpolation. The person who teaches men to break the commandments is undoubtedly Paul, and in order to furnish a text against Paul's followers, the "Nicolaitans," Jesus is made to declare that he came not to destroy one tittle of the law, but to fulfil the whole in every particular. Such an utterance is in manifest contradiction to the spirit of Jesus' teaching, as shown in the very same chapter, and throughout a great part of the same gospel. He who taught in his own name and not as the scribes, who proclaimed himself Lord over the Sabbath, and who manifested from first to last a more than Essenian contempt for rites and ceremonies, did not come to fulfil the law of Mosaism, but to supersede it. Nor can any inference adverse to this conclusion be drawn from the injunction to the disciples (Matt. x. 5-7) not to preach to Gentiles and Samaritans, but only "to the lost sheep of the house of Israel"; for this remark is placed before the beginning of Jesus' Messianic career, and the reason assigned for the restriction is merely that the disciples will not have time even to preach to all the Jews before the coming of the Messiah, whose approach Jesus was announcing (Matt. x. 23)

These examples show that we must use caution in weighing the testimony even of the first gospel, and must not too hastily cite it as proof that Jesus supposed his mission to be restricted to the Jews. When we come to consider what happened a few years after the death of Jesus, we shall be still less ready to insist upon the view defended by our anonymous author. Paul, according to his own confession, persecuted the Christians unto death. Now what, in the theories or in the practice of the Jewish disciples of Jesus, could have moved Paul to such fanatic behaviour? Certainly not their spiritual interpretation of Mosaism, for Paul himself belonged to the liberal school of Gamaliel, to the views of which the teachings and practices of Peter, James, and John might easily be accommodated. Probably not their belief in Jesus as the Messiah, for at the riot in which Stephen was murdered and all the Hellenist disciples driven from Jerusalem, the Jewish disciples were allowed to remain in the city unmolested. (See Acts viii. 1, 14.) This marked difference of treatment indicates that Paul regarded Stephen and his friends as decidedly more heretical and obnoxious than Peter, James, and John, whom, indeed, Paul's own master Gamaliel had recently (Acts v. 34) defended before the council. And this inference is fully confirmed by the account of Stephen's death, where his murderers charge him with maintaining that Jesus had founded a new religion which was destined entirely to supersede and replace Judaism (Acts vi. 14). The Petrine disciples never held this view of the mission of Jesus; and to this difference it is undoubtedly owing that Paul and his companions forbore to disturb them. It would thus appear that even previous to Paul's conversion, within five or six years after the death of Jesus, there was a prominent party among the disciples which held that the new religion was not a modification but an abrogation of Judaism; and their name "Hellenists" sufficiently shows either that there were Gentiles among them or that they held fellowship with Gentiles. It was this which aroused Paul to persecution, and upon his sudden conversion it was with these Hellenistic doctrines that he fraternized, taking little heed of the Petrine disciples (Galatians i. 17), who were hardly more than a Jewish sect.

Now the existence of these Hellenists at Jerusalem so soon after the death of Jesus is clear proof that he had never distinctly and irrevocably pronounced against the admission of Gentiles to the Messianic kingdom, and it makes it very probable that the downfall of Mosaism as a result of his preaching was by no means unpremeditated. While, on the other hand, the obstinacy of the Petrine party in adhering to Jewish customs shows equally that Jesus could not have unequivocally committed himself in favour of a new gospel for the Gentiles. Probably Jesus was seldom brought into direct contact with others than Jews, so that the questions concerning the admission of Gentile converts did not come up during his lifetime; and thus the way was left open for the controversy which soon broke out between the Petrine party and Paul. Nevertheless, though Jesus may never have definitely pronounced upon this point, it will hardly be denied that his teaching, even as reported in the first gospel, is in its utter condemnation of formalism far more closely allied to the Pauline than to the Petrine doctrines. In his hands Mosaism became spiritualized until it really lost its identity, and was transformed into a code fit for the whole Roman world. And we do not doubt that if any one had asked Jesus whether circumcision were an essential prerequisite for admission to the Messianic kingdom, he would have given the same answer which Paul afterwards gave. We agree with Zeller and Strauss that, "as Luther was a more liberal spirit than the Lutheran divines of the succeeding generation, and Sokrates a more profound thinker than Xenophon or Antisthenes, so also Jesus must be credited with having raised himself far higher above the narrow prejudices of his nation than those of his disciples who could scarcely understand the spread of Christianity among the heathen when it had become an accomplished fact."

January, 1870.

IV.

THE CHRIST OF DOGMA.[22]

The meagreness of our information concerning the historic career of Jesus stands in striking contrast with the mass of information which lies within our reach concerning the primitive character of Christologic speculation. First we have the four epistles of Paul, written from twenty to thirty years after the crucifixion, which, although they tell us next to nothing about what Jesus did, nevertheless give us very plain information as to the impression which he made. Then we have the Apocalypse, written by John, A. D. 68, which exhibits the Messianic theory entertained by the earliest disciples. Next we have the epistles to the Hebrews, Philippians, Colossians, and Ephesians, besides the four gospels, constituting altogether a connected chain of testimony to the progress of Christian doctrine from the destruction of Jerusalem to the time of the Quartodeciman controversy (A. D. 70-170). Finally, there is the vast collection of apocryphal, heretical, and patristic literature, from the writings of Justin Martyr, the pseudo-Clement, and the pseudo-Ignatius, down to the time of the Council of Nikaia, when the official theories of Christ's person assumed very nearly the shape which they have retained, within the orthodox churches of Christendom, down to the present day. As we pointed out in the foregoing essay, while all this voluminous literature throws but an uncertain light upon the life and teachings of the founder of Christianity, it nevertheless furnishes nearly all the data which we could desire for knowing what the early Christians thought of the master of their faith. Having given a brief account of the historic career of Jesus, so far as it can now be determined, we propose here to sketch the rise and progress of Christologic doctrine, in its most striking features, during the first three centuries. Beginning with the apostolic view of the human Messiah sent to deliver Judaism from its spiritual torpor, and prepare it for the millennial kingdom, we shall briefly trace the progressive metamorphosis of this conception until it completely loses its identity in the Athanasian theory, according to which Jesus was God himself, the Creator of the universe, incarnate in human flesh.

The earliest dogma held by the apostles concerning Jesus was that of his resurrection from the grave after death. It was not only the earliest, but the most essential to the success of the new religion. Christianity might have overspread the Roman Empire, and maintained its hold upon men's faith until to-day, without the dogmas of the incarnation and the Trinity; but without the

---

[22] Saint-Paul, par Ernest Renan. Paris, 1869. Histoire du Dogme de la Divinite de Jesus-Christ, par Albert Reville. Paris, 1869. The End of the World and the Day of Judgment. Two Discourses by the Rev. W. R. Alger. Boston: Roberts Brothers, 1870.

dogma of the resurrection it would probably have failed at the very outset. Its lofty morality would not alone have sufficed to insure its success. For what men needed then, as indeed they still need, and will always need, was not merely a rule of life and a mirror to the heart, but also a comprehensive and satisfactory theory of things, a philosophy or theosophy. The times demanded intellectual as well as moral consolation; and the disintegration of ancient theologies needed to be repaired, that the new ethical impulse imparted by Christianity might rest upon a plausible speculative basis. The doctrine of the resurrection was but the beginning of a series of speculative innovations which prepared the way for the new religion to emancipate itself from Judaism, and achieve the conquest of the Empire. Even the faith of the apostles in the speedy return of their master the Messiah must have somewhat lost ground, had it not been supported by their belief in his resurrection from the grave and his consequent transfer from Sheol, the gloomy land of shadows, to the regions above the sky.

The origin of the dogma of the resurrection cannot be determined with certainty. The question has, during the past century, been the subject of much discussion, upon which it is not necessary for us here to comment. Such apparent evidence as there is in favour of the old theory of Jesus' natural recovery from the effects of the crucifixion may be found in Salvador's "Jesus-Christ et sa Doctrine"; but, as Zeller has shown, the theory is utterly unsatisfactory. The natural return of Jesus to his disciples never could have given rise to the notion of his resurrection, since the natural explanation would have been the more obvious one; besides which, if we were to adopt this hypothesis, we should be obliged to account for the fact that the historic career of Jesus ends with the crucifixion. The most probable explanation, on the whole, is the one suggested by the accounts in the gospels, that the dogma of the resurrection is due originally to the excited imagination of Mary of Magdala.[23] The testimony of Paul may also be cited in favour of this view, since he always alludes to earlier Christophanies in just the same language which he uses in describing his own vision on the road to Damascus.

But the question as to how the belief in the resurrection of Jesus originated is of less importance than the question as to how it should have produced the effect that it did. The dogma of the resurrection has, until recent times, been so rarely treated from the historical point of view, that the student of history at first finds some difficulty in thoroughly realizing its import to the minds of those who first proclaimed it. We cannot hope to understand it without bearing in mind the theories of the Jews and early Christians concerning the structure of the world and the cosmic location of departed souls. Since the time of Copernicus modern Christians no longer attempt to locate heaven and hell; they are conceived merely as mysterious places remote from the earth. The theological universe no longer corresponds to that which

---

[23] See Taine, De l'Intelligence, II. 192.

physical science presents for our contemplation. It was quite different with the Jew. His conception of the abode of Jehovah and the angels, and of departed souls, was exceedingly simple and definite. In the Jewish theory the universe is like a sort of three-story house. The flat earth rests upon the waters, and under the earth's surface is the land of graves, called Sheol, where after death the souls of all men go, the righteous as well as the wicked, for the Jew had not arrived at the doctrine of heaven and hell. The Hebrew Sheol corresponds strictly to the Greek Hades, before the notions of Elysium and Tartarus were added to it,—a land peopled with flitting shadows, suffering no torment, but experiencing no pleasure, like those whom Dante met in one of the upper circles of his Inferno. Sheol is the first story of the cosmic house; the earth is the second. Above the earth is the firmament or sky, which, according to the book of Genesis (chap. i. v. 6, Hebrew text), is a vast plate hammered out by the gods, and supports a great ocean like that upon which the earth rests. Rain is caused by the opening of little windows or trap-doors in the firmament, through which pours the water of this upper ocean. Upon this water rests the land of heaven, where Jehovah reigns, surrounded by hosts of angels. To this blessed land two only of the human race had ever been admitted,—Enoch and Elijah, the latter of whom had ascended in a chariot of fire, and was destined to return to earth as the herald and forerunner of the Messiah. Heaven forms the third story of the cosmic house. Between the firmament and the earth is the air, which is the habitation of evil demons ruled by Satan, the "prince of the powers of the air."

Such was the cosmology of the ancient Jew; and his theology was equally simple. Sheol was the destined abode of all men after death, and no theory of moral retribution was attached to the conception. The rewards and punishments known to the authors of the Pentateuch and the early Psalms are all earthly rewards and punishments. But in course of time the prosperity of the wicked and the misfortunes of the good man furnished a troublesome problem for the Jewish thinker; and after the Babylonish Captivity, we find the doctrine of a resurrection from Sheol devised in order to meet this case. According to this doctrine—which was borrowed from the Zarathustrian theology of Persia—the Messiah on his arrival was to free from Sheol all the souls of the righteous, causing them to ascend reinvested in their bodies to a renewed and beautiful earth, while on the other hand the wicked were to be punished with tortures like those of the valley of Hinnom, or were to be immersed in liquid brimstone, like that which had rained upon Sodom and Gomorrah. Here we get the first announcement of a future state of retribution. The doctrine was peculiarly Pharisaic, and the Sadducees, who were strict adherents to the letter of Mosaism, rejected it to the last. By degrees this doctrine became coupled with the Messianic theories of the Pharisees. The loss of Jewish independence under the dominion of Persians, Macedonians, and Romans, caused the people to look ever more earnestly toward the expected time when the Messiah should appear in Jerusalem to deliver them from their oppressors. The moral doctrines of the Psalms and earlier prophets assumed an increasingly political aspect. The Jews were the righteous "under a cloud," whose sufferings were symbolically depicted by the younger Isaiah as the afflictions of the "servant of Jehovah"; while on the other hand, the "wicked" were the Gentile oppressors of the holy people. Accordingly the Messiah, on his arrival, was to sit in judgment in the valley of Jehoshaphat, rectifying the wrongs of his chosen ones, condemning the Gentile tyrants to the torments of Gehenna, and raising from Sheol all those Jews who had lived and died during the evil times before his coming. These were to find in the Messianic kingdom the compensation for the ills which they had suffered in their first earthly existence. Such are the main outlines of the theory found in the Book of Enoch, written about B. C. 100, and it is adopted in the Johannine Apocalypse, with little variation, save in the recognition of Jesus as the Messiah, and in the transferrence to his second coming of all these wonderful proceedings. The manner of the Messiah's coming had been variously imagined. According to an earlier view, he was to enter Jerusalem as a King of the house of David, and therefore of human lineage. According to a later view, presented in the Book of Daniel, he was to descend from the sky, and appear among the clouds. Both these views were adopted by the disciples of Jesus, who harmonized them by referring the one to his first and the other to his second appearance.

Now to the imaginations of these earliest disciples the belief in the resurrection of Jesus presented itself as a needful guarantee of his Messiahship. Their faith, which must have been shaken by his execution and descent into Sheol, received welcome confirmation by the springing up of the belief that he had been again seen upon the face of the earth. Applying the imagery of Daniel, it became a logical conclusion that he must have ascended into the sky, whence he might shortly be expected to make his appearance, to enact the scenes foretold in prophecy. That such was the actual process of inference is shown by the legend of the Ascension in the first chapter of the "Acts," and especially by the words, "This Jesus who hath been taken up from you into heaven, will come in the same manner in which ye beheld him going into heaven." In the Apocalypse, written A. D. 68, just after the death of Nero, this second coming is described as something immediately to happen, and the colours in which it is depicted show how closely allied were the Johannine notions to those of the Pharisees. The glories of the New Jerusalem are to be reserved for Jews, while for the Roman tyrants of Judaea is reserved a fearful retribution. They are to be trodden underfoot by the Messiah, like grapes in a wine-press, until the gushing blood shall rise to the height of the horse's bridle.

In the writings of Paul the dogma of the resurrection assumes a very different aspect. Though Paul, like the older apostles, held that Jesus, as the Messiah, was to return to the earth within a few years, yet to his catholic mind this anticipated event had become divested of its narrow Jewish significance. In the eyes of Paul, the religion preached by Jesus was an abrogation of Mosaism, and the truths contained in it were a free gift to the Gentile as well as to the

Jewish world. According to Paul, death came into the world as a punishment for the sin of Adam. By this he meant that, had it not been for the original transgression, all men escaping death would either have remained upon earth or have been conveyed to heaven, like Enoch and Elijah, in incorruptible bodies. But in reality as a penance for disobedience, all men, with these two exceptions, had suffered death, and been exiled to the gloomy caverns of Sheol. The Mosaic ritual was powerless to free men from this repulsive doom, but it had nevertheless served a good purpose in keeping men's minds directed toward holiness, preparing them, as a schoolmaster would prepare his pupils, to receive the vitalizing truths of Christ. Now, at last, the Messiah or Christ had come as a second Adam, and being without sin had been raised by Jehovah out of Sheol and taken up into heaven, as testimony to men that the power of sin and death was at last defeated. The way henceforth to avoid death and escape the exile to Sheol was to live spiritually like Jesus, and with him to be dead to sensual requirements. Faith, in Paul's apprehension, was not an intellectual assent to definitely prescribed dogmas, but, as Matthew Arnold has well pointed out, it was an emotional striving after righteousness, a developing consciousness of God in the soul, such as Jesus had possessed, or, in Paul's phraseology, a subjugation of the flesh by the spirit. All those who should thus seek spiritual perfection should escape the original curse. The Messiah was destined to return to the earth to establish the reign of spiritual holiness, probably during Paul's own lifetime (I Cor. xv. 51). Then the true followers of Jesus should be clothed in ethereal bodies, free from the imperfections of "the flesh," and should ascend to heaven without suffering death, while the righteous dead should at the same time be released from Sheol, even as Jesus himself had been released.

To the doctrine of the resurrection, in which ethical and speculative elements are thus happily blended by Paul, the new religion doubtless owed in great part its rapid success. Into an account of the causes which favoured the spreading of Christianity, it is not our purpose to enter at present. But we may note that the local religions of the ancient pagan world had partly destroyed each other by mutual intermingling, and had lost their hold upon people from the circumstance that their ethical teaching no longer corresponded to the advanced ethical feeling of the age. Polytheism, in short, was outgrown. It was outgrown both intellectually and morally. People were ceasing to believe in its doctrines, and were ceasing to respect its precepts. The learned were taking refuge in philosophy, the ignorant in mystical superstitions imported from Asia. The commanding ethical motive of ancient republican times had been patriotism,—devotion to the interests of the community. But Roman dominion had destroyed patriotism as a guiding principle of life, and thus in every way the minds of men were left in a sceptical, unsatisfied state,—craving after a new theory of life, and craving after a new stimulus to right action. Obviously the only theology which could now be satisfactory to philosophy or to common-sense was some form of monotheism;—some system of doctrines which should represent all men as spiritually subjected to the will of a single God, just as they were subjected to the temporal authority of the Emperor. And similarly the only system of ethics which could have a chance of prevailing must be some system which should clearly prescribe the mutual duties of all men without distinction of race or locality. Thus the spiritual morality of Jesus, and his conception of God as a father and of all men as brothers, appeared at once to meet the ethical and speculative demands of the time.

Yet whatever effect these teachings might have produced, if unaided by further doctrinal elaboration, was enhanced myriadfold by the elaboration which they received at the hands of Paul. Philosophic Stoics and Epicureans had arrived at the conception of the brotherhood of men, and the Greek hymn of Kleanthes had exhibited a deep spiritual sense of the fatherhood of God. The originality of Christianity lay not so much in its enunciation of new ethical precepts as in the fact that it furnished a new ethical sanction,—a commanding incentive to holiness of living. That it might accomplish this result, it was absolutely necessary that it should begin by discarding both the ritualism and the narrow theories of Judaism. The mere desire for a monotheistic creed had led many pagans, in Paul's time, to embrace Judaism, in spite of its requirements, which to Romans and Greeks were meaningless, and often disgusting; but such conversions could never have been numerous. Judaism could never have conquered the Roman world; nor is it likely that the Judaical Christianity of Peter, James, and John would have been any more successful. The doctrine of the resurrection, in particular, was not likely to prove attractive when accompanied by the picture of the Messiah treading the Gentiles in the wine-press of his righteous indignation. But here Paul showed his profound originality The condemnation of Jewish formalism which Jesus had pronounced, Paul turned against the older apostles, who insisted upon circumcision. With marvellous flexibility of mind, Paul placed circumcision and the Mosaic injunctions about meats upon a level with the ritual observances of pagan nations, allowing each feeble brother to perform such works as might tickle his fancy, but bidding all take heed that salvation was not to be obtained after any such mechanical method, but only by devoting the whole soul to righteousness, after the example of Jesus.

This was the negative part of Paul's work. This was the knocking down of the barriers which had kept men, and would always have kept them, from entering into the kingdom of heaven. But the positive part of Paul's work is contained in his theory of the salvation of men from death through the second Adam, whom Jehovah rescued from Sheol for his sinlessness. The resurrection of Jesus was the visible token of the escape from death which might be achieved by all men who, with God's aid, should succeed in freeing themselves from the burden of sin which had encumbered all the children of Adam. The end of the world was at hand, and they who would live with Christ must figuratively die with Christ, must become dead to sin. Thus to the pure and spiritual ethics contained in the teachings of Jesus, Paul added an incalculably powerful incentive to right action, and a theory of life calculated to satisfy the speculative necessities of the pagan or Gentile world. To the educated and sceptical Athenian, as to the critical scholar of modern times, the physical resurrection of Jesus from the grave, and his ascent through the vaulted floor of heaven, might seem foolishness or naivete. But to the average Greek or Roman the conception presented no serious difficulty. The cosmical theories upon which the conception was founded were essentially the same among Jews and Gentiles, and indeed were but little modified until the establishment of the Copernican astronomy. The doctrine of the Messiah's second coming was also received without opposition, and for about a century men lived in continual anticipation of that event, until hope long deferred produced its usual results; the writings in which that event was predicted were gradually explained away, ignored, or stigmatized as uncanonical; and the Church ended by condemning as a heresy the very doctrine which Paul and the Judaizing apostles, who agreed in little else, had alike made the basis of their speculative teachings. Nevertheless, by the dint of allegorical interpretation, the belief has maintained an obscure existence even down to the present time; the Antiochus of the Book of Daniel and the Nero of the Apocalypse having given place to the Roman Pontiff or to the Emperor of the French.

But as the millenarism of the primitive Church gradually died out during the second century, the essential principles involved in it lost none of their hold on men's minds. As the generation contemporary with Paul died away and was gathered into Sheol, it became apparent that the original theory must be somewhat modified, and to this question the author of the second epistle to the Thessalonians addresses himself. Instead of literal preservation from death, the doctrine of a resurrection from the grave was gradually extended to the case of the new believers, who were to share in the same glorious revival with the righteous of ancient times. And thus by slow degrees the victory over death, of which the resurrection of Jesus was a symbol and a witness, became metamorphosed into the comparatively modern doctrine of the rest of the saints in heaven, while the banishment of the unrighteous to Sheol was made still more dreadful by coupling with the vague conception of a gloomy subterranean cavern the horrible imagery of the lake of fire and brimstone borrowed from the apocalyptic descriptions of Gehenna. But in this modification of the original theory, the fundamental idea of a future state of retribution was only the more distinctly emphasized; although, in course of time, the original incentive to righteousness supplied by Paul was more and more subordinated to the comparatively degrading incentive involved in the fear of damnation. There can hardly be a doubt that the definiteness and vividness of the Pauline theory of a future life contributed very largely to the rapid spread of the Christian religion; nor can it be doubted that to the desire to be holy like Jesus, in order to escape death and live with Jesus, is due the elevating ethical influence which, even in the worst times of ecclesiastic degeneracy, Christianity has never failed to exert. Doubtless, as Lessing long, ago observed, the notion of future reward and punishment needs to be eliminated in order that the incentive to holiness may be a perfectly pure one. The highest virtue is that which takes no thought of reward or punishment; but for a conception of this sort the mind of antiquity was not ready, nor is the average mind of to-day yet ready; and the sudden or premature dissolution of the Christian theory—which is fortunately impossible—might perhaps entail a moral retrogradation.

The above is by no means intended as a complete outline of the religious philosophy of Paul. We have aimed only at a clear definition of the character and scope of the doctrine of the resurrection of Jesus, at the time when it was first elaborated. We have now to notice the influence of that doctrine upon the development of Christologic speculation.

In neither or the four genuine epistles of Paul is Jesus described as superhuman, or as differing in nature from other men, save in his freedom from sin. As Baur has shown, "the proper nature of the Pauline Christ is human. He is a man, but a spiritual man, one in whom spirit or pneuma was the essential principle, so that he was spirit as well as man. The principle of an ideal humanity existed before Christ in the bright form of a typical man, but was manifested to mankind in the person of Christ." Such, according to Baur, is Paul's interpretation of the Messianic idea. Paul knows nothing of the miracles, of the supernatural conception, of the incarnation, or of the Logos. The Christ whom he preaches is the man Jesus, the founder of a new and spiritual order of humanity, as Adam was the father of humanity after the flesh. The resurrection is uniformly described by him as a manifestation of the power of Jehovah, not of Jesus himself. The later conception of Christ bursting the barred gates of Sheol, and arising by his own might to heaven, finds no warrant in the expressions of Paul. Indeed, it was essential to Paul's theory of the Messiah as a new Adam, that he should be human and not divine; for the escape of a divine being from Sheol could afford no precedent and furnish no assurance of the future escape of human beings. It was expressly because the man Jesus had been rescued from the grave because of his spirituality, that other men might hope, by becoming spiritual like him, to be rescued also. Accordingly Paul is careful to state that "since through man came death, through man came also the resurrection of the dead" (I Cor. xv. 21); a passage which would look like an express denial of Christ's superhuman character, were it probable that any of Paul's contemporaries had ever conceived of Jesus as other than essentially human.

But though Paul's Christology remained in this primitive stage, it contained the germs of a more advanced theory. For even Paul conceived of Jesus as a man wholly exceptional in spiritual character; or, in the phraseology of the time, as consisting to a larger extent of pneuma than any man who had lived before him. The question was sure to arise, Whence came this pneuma or spiritual quality? Whether the question ever distinctly presented itself to Paul's mind cannot be determined. Probably it did not. In those writings of his which have come down to us, he shows himself careless of metaphysical considerations. He is mainly concerned with exhibiting the unsatisfactory character of Jewish Christianity, and with inculcating a spiritual morality, to which the doctrine of Christ's resurrection is made to supply a surpassingly powerful sanction. But attempts to solve the problem were not long in coming. According to a very early tradition, of which the obscured traces remain in the synoptic gospels, Jesus received the pneuma at the time of his baptism, when the Holy Spirit, or visible manifestation of the essence of Jehovah, descended upon him and became incarnate in him. This theory, however, was exposed to the objection that it implied a sudden and entire transformation of an ordinary man into a person inspired or possessed by the Deity. Though long maintained by the Ebionites or primitive Christians, it was very soon rejected by the great body of the Church, which asserted instead that Jesus had been inspired by the Holy Spirit from the moment of his conception. From this it was but a step to the theory that Jesus was actually begotten by or of the Holy Spirit; a notion which the Hellenic mind, accustomed to the myths of Leda, Anchises, and others, found no difficulty in entertaining. According to the Gospel of the Hebrews, as cited by Origen, the Holy Spirit was the mother of Jesus, and Joseph was his father. But according to the prevailing opinion, as represented in the first and third synoptists, the relationship was just the other way. With greater apparent plausibility, the divine aeon was substituted for the human father, and a myth sprang up, of which the materialistic details furnished to the opponents of the new religion an opportunity for making the most gross and exasperating insinuations. The dominance of this theory marks the era at which our first and third synoptic gospels were composed,—from sixty to ninety years after the death of Jesus. In the luxuriant mythologic growth there exhibited, we may yet trace the various successive phases of Christologic speculation but imperfectly blended. In "Matthew" and "Luke" we find the original Messianic theory exemplified in the genealogies of Jesus, in which, contrary to historic probability (cf. Matt. xxii. 41-46), but in accordance with a time-honoured tradition, his pedigree is traced back to David; "Matthew" referring him to the royal line of Judah, while "Luke" more cautiously has recourse to an assumed younger branch. Superposed upon this primitive mythologic stratum, we find, in the same narratives, the account of the descent of the pneuma at the time of the baptism; and crowning the whole, there are the two accounts of the nativity which, though conflicting in nearly all their details, agree in representing the divine pneuma as the father of Jesus. Of these three stages of Christology, the last becomes entirely irreconcilable with the first; and nothing can better illustrate the uncritical character of the synoptists than the fact that the assumed descent of Jesus from David through his father Joseph is allowed to stand side by side with the account of the miraculous conception which completely negatives it. Of this difficulty "Matthew" is quite unconscious, and "Luke," while vaguely noticing it (iii. 23), proposes no solution, and appears undisturbed by the contradiction.

Thus far the Christology with which we have been dealing is predominantly Jewish, though to some extent influenced by Hellenic conceptions. None of the successive doctrines presented in Paul, "Matthew," and "Luke" assert or imply the pre-existence of Jesus. At this early period he was regarded as a human being raised to participation in certain attributes of divinity; and this was as far as the dogma could be carried by the Jewish metaphysics. But soon after the date of our third gospel, a Hellenic system of Christology arose into prominence, in which the problem was reversed, and Jesus was regarded as a semi-divine being temporarily lowered to participation in certain attributes of humanity. For such a doctrine Jewish mythology supplied no precedents; but the Indo-European mind was familiar with the conception of deity incarnate in human form, as in the avatars of Vishnu, or even suffering III the interests of humanity, as in the noble myth of Prometheus. The elements of Christology pre-existing in the religious conceptions of Greece, India, and Persia, are too rich and numerous to be discussed here. A very full account of them is given in Mr. R. W. Mackay's acute and learned treatise on the "Religious Development of the Greeks and Hebrews{.}"

It was in Alexandria, where Jewish theology first came into contact with Hellenic and Oriental ideas, that the way was prepared for the dogma of Christ's pre-existence. The attempt to rationalize the conception of deity as embodied in the Jehovah of the Old Testament gave rise to the class of opinions described as Gnosis, or Gnosticism. The signification of Gnosis is simply "rationalism,"—the endeavour to harmonize the materialistic statements of an old mythology with the more advanced spiritualistic philosophy of the time. The Gnostics rejected the conception of an anthropomorphic deity who had appeared visibly and audibly to the patriarchs; and they were the authors of the doctrine, very widely spread during the second and third centuries, that God could not in person have been the creator of the world. According to them, God, as pure spirit, could not act directly upon vile and gross matter. The difficulty which troubled them was curiously analogous to that which disturbed the Cartesians and the followers of Leibnitz in the seventeenth century; how was spirit to act upon matter, without ceasing, pro tanto, to be spirit? To evade this difficulty, the Gnostics postulated a series of emanations from God, becoming successively less and less spiritual and more and more material, until at the lowest end of the scale was reached the Demiurgus or Jehovah of the Old Testament, who created the world and appeared, clothed in material form, to the patriarchs. According to some of the Gnostics this lowest aeon or emanation was identical with the Jewish Satan, or the Ahriman of the Persians, who is called "the prince of this world," and the creation of the world was an essentially evil act. But all did not share in these extreme opinions. In the prevailing, theory, this last of the divine emanations was identified with the "Sophia," or personified "Wisdom," of the Book of Proverbs (viii. 22-30), who is described as present with God before the foundation of the world. The totality of these aeons constituted the pleroma, or "fulness of God" (Coloss. i. 20; Eph. i. 23), and in a corollary which bears unmistakable marks of Buddhist influence, it was argued that, in the final consummation of things, matter should be eliminated and all spirit reunited with God, from whom it had primarily flowed.

It was impossible that such views as these should not soon be taken up and applied to the fluctuating Christology of the time. According to the "Shepherd of Hermas," an apocalyptic writing nearly contemporary with the gospel of "Mark," the aeon or son of God who existed previous to the creation was not the Christ, or the Sophia, but the Pneuma or Holy Spirit, represented in the Old Testament as the "angel of Jehovah." Jesus, in reward for his perfect goodness, was admitted to a share in the privileges of this Pneuma (Reville, p. 39). Here, as M. Reville observes, though a Gnostic idea is adopted, Jesus is nevertheless viewed as ascending humanity, and not as descending divinity. The author of the "Clementine Homilies" advances a step farther, and clearly assumes the pre-existence of Jesus, who, in his opinion, was the pure, primitive man, successively incarnate in Adam, Enoch, Noah, Abraham, Isaac, Jacob, Moses, and finally in the Messiah or Christ. The author protests, in vehement language, against those Hellenists who, misled by their polytheistic associations, would elevate Jesus into a god. Nevertheless, his own hypothesis of pre-existence supplied at once the requisite fulcrum for those Gnostics who wished to reconcile a strict monotheism with the ascription of divine attributes to Jesus. Combining with this notion of pre-existence the pneumatic or spiritual quality attributed to Jesus in the writings of Paul, the Gnosticizing Christians maintained that Christ was an aeon or emanation from God, redeeming men from the consequences entailed by their imprisonment in matter. At this stage of Christologic speculation appeared the anonymous epistle to the "Hebrews," and the pseudo-Pauline epistles to the "Colossians," "Ephesians," and "Philippians" (A. D. 130). In these epistles, which originated among the Pauline Christians, the Gnostic theosophy is skilfully applied to the Pauline conception of the scope and purposes of Christianity. Jesus is described as the creator of the world (Coloss. i. 16), the visible image of the invisible God, the chief and ruler of the "throues, dominions, principalities, and powers," into which, in Gnostic phraseology, the emanations of God were classified. Or, according to "Colossians" and "Philippians," all the aeons are summed up in him, in whom dwells the pleroma, or "fulness of God." Thus Jesus is elevated quite above ordinary humanity, and a close approach is made to ditheism, although he is still emphatically subordinated to God by being made the creator of the world,—an office then regarded as incompatible with absolute divine perfection. In the celebrated passage, "Philippians" ii. 6-11, the aeon Jesus is described as being the form or visible manifestation of God, yet as humbling himself by taking on the form or semblance of humanity, and suffering death, in return for which he is to be exalted even above the archangels. A similar view is taken in "Hebrews"; and it is probable that to the growing favour with which these doctrines were received, we owe the omission of the miraculous conception from the gospel of "Mark,"—a circumstance which has misled some critics into assigning to that gospel an earlier date than to "Matthew" and "Luke." Yet the fact that in this gospel Jesus is implicitly ranked above the angels (Mark xiii. 32), reveals a later stage of Christologic doctrine than that reached by the first and third synoptists; and it is altogether probable that, in accordance with the noticeable conciliatory disposition of this evangelist, the supernatural conception is omitted out of deference to the Gnosticizing theories of "Colossians" and "Philippians," in which this materialistic doctrine seems to have had no assignable place. In "Philippians" especially, many expressions seem to verge upon Docetism, the extreme form of Gnosticism, according to which the human body of Jesus was only a phantom. Valentinus, who was contemporary with the Pauline writers of the second century, maintained that Jesus was not born of Mary by any process of conception, but merely passed through her, as light traverses a translucent substance. And finally Marcion (A. D. 140) carried the theory to its extreme limits by declaring that Jesus was the pure Pneuma or Spirit, who contained nothing in common with carnal humanity.

The pseudo-Pauline writers steered clear of this extravagant doctrine, which erred by breaking entirely with historic tradition, and was consequently soon condemned as heretical. Their language, though unmistakably Gnostic, was sufficiently neutral and indefinite to allow of their combination with earlier and later expositions of dogma, and they were therefore eventually received into the canon, where they exhibit a stage of opinion midway between that of Paul and that of the fourth gospel.

For the construction of a durable system of Christology, still further elaboration was necessary. The pre-existence of Jesus, as an emanation from God, in whom were summed up the attributes of the pleroma or full scale of Gnostic aeons, was now generally conceded. But the relation of this pleroqma to the Godhead of which it was the visible manifestation, needed to be more accurately defined. And here recourse was had to the conception of the "Logos,"—a notion which Philo had borrowed from Plato, lending to it a theosophic significance. In the Platonic metaphysics objective existence was attributed to general terms, the signs of general notions. Besides each particular man, horse, or tree, and besides all men, horses, and trees, in the aggregate, there was supposed to exist an ideal Man, Horse, and Tree. Each particular man, horse, or tree consisted of abstract existence plus a portion of the ideal man, horse, or tree. Sokrates, for instance, consisted of Existence, plus Animality, plus Humanity, plus Sokraticity. The visible world of particulars thus existed only by virtue of its participation in the attributes of the ideal world of universals. God created the world by encumbering each idea with an envelopment or clothing of visible matter; and since matter is vile or imperfect, all things are more or less perfect as they partake more or less fully of the idea. The pure unencumbered idea, the "Idea of ideas," is the Logos, or divine

Reason, which represents the sum-total of the activities which sustain the world, and serves as a mediator between the absolutely ideal God and the absolutely non-ideal matter. Here we arrive at a Gnostic conception, which the Philonists of Alexandria were not slow to appropriate. The Logos, or divine Reason, was identified with the Sophia, or divine Wisdom of the Jewish Gnostics, which had dwelt with God before the creation of the world. By a subtle play upon the double meaning of the Greek term (logos = "reason" or "word"), a distinction was drawn between the divine Reason and the divine Word. The former was the archetypal idea or thought of God, existing from all eternity; the latter was the external manifestation or realization of that idea which occurred at the moment of creation, when, according to Genesis, God SPOKE, and the world was.

In the middle of the second century, this Philonian theory was the one thing needful to add metaphysical precision to the Gnostic and Pauline speculations concerning the nature of Jesus. In the writings of Justin Martyr (A. D. 150-166), Jesus is for the first time identified with the Philonian Logos or "Word of God." According to Justin, an impassable abyss exists between the Infinite Deity and the Finite World; the one cannot act upon the other; pure spirit cannot contaminate itself by contact with impure matter. To meet this difficulty, God evolves from himself a secondary God, the Logos,—yet without diminishing himself any more than a flame is diminished when it gives birth to a second flame. Thus generated, like light begotten of light (lumen de lumine), the Logos creates the world, inspires the ancient prophets with their divine revelations, and finally reveals himself to mankind in the person of Christ. Yet Justin sedulously guards himself against ditheism, insisting frequently and emphatically upon the immeasurable inferiority of the Logos as compared with the actual God (gr o ontws qeos).

We have here reached very nearly the ultimate phase of New Testament speculation concerning Jesus. The doctrines enunciated by Justin became eventually, with slight modification, the official doctrines of the Church; yet before they could thus be received, some further elaboration was needed. The pre-existing Logos-Christ of Justin was no longer the human Messiah of the first and third gospels, born of a woman, inspired by the divine Pneuma, and tempted by the Devil. There was danger that Christologic speculation might break quite loose from historic tradition, and pass into the metaphysical extreme of Docetism. Had this come to pass, there might perhaps have been a fatal schism in the Church. Tradition still remained Ebionitish; dogma had become decidedly Gnostic; how were the two to be moulded into harmony with each other? Such was the problem which presented itself to the author of the fourth gospel (A. D. 170-180). As M. Reville observes, "if the doctrine of the Logos were really to be applied to the person of Jesus, it was necessary to remodel the evangelical history." Tradition must be moulded so as to fit the dogma, but the dogma must be restrained by tradition from running into Docetic extravagance. It must be shown historically how "the Word became flesh" and dwelt on earth (John i. 14), how the deeds of Jesus of Nazareth were the deeds of the incarnate Logos, in whom was exhibited the pleroma or fulness of the divine attributes. The author of the fourth gospel is, like Justin, a Philonian Gnostic; but he differs from Justin in his bold and skilful treatment of the traditional materials supplied by the earlier gospels. The process of development in the theories and purposes of Jesus, which can be traced throughout the Messianic descriptions of the first gospel, is entirely obliterated in the fourth. Here Jesus appears at the outset as the creator of the world, descended from his glory, but destined soon to be reinstated. The title "Son of Man" has lost its original significance, and become synonymous with "Son of God." The temptation, the transfiguration, the scene in Gethsemane, are omitted, and for the latter is substituted a Philonian prayer. Nevertheless, the author carefully avoids the extremes of Docetism or ditheism. Not only does he represent the human life of Jesus as real, and his death as a truly physical death, but he distinctly asserts the inferiority of the Son to the Father (John xiv. 28). Indeed, as M. Reville well observes, it is part of the very notion of the Logos that it should be imperfect relatively to the absolute God; since it is only its relative imperfection which allows it to sustain relations to the world and to men which are incompatible with absolute perfection, from the Philonian point of view. The Athanasian doctrine of the Trinity finds no support in the fourth gospel, any more than in the earlier books collected in the New Testament.

The fourth gospel completes the speculative revolution by which the conception of a divine being lowered to humanity was substituted for that of a human being raised to divinity. We have here travelled a long distance from the risen Messiah of the genuine Pauline epistles, or the preacher of righteousness in the first gospel. Yet it does not seem probable that the Church of the third century was thoroughly aware of the discrepancy. The authors of the later Christology did not regard themselves as adding new truths to Christianity, but merely as giving a fuller and more consistent interpretation to what must have been known from the outset. They were so completely destitute of the historic sense, and so strictly confined to the dogmatic point of view, that they projected their own theories back into the past, and vituperated as heretics those who adhered to tradition in its earlier and simpler form. Examples from more recent times are not wanting, which show that we are dealing here with an inveterate tendency of the human mind. New facts and new theories are at first condemned as heretical or ridiculous; but when once firmly established, it is immediately maintained that every one knew them before. After the Copernican astronomy had won the day, it was tacitly assumed that the ancient Hebrew astronomy was Copernican, and the Biblical conception of the universe as a kind of three-story house was ignored, and has been, except by scholars, quite forgotten. When the geologic evidence of the earth's immense antiquity could no longer be gainsaid, it was suddenly ascertained that the Bible had from the outset asserted that antiquity; and in our own day we have seen an elegant popular writer perverting the testimony of the rocks and distorting the Elohistic cosmogony of the Pentateuch, until the twain have been made to furnish what Bacon long ago described as "a heretical religion and a false philosophy." Now just as in the popular thought of the present day the ancient Elohist is accredited with a knowledge of modern geology and astronomy, so in the opinion of the fourth evangelist and his contemporaries the doctrine of the Logos-Christ was implicitly contained in the Old Testament and in the early traditions concerning Jesus, and needed only to be brought into prominence by a fresh interpretation. Hence arose the fourth gospel, which was no more a conscious violation of historic data than Hugh Miller's imaginative description of the "Mosaic Vision of Creation." Its metaphysical discourses were readily accepted as equally authentic with the Sermon on the Mount. Its Philonian doctrines were imputed to Paul and the apostles, the pseudo-Pauline epistles furnishing the needful texts. The Ebionites—who were simply Judaizing Christians, holding in nearly its original form the doctrine of Peter, James, and John—were ejected from the Church as the most pernicious of heretics; and so completely was their historic position misunderstood and forgotten, that, in order to account for their existence, it became necessary to invent an eponymous heresiarch, Ebion, who was supposed to have led them astray from the true faith!

The Christology of the fourth gospel is substantially the same as that which was held in the next two centuries by Tertullian, Clement of Alexandria, Origen, and Arius. When the doctrine of the Trinity was first announced by Sabellius (A. D. 250-260), it was formally condemned as heretical, the Church being not yet quite prepared to receive it. In 269 the Council of Antioch solemnly declared that the Son was NOT consubstantial with the Father,—a declaration which, within sixty years, the Council of Nikaia was destined as solemnly to contradict. The Trinitarian Christology struggled long for acceptance, and did not finally win the victory until the end of the fourth century. Yet from the outset its ultimate victory was hardly doubtful. The peculiar doctrines of the fourth gospel could retain their integrity only so long as Gnostic ideas were prevalent. When Gnosticism declined in importance, and its theories faded out of recollection, its peculiar phraseology received of necessity a new interpretation. The doctrine that God could not act directly upon the world sank gradually into oblivion as the Church grew more and more hostile to the Neo-Platonic philosophy. And when this theory was once forgotten, it was inevitable that the Logos, as the creator of the world, should be raised to an equality or identity with God himself. In the view of the fourth evangelist, the Creator was necessarily inferior to God; in the view of later ages, the Creator could be none other than God. And so the very phrases which had most emphatically asserted the subordination of the Son were afterward interpreted as asserting his absolute divinity. To the Gnostic formula, lumen de lumine, was added the Athanasian scholium, Deum verum de Deo vero; and the Trinitarian dogma of the union of persons in a single Godhead became thus the only available logical device for preserving the purity of monotheism.

February, 1870.

V.

A WORD ABOUT MIRACLES.[24]

It is the lot of every book which attempts to treat the origin and progress of Christianity in a sober and scientific spirit, to meet with unsparing attacks. Critics in plenty are always to be found, who, possessed with the idea that the entire significance and value of the Christian religion are demolished unless we regard it as a sort of historical monstrosity, are only too eager to subject the offending work to a scathing scrutiny, displaying withal a modicum of righteous indignation at the unblushing heresy of the author, not unmixed with a little scornful pity at his inability to believe very preposterous stories upon very meagre evidence. "Conservative" polemics of this sort have doubtless their function. They serve to purge scientific literature of the awkward and careless statements too often made by writers not sufficiently instructed or cautious, which in the absence of hostile criticism might get accepted by the unthinking reader along with the truths which they accompany. Most scientific and philosophical works have their defects; and it is fortunate that there is such a thing as dogmatic ardour in the world, ever sharpening its wits to the utmost, that it may spy each lurking inaccuracy and ruthlessly drag it to light. But this useful spirit is wont to lead those who are inspired by it to shoot beyond the mark, and after pointing out the errors of others, to commit fresh mistakes of their own. In the skilful criticism of M. Renan's work on the Apostles, in No. 29 of the "Fortnightly Review" there is now and then a vulnerable spot through which a controversial shaft may perhaps be made to pierce.

It may be true that Lord Lyttelton's tract on the Conversion of St. Paul, as Dr. Johnson and Dr. Rogers have said, has never yet been refuted; but if I may judge from my own recollection of the work, I should say that this must be because no competent writer ever thought it worth his pains to criticize it. Its argument contains about as much solid consistency as a distended balloon, and collapses as readily at the first puncture. It attempts to prove, first, that the conversion of St. Paul cannot be made intelligible except on the assumption that there was a miracle in the case; and secondly, that if Paul was converted by a miracle, the truth of Christianity is impregnable. Now, if the first of these points be established, the demonstration is not yet complete, for the second point must be proved independently. But if the first point be overthrown, the second loses its prop, and falls likewise.

Great efforts are therefore made to show that no natural influences could have intervened to bring about a change in the feelings of Paul. He was violent,

---

[24] These comments on Mr. Henry Rogers's review of M. Renan's Les Apotres, contained in a letter to Mr. Lewes, were shortly afterwards published by him in the Fortnightly Review, September 15, 1866,

"thorough," unaffected by pity or remorse; and accordingly he could not have been so completely altered as he was, had he not actually beheld the risen Christ: such is the argument which Mr. Rogers deems so conclusive. I do not know that from any of Paul's own assertions we are entitled to affirm that no shade of remorse had ever crossed his mind previous to the vision near Damascus. But waiving this point, I do maintain that, granting Paul's feelings to have been as Mr. Rogers thinks they were, his conversion is inexplicable, even on the hypothesis of a miracle. He that is determined not to believe, will not believe, though one should rise from the dead. To make Paul a believer, it was not enough that he should meet his Lord face to face he must have been already prepared to believe. Otherwise he would have easily found means of explaining the miracle from his own point of view. He would certainly have attributed it to the wiles of the demon, even as the Pharisees are said to have done with regard to the miraculous cures performed by Jesus. A "miraculous" occurrence in those days did not astonish as it would at present. "Miracles" were rather the order of the day, and in fact were lavished with such extreme bounty on all hands, that their convincing power was very slight. Neither side ever thought of disputing the reality of the miracles supposed to be performed on the other; but each side considered the miracles of its antagonist to be the work of diabolic agencies. Such being the case, it is useless to suppose that Paul could have distinguished between a true and a false miracle, or that a real miracle could of itself have had any effect in inducing him to depart from his habitual course of belief and action. As far as Paul's mental operations were concerned, it could have made no difference whether he met with his future Master in person, or merely encountered him in a vision. The sole point to be considered is whether or not he BELIEVED in the Divine character and authority of the event which had happened. What the event might have really been was of no practical consequence to him or to any one else. What he believed it to be was of the first importance. And since he did believe that he had been divinely summoned to cease persecuting, and commence preaching the new faith, it follows that his state of mind must have been more or less affected by circumstances other than the mere vision. Had he not been ripe for change, neither shadow nor substance could have changed him.

This view of the case is by no means so extravagant as Mr. Rogers would have us suppose. There is no reason for believing that Paul's character was essentially different afterwards from what it had been before. The very fervour which caused him, as a Pharisee, to exclude all but orthodox Jews from the hope of salvation, would lead him, as a Christian, to carry the Christian idea to its extreme development, and admit all persons whatever to the privileges of the Church. The same zeal for the truth which had urged him to persecute the Christians unto the death afterwards led him to spare no toil and shun no danger which might bring about the triumph of their cause. It must not be forgotten that the persecutor and the martyr are but one and the same man under different circumstances. He who is ready to die for his own faith will sometimes think it fair to make other men die for theirs. Men of a vehement and fiery temperament, moreover,—such as Paul always was,—never change their opinions slowly, never rest in philosophic doubt, never take a middle course. If they leave one extreme for an instant, they are drawn irresistibly to the other; and usually very little is needed to work the change. The conversion of Omar is a striking instance in point, and has been cited by M. Renan himself. The character of Omar bears a strong likeness to that of Paul. Previous to his conversion, he was a conscientious and virulent persecutor of Mohammedanism.[25] After his conversion, he was Mohammed's most efficient disciple, and it may be safely asserted that for disinterestedness and self-abnegation he was not inferior to the Apostle of the Gentiles. The change in his case was, moreover, quite as sudden and unexpected as it was with Paul; it was neither more nor less incomprehensible; and if Paul's conversion needs a miracle to explain it, Omar's must need one likewise. But in truth, there is no difficulty in the case, save that which stupid dogmatism has created. The conversions of Paul and Omar are paralleled by innumerable events which occur in every period of religious or political excitement. Far from being extraordinary, or inexplicable on natural grounds, such phenomena are just what might occasionally be looked for.

But, says Mr. Rogers, "is it possible for a moment to imagine the doting and dreaming victim of hallucinations (which M. Renan's theory represents Paul) to be the man whose masculine sense, strong logic, practical prudence, and high administrative talent appear in the achievements of his life, and in the Epistles he has left behind him?" M. Renan's theory does not, however, represent Paul as the "victim of hallucinations "to a greater degree than Mohammed. The latter, as every one knows, laboured during much of his life under almost constant "hallucination"; yet "masculine sense, strong logic," etc., were qualities quite as conspicuous in him as in St. Paul.

Here, as throughout his essay, Mr. Rogers shows himself totally unable to comprehend the mental condition of men in past ages. If an Apostle has a dream or sees a vision, and interprets it according to the ideas of his time and country, instead of according to the ideas of scientific England in the nineteenth century Mr. Rogers thinks he must needs be mad: and when according to the well-known law that mental excitement is contagious,[26] several persons are said to have concurred in interpreting some phenomenon supernaturally, Mr. Rogers cannot see why so many people should all go mad at once! "To go mad," in fact is his favourite designation for a mental act, which nearly all the human race have habitually performed in all ages; the act of mistaking subjective impressions for outward realities. The disposition to regard all strange phenomena as manifestations of supernatural power was

---

[25] Saint-Hilaire: Mahomet et le Coran, p. 109.
[26] Hecker's Epidemics of the Middle Ages, pp. 87-152.

universally prevalent in the first century of Christianity, and long after. Neither greatness of intellect nor thoroughness of scepticism gave exemption. Even Julius Caesar, the greatest practical genius that ever lived, was somewhat superstitious, despite his atheism and his Vigorous common-sense. It is too often argued that the prevalence of scepticism in the Roman Empire must have made men scrupulous about accepting miracles. By no means. Nothing but physical science ever drives out miracles: mere doctrinal scepticism is powerless to do it. In the age of the Apostles, little if any radical distinction was drawn between a miracle and an ordinary occurrence. No one supposed a miracle to be an infraction of the laws of nature, for no one had a clear idea that there were such things as laws of nature. A miracle was simply an extraordinary act, exhibiting the power of the person who performed it. Blank, indeed, would the evangelists have looked, had any one told them what an enormous theory of systematic meddling with nature was destined to grow out of their beautiful and artless narratives.

The incapacity to appreciate this frame of mind renders the current arguments in behalf of miracles utterly worthless. From the fact that Celsus and others never denied the reality of the Christian miracles, it is commonly inferred that those miracles must have actually happened. The same argument would, however, equally apply to the miracles of Apollonius and Simon Magus, for the Christians never denied the reality of these. What these facts really prove is that the state of human intelligence was as I have just described it: and the inference to be drawn from them is that no miraculous account emanating from an author of such a period is worthy of serious attention. When Mr. Rogers supposes that if the miracles had not really happened they would have been challenged, he is assuming that a state of mind existed in which it was possible for miracles to be challenged; and thus commits an anachronism as monstrous as if he had attributed the knowledge of some modern invention, such as steamboats, to those early ages.

Mr. Rogers seems to complain of M. Renan for "quietly assuming" that miracles are invariably to be rejected. Certainly a historian of the present day who should not make such an assumption would betray his lack of the proper qualifications for his profession. It is not considered necessary for every writer to begin his work by setting out to prove the first principles of historical criticism. They are taken for granted. And, as M. Renan justly says, a miracle is one of those things which must be disbelieved until it is proved. The onus probandi lies on the assertor of a fact which conflicts with universal experience. Nevertheless, the great number of intelligent persons who, even now, from dogmatic reasons, accept the New Testament miracles, forbids that they should be passed over in silence like similar phenomena elsewhere narrated. But, in the present state of historical science, the arguing against miracles is, as Colet remarked of his friend Erasmus's warfare against the Thomists and Scotists of Cambridge, "a contest more necessary than glorious or difficult." To be satisfactorily established, a miracle needs at least to be recorded by an eyewitness; and the mental attainments of the witness need to be thoroughly known besides. Unless he has a clear conception of the difference between the natural and the unnatural order of events, his testimony, however unimpeachable on the score of honesty, is still worthless. To say that this condition was fulfilled by those who described the New Testament miracles, would be absurd. And in the face of what German criticism has done for the early Christian documents, it would be an excess of temerity to assert that any one of the supernatural accounts contained in them rests on contemporary authority. Of all history, the miraculous part should be attested by the strongest testimony, whereas it is invariably attested by the weakest. And the paucity of miracles wherever we have contemporary records, as in the case of primitive Islamism, is a most significant fact.

In attempting to defend his principle of never accepting a miracle, M. Renan has indeed got into a sorry plight, and Mr. Rogers, in controverting him, has not greatly helped the matter. By stirring M. Renan's bemuddled pool, Mr. Rogers has only bemuddled it the more. Neither of these excellent writers seems to suspect that transmutation of species, the geologic development of the earth, and other like phenomena do not present features conflicting with ordinary experience. Sir Charles Lyell and Mr. Darwin would be greatly astonished to be told that their theories of inorganic and organic evolution involved any agencies not known to exist in the present course of nature. The great achievement of these writers has been to show that all past changes of the earth and its inhabitants are to be explained as resulting from the continuous action of causes like those now in operation, and that throughout there has been nothing even faintly resembling a miracle. M. Renan may feel perfectly safe in extending his principle back to the beginning of things; and Mr. Rogers's argument, even if valid against M. Renan, does not help his own case in the least.

On some points, indeed, M. Renan has laid himself open to severe criticism, and on other points he has furnished good handles for his orthodox opponents. His views in regard to the authorship of the Fourth Gospel and the Acts are not likely to be endorsed by many scholars; and his revival of the rationalistic absurdities of Paulus merits in most instances all that Mr. Rogers has said about it. As was said at the outset, orthodox criticisms upon heterodox books are always welcome. They do excellent service. And with the feeling which impels their authors to defend their favourite dogmas with every available weapon of controversy I for one can heartily sympathize. Their zeal in upholding what they consider the truth is greatly to be respected and admired. But so much cannot always be said for the mode of argumentation they adopt, which too often justifies M. Renan's description, when he says, "Raisonnements triomphants sur des choses que l'adversaire n'a pas dites, cris de victoire sur des erreurs qu'il n'a pas commises, rien ne parait deloyal a celui qui croft tenir en main les interets de la verite absolue."

August, 1866.

VI.

DRAPER ON SCIENCE AND RELIGION.[27]

Some twelve years ago, Dr. Draper published a bulky volume entitled "A History of the Intellectual Development of Europe," in which his professed purpose was to show that nations or races pass through certain definable epochs of development, analogous to the periods of infancy, childhood, youth, manhood, and old age in individuals. But while announced with due formality, the carrying out of the argument was left for the most part to the headings and running-titles of the several chapters, while in the text the author peacefully meandered along down the stream of time, giving us a succession of pleasant though somewhat threadbare anecdotes, as well as a superabundance of detached and fragmentary opinions on divers historical events, having apparently quite forgotten that he had started with a thesis to prove. In the arrangement of his "running heads," some points were sufficiently curious to require a word of explanation, as, for example, when the early ages of Christianity were at one time labelled as an epoch of progress and at another time as an epoch of decrepitude. But the argument and the contents never got so far en rapport with each other as to clear up such points as this. On the contrary, each kept on the even tenour of its way without much regard to the other. From the titles of the chapters one was led to expect some comprehensive theory of European civilization continuously expounded. But the text merely showed a great quantity of superficial and second-hand information, serving to illustrate the mental idiosyncrasies of the author. Among these idiosyncrasies might be noted a very inadequate understanding of the part played by Rome in the work of civilization, a singular lack of appreciation of the political and philosophical achievements of Greece under Athenian leadership, a strong hostility to the Catholic Church, a curious disposition to overrate semi-barbarous. or abortive civilizations, such as those of the old Asiatic and native American communities, at the expense of Europe, and, above all, an undiscriminating admiration for everything, great or small, that has ever worn the garb of Islam or been associated with the career of the Saracens. The discovery that in some respects the Mussulmans of the Middle Ages were more highly cultivated than their Christian contemporaries, has made such an impression on Dr. Draper's mind that it seems to be as hard for him to get rid of it as it was for Mr. Dick to keep the execution of Charles I. out of his "Memorial." Even in an essay on the "Civil Policy of America," the turbaned sage figures quite prominently; and it is needless to add that he

---

[27] History of the Conflict between Religion and Science. by John William Draper, M. D., LL. D. Fourth edition. New York: D. Appleton & Co. 1875. 12mo, pp. xxii., 373. (International Scientific Series, XII.)

reappears, as large as life, when the subject of discussion is the attitude of science toward religion.

Speaking briefly with regard to this matter, we may freely admit that the work done by the Arabs, in scientific inquiry as well as in the making of events, was very considerable. It was a work, too, the value of which is not commonly appreciated in the accounts of European history written for the general reader, and we have no disposition to find fault with Dr. Draper for describing it with enthusiasm. The philosophers of Bagdad and Cordova did excellent service in keeping alive the traditions of Greek physical inquiry at a time when Christian thinkers were too exclusively occupied with transcendental speculations in theology and logic. In some departments, as in chemistry and astronomy, they made original discoveries of considerable value; and if we turn from abstract knowledge to the arts of life, it cannot be denied that the mediaeval Mussulmans had reached a higher plane of material comfort than their Christian contemporaries. In short, the work of all kinds done by these people would furnish the judicious advocate of the claims of the Semitic race with materials for a pleasing and instructive picture. Dr. Draper, however, errs, though no doubt unintentionally, by so presenting the case as to leave upon the reader's mind the impression that all this scientific and practical achievement was the work of Islamism, and that the Mohammedan civilization was of a higher type than the Christian. It is with an apparent feeling of regret that he looks upon the ousting of the Moors from dominion in Spain; but this is a mistaken view. As regards the first point, it is a patent fact that scientific inquiry was conducted at the cost of as much theological obloquy in the Mohammedan as in the Christian world. It is true there was more actual tolerance of heresy on the part of Moslem governments than was customary in Europe in those days; but this is a superficial fact, which does not indicate any superiority in Moslem popular sentiment. The caliphate or emirate was a truly absolute despotism, such as the Papacy has never been, and the conduct of a sceptical emir in encouraging scientific inquiry goes but little way toward proving anything like a general prevalence of tolerance or of free-thinking. And this brings us to the second point,—that Mohammedan civilization was, on the whole, rather a skin-deep affair. It was superficial because of that extreme severance between government and people which has never existed in European nations within historic times, but which has always existed among the principal races that have professed Moslemism. Nowhere in the Mohammedan world has there ever been what we call a national life, and nowhere do we find in its records any trace of such an intellectual impulse, thrilling through every fibre of the people and begetting prodigious achievements in art, poetry, and philosophy, as was awakened in Europe in the thirteenth century and again in the fifteenth. Under the peculiar form of unlimited material and spiritual despotism exemplified in the caliphate, a few men may discover gases or comment on Aristotle, but no general movement toward political progress or philosophical inquiry is possible. Such a society is rigid and inorganic at bottom, whatever scanty signs of flexibility and life it may show at the surface. There is no better illustration of this, when well considered, than the fact that Moorish civilization remained, politically and intellectually, a mere excrescence in Spain, after having been fastened down over half the country for nearly eight centuries.

But we are in danger of forgetting our main theme, as Dr. Draper seems to do, while we linger with him over these interesting wayside topics. We may perhaps be excused, however, if we have not yet made any very explicit allusion to the "Conflict between Religion and Science," because this work seems to be in the main a repetition en petit of the "Intellectual Development of Europe," and what we have said will apply as well to one as to the other. In the little book, as in the big one, we hear a great deal about the Arabs, and something about Columbus and Galileo, who made men accept sundry truths in the teeth of clerical opposition; and, as before, we float gently down the current of history without being over well-informed as to the precise didactic purpose of our voyage. Here, indeed, even our headings and running-titles do not materially help us, for though we are supposed to be witnessing, or mayhap assisting in, a perennial conflict between "science" and "religion," we are nowhere enlightened as to what the cause or character of this conflict is, nor are we enabled to get a good look at either of the parties to the strife. With regard to it "religion" especially are we left in the dark. What this dreadful thing is towards which "science" is always playing the part of Herakles towards the Lernaean Hydra, we are left to gather from the course of the narrative. Yet, in a book with any valid claim to clearsightedness, one would think such a point as this ought to receive very explicit preliminary treatment.

The course of the narrative, however, leaves us in little doubt as to what Dr. Draper means by a conflict between science and religion. When he enlarges on the trite story of Galileo, and alludes to the more modern quarrel between the Church and the geologists, and does this in the belief that he is thereby illustrating an antagonism between religion and science, it is obvious that he identifies the cause of the anti-geologists and the persecutors of Galileo with the cause of religion. The word "religion" is to him a symbol which stands for unenlightened bigotry or narrow-minded unwillingness to look facts in the face. Such a conception of religion is common enough, and unhappily a great deal has been done to strengthen it by the very persons to whom the interests of religion are presumed to be a professional care. It is nevertheless a very superficial conception, and no book which is vitiated by it can have much philosophic value. It is simply the crude impression which, in minds unaccustomed to analysis, is left by the fact that theologians and other persons interested in religion are usually alarmed at new scientific truths, and resist them with emotions so highly wrought that they are not only incapable of estimating evidence, but often also have their moral sense impaired, and fight with foul means when fair ones fail. If we reflect carefully on this class of phenomena, we shall see that something besides mere pride of opinion is involved in the struggle. At the bottom of changing theological beliefs there lies something which men perennially value, and for the sake of which they cling to the beliefs as long as possible. That which they value is not itself a matter of belief, but it is a matter of conduct; it is the searching after goodness,—after a higher life than the mere satisfaction of individual desires. All animals seek for fulness of life; but in civilized man this craving has acquired a moral significance, and has become a spiritual aspiration; and this emotional tendency, more or less strong in the human race, we call religious feeling or religion. Viewed in this light, religion is not only something that mankind is never likely to get rid of, but it is incomparably the most noble as well as the most useful attribute of humanity.

Now, this emotional prompting toward completeness of life requires, of course, that conduct should be guided, as far as possible, in accordance with a true theory of the relations of man to the world in which he lives. Hence, at any given era the religious feeling will always be found enlisted in behalf of some theory of the universe. At any time, whatever may be their shortcomings in practice, religious men will aim at doing right according to their conceptions of the order of the world. If men's conceptions of the order of nature remained constant, no apparent conflict between their religious feelings and their knowledge need ever arise. But with the first advance in our knowledge of nature the case is altered. New and strange theories are naturally regarded with fear and dislike by persons who have always been accustomed to find the sanction and justification of their emotional prompting toward righteousness in old familiar theories which the new ones are seeking to supplant. Such persons oppose the new doctrine because their engrained mental habits compel them to believe that its establishment will in some way lower men's standard of life, and make them less careful of their spiritual welfare. This is the case, at all events, when theologians oppose scientific conclusions on religious grounds, and not simply from mental dulness or rigidity. And, in so far as it is religious feeling which thus prompts resistance to scientific innovation, it may be said, with some appearance of truth, that there is a conflict between religion and science.

But there must always be two parties to a quarrel, and our statement has to be modified as soon as we consider what the scientific innovator impugns. It is not the emotional prompting toward righteousness, it is not the yearning to live im Guten, Ganzen, Wahren, that he seeks to weaken; quite likely he has all this as much at heart as the theologian who vituperates him. Nor is it true that his discoveries, in spite of him, tend to destroy this all-important mental attitude. It would be ridiculous to say that the fate of religious feeling is really involved in the fate of grotesque cosmogonies and theosophies framed in the infancy of men's knowledge of nature; for history shows us quite the contrary. Religious feeling has survived the heliocentric theory and the discoveries of geologists; and it will be none the worse for the establishment of Darwinism. It is the merest truism to say that religion strikes its roots deeper down into human nature than speculative opinion, and is accordingly independent of any particular set of beliefs. Since, then, the scientific innovator does not, either voluntarily or involuntarily, attack religion, it follows that there can be no such "conflict" as that of which Dr. Draper has undertaken to write the history. The real contest is between one phase of science and another; between the more-crude knowledge of yesterday and the less-crude knowledge of to-day. The contest, indeed, as presented in history, is simply the measure of the difficulty which men find in exchanging old views for new ones. All along, the practical question has been, whether we should passively acquiesce in the crude generalizations of our ancestors or venture actively to revise them. But as for the religious sentiment, the perennial struggle in which it has been engaged has not been with scientific inquiry, but with the selfish propensities whose tendency is to make men lead the lives of brutes.

The time is at hand when the interests of religion can no longer be supposed to be subserved by obstinate adherence to crude speculations bequeathed to us from pre-scientific antiquity. One good result of the doctrine of evolution, which is now gaining sway in all departments of thought, is the lesson that all our opinions must be held subject to continual revision, and that with none of them can our religious interests be regarded as irretrievably implicated. To any one who has once learned this lesson, a book like Dr. Draper's can be neither interesting nor useful. He who has not learned it can derive little benefit from a work which in its very title keeps open an old and baneful source of error and confusion.

November. 1875.

VII.

NATHAN THE WISE.[28]

The fame of Lessing is steadily growing. Year by year he is valued more highly, and valued by a greater number of people. And he is destined, like his master and forerunner Spinoza, to receive a yet larger share of men's reverence and gratitude when the philosophic spirit which he lived to illustrate shall have become in some measure the general possession of the civilized part of mankind. In his own day, Lessing, though widely known and greatly admired, was little understood or appreciated. He was known to be a learned antiquarian, a terrible controversialist, and an incomparable writer. He was regarded as a brilliant ornament to Germany; and a paltry Duke of Brunswick thought a few hundred thalers well spent in securing the glory of having such a man to reside at his provincial court. But the majority of Lessing's contemporaries understood him as little perhaps as did the Duke of Brunswick. If anything were needed to prove this, it would he the uproar which was made over the publication of the "Wolfenbuttel Fragments," and the curious exegesis which was applied to the poem of "Nathan" on its first appearance. In order to understand the true character of this great poem, and of Lessing's religious opinions as embodied in it, it will be necessary first to consider the memorable theological controversy which preceded it.

During Lessing's residence at Hamburg, he had come into possession of a most important manuscript, written by Hermann Samuel Reimarus, a professor of Oriental languages, and bearing the title of an "Apology for the Rational Worshippers of God." Struck with the rigorous logic displayed in its arguments, and with the quiet dignity of its style, while yet unable to accept its most general conclusions, Lessing resolved to publish the manuscript, accompanying it with his own comments and strictures. Accordingly in 1774, availing himself of the freedom from censorship enjoyed by publications drawn from manuscripts deposited in the Ducal Library at Wolfenbuttel, of which he was librarian, Lessing published the first portion of this work, under the title of "Fragments drawn from the Papers of an Anonymous Writer." This first Fragment, on the "Toleration of Deists," awakened but little opposition; for the eighteenth century, though intolerant enough, did not parade its bigotry, but rather saw fit to disclaim it. A hundred years before, Rutherford, in his "Free Disputation," had declared "toleration of alle religions to bee not farre removed from blasphemie." Intolerance was then a thing to be proud of, but in

---

[28] Nathan the Wise: A Dramatic Poem, by Gotthold Ephraim Lessing. Translated by Ellen Frothingham. Preceded by a brief account of the poet and his works, and followed by an essay on the poem by Kuno Fischer. Second edition. New York: Leypoldt & Holt. 1868. Le Christianisme Moderne. etude sur Lessing. Par Ernest Fontanes. Paris: Bailliere. 1867.

Lessing's time some progress had been achieved, and men began to think it a good thing to seem tolerant. The succeeding Fragments were to test this liberality and reveal the flimsiness of the stuff of which it was made. When the unknown disputant began to declare "the impossibility of a revelation upon which all men can rest a solid faith," and when he began to criticize the evidences of Christ's resurrection, such a storm burst out in the theological world of Germany as had not been witnessed since the time of Luther. The recent Colenso controversy in England was but a gentle breeze compared to it. Press and pulpit swarmed with "refutations," in which weakness of argument and scantiness of erudition were compensated by strength of acrimony and unscrupulousness of slander. Pamphlets and sermons, says M. Fontanes, "were multiplied, to denounce the impious blasphemer, who, destitute alike of shame and of courage, had sheltered himself behind a paltry fiction, in order to let loose upon society an evil spirit of unbelief." But Lessing's artifice had been intended to screen the memory of Reimarus, rather than his own reputation. He was not the man to quail before any amount of human opposition; and it was when the tempest of invective was just at its height that he published the last and boldest Fragment of all,—on "the Designs of Jesus and his Disciples."

The publication of these Fragments led to a mighty controversy. The most eminent, both for uncompromising zeal and for worldly position, of those who had attacked Lessing, was Melchior Goetze, "pastor primarius" at the Hamburg Cathedral. Though his name is now remembered only because of his connection with Lessing, Goetze was not destitute of learning and ability. He was a collector of rare books, an amateur in numismatics, and an antiquarian of the narrow-minded sort. Lessing had known him while at Hamburg, and had visited him so constantly as to draw forth from his friends malicious insinuations as to the excellence of the pastor's white wine. Doubtless Lessing, as a wise man, was not insensible to the attractions of good Moselle; but that which he chiefly liked in this theologian was his logical and rigorously consistent turn of mind. "He always," says M. Fontanes, "cherished a holy horror of loose, inconsequent thinkers; and the man of the past, the inexorable guardian of tradition, appeared to him far more worthy of respect than the heterodox innovator who stops in mid-course, and is faithful neither to reason nor to faith."

But when Lessing published these unhallowed Fragments, the hour of conflict had sounded, and Goetze cast himself into the arena with a boldness and impetuosity which Lessing, in his artistic capacity, could not fail to admire. He spared no possible means of reducing his enemy to submission. He aroused against him all the constituted authorities, the consistories, and even the Aulic Council of the Empire, and he even succeeded in drawing along with him the chief of contemporary rationalists, Semler, who so far forgot himself as to declare that Lessing, for what he had done, deserved to be sent to the madhouse. But with all Goetze's orthodox valour, he was no match for the antagonist whom he had excited to activity. The great critic replied with pamphlet after pamphlet, invincible in logic and erudition, sparkling with wit, and irritating in their utter coolness. Such pamphlets had not been seen since Pascal published the "Provincial Letters." Goetze found that he had taken up arms against a master in the arts of controversy, and before long he became well aware that he was worsted. Having brought the case before the Aulic Council, which consisted in great part of Catholics, the stout pastor, forgetting that judgment had not yet been rendered, allowed himself to proclaim that all who do not recognize the Bible as the only source of Christianity are not fit to be called Christians at all. Lessing was not slow to profit by this unlucky declaration. Questioned, with all manner of ferocious vituperation, by Goetze, as to what sort of Christianity might have existed prior to and independently of the New Testament canon, Lessing imperturbably answered: "By the Christian religion I mean all the confessions of faith contained in the collection of creeds of the first four centuries of the Christian Church, including, if you wish it, the so-called creed of the apostles, as well as the creed of Athanasius. The content of these confessions is called by the earlier Fathers the regula fidei, or rule of faith. This rule of faith is not drawn from the writings of the New Testament. It existed before any of the books in the New Testament were written. It sufficed not only for the first Christians of the age of the apostles, but for their descendants during four centuries. And it is, therefore, the veritable foundation upon which the Church of Christ is built; a foundation not based upon Scripture." Thus, by a master-stroke, Lessing secured the adherence of the Catholics constituting a majority of the Aulic Council of the Empire. Like Paul before him, he divided the Sanhedrim. So that Goetze, foiled in his attempts at using violence, and disconcerted by the patristic learning of one whom he had taken to be a mere connoisseur in art and writer of plays for the theatre, concluded that discretion was the surest kind of valour, and desisted from further attacks.

  Lessing's triumph came opportunely; for already the ministry of Brunswick had not only confiscated the Fragments, but had prohibited him from publishing anything more on the subject without first obtaining express authority to do so. His last replies to Goetze were published at Hamburg; and as he held himself in readiness to depart from Wolfenbuttel, he wrote to several friends that he had conceived the design of a drama, with which he would tear the theologians in pieces more than with a dozen Fragments. "I will try and see," said he, "if they will let me preach in peace from my old pulpit, the theatre." In this way originated "Nathan the Wise." But it in no way answered to the expectations either of Lessing's friends or of his enemies. Both the one and the other expected to see the controversy with Goetze carried on, developed, and generalized in the poem. They looked for a satirical comedy, in which orthodoxy should be held up for scathing ridicule, or at least for a direful tragedy, the moral of which, like that of the great poem of Lucretius, should be

"Tantum religio potuit suadere malorum." Had Lessing produced such a poem, he would doubtless have gratified his free-thinking friends and wreaked due literary vengeance upon his theological persecutors. He would, perhaps, have given articulate expression to the radicalism of his own time, and, like Voltaire, might have constituted himself the leader of the age, the incarnation of its most conspicuous tendencies. But Lessing did nothing of the kind; and the expectations formed of him by friends and enemies alike show how little he was understood by either. "Nathan the Wise" was, as we shall see, in the eighteenth century an entirely new phenomenon; and its author was the pioneer of a quite new religious philosophy.

Reimarus, the able author of the Fragments, in his attack upon the evidences of revealed religion, had taken the same ground as Voltaire and the old English deists. And when we have said this, we have sufficiently defined his position, for the tenets of the deists are at the present day pretty well known, and are, moreover, of very little vital importance, having long since been supplanted by a more just and comprehensive philosophy. Reimarus accepted neither miracles nor revelation; but in accordance with the rudimentary state of criticism in his time, he admitted the historical character of the earliest Christian records, and was thus driven to the conclusion that those writings must have been fraudulently composed. How such a set of impostors as the apostles must on this hypothesis have been, should have succeeded in inspiring large numbers of their contemporaries with higher and grander religious notions than had ever before been conceived; how they should have laid the foundations of a theological system destined to hold together the most enlightened and progressive portion of human society for seventeen or eighteen centuries,—does not seem to have entered his mind. Against such attacks as this, orthodoxy was comparatively safe; for whatever doubt might be thrown upon some of its leading dogmas, the system as a whole was more consistent and rational than any of the theories which were endeavouring to supplant it. And the fact that nearly all the great thinkers of the eighteenth century adopted this deistic hypothesis, shows, more than anything else, the crudeness of their psychological knowledge, and their utter lack of what is called "the historical sense."

Lessing at once saw the weak point in Reimarus's argument, but his method of disposing of it differed signally from that adopted by his orthodox contemporaries. The more advanced German theologians of that day, while accepting the New Testament records as literally historical, were disposed to rationalize the accounts of miracles contained in them, in such a way as to get rid of any presumed infractions of the laws of nature. This method of exegesis, which reached its perfection in Paulus, is too well known to need describing. Its unsatisfactory character was clearly shown, thirty years ago, by Strauss, and it is now generally abandoned, though some traces of it may still be seen in the recent works of Renan. Lessing steadily avoided this method of interpretation. He had studied Spinoza to some purpose, and the outlines of Biblical criticism laid down by that remarkable thinker Lessing developed into a system wonderfully like that now adopted by the Tubingen school. The cardinal results which Baur has reached within the past generation were nearly all hinted at by Lessing, in his commentaries on the Fragments. The distinction between the first three, or synoptic gospels, and the fourth, the later age of the fourth, and the method of composition of the first three, from earlier documents and from oral tradition, are all clearly laid down by him. The distinct points of view from which the four accounts were composed, are also indicated,—the Judaizing disposition of "Matthew," the Pauline sympathies of "Luke," the compromising or Petrine tendencies of "Mark," and the advanced Hellenic character of "John." Those best acquainted with the results of modern criticism in Germany will perhaps be most surprised at finding such speculations in a book written many years before either Strauss or Baur were born.

But such results, as might have been expected, did not satisfy the pastor Goetze or the public which sympathized with him. The valiant pastor unhesitatingly declared that he read the objections which Lessing opposed to the Fragmentist with more horror and disgust than the Fragments themselves; and in the teeth of the printed comments he declared that the editor was craftily upholding his author in his deistical assault upon Christian theology. The accusation was unjust, because untrue. There could be no genuine cooperation between a mere iconoclast like Reimarus, and a constructive critic like Lessing. But the confusion was not an unnatural one on Goetze's part, and I cannot agree with M. Fontanes in taking it as convincing proof of the pastor's wrong-headed perversity. It appears to me that Goetze interpreted Lessing's position quite as accurately as M. Fontanes. The latter writer thinks that Lessing was a Christian of the liberal school since represented by Theodore Parker in this country and by M. Reville in France; that his real object was to defend and strengthen the Christian religion by relieving it of those peculiar doctrines which to the freethinkers of his time were a stumbling-block and an offence. And, in spite of Lessing's own declarations, he endeavours to show that he was an ordinary theist,—a follower of Leibnitz rather than of Spinoza. But I do not think he has made out his case. Lessing's own confession to Jacobi is unequivocal enough, and cannot well be argued away. In that remarkable conversation, held toward the close of his life, he indicates clearly enough that his faith was neither that of the ordinary theist, the atheist, nor the pantheist, but that his religious theory of the universe was identical with that suggested by Spinoza, adopted by Goethe, and recently elaborated in the first part of the "First Principles" of Mr. Herbert Spencer. Moreover, while Lessing cannot be considered an antagonist of Christianity, neither did he assume the attitude of a defender. He remained outside the theological arena; looking at theological questions from the point of view of a layman, or rather, as M. Cherbuliez has happily expressed it, of a Pagan. His mind was of decidedly antique structure. He had the virtues of paganism: its sanity, its calmness, and its probity; but of the tenderness of Christianity, and its quenchless aspirations after an indefinable ideal, of that feeling which has incarnated itself in Gothic cathedrals, masses and oratorios, he exhibited but scanty traces. His intellect was above all things self-consistent and incorruptible. He had that imperial good-sense which might have formed the ideal alike of Horace and of Epictetus. No clandestine preference for certain conclusions could make his reason swerve from the straight paths of logic. And he examined and rejected the conclusions of Reimarus in the same imperturbable spirit with which he examined and rejected the current theories of the French classic drama.

Such a man can have had but little in common with a preacher like Theodore Parker, or with a writer like M. Fontanes, whose whole book is a noble specimen of lofty Christian eloquence. His attribute was light, not warmth. He scrutinized, but did not attack or defend. He recognized the transcendent merits of the Christian faith, but made no attempt to reinstate it where it had seemed to suffer shock. It was therefore with the surest of instincts, with that same instinct of self-preservation which had once led the Church to anathematize Galileo, that Goetze. proclaimed Lessing a more dangerous foe to orthodoxy than the deists who had preceded him. Controversy, he doubtless thought, may be kept up indefinitely, and blows given and returned forever; but before the steady gaze of that scrutinizing eye which one of us shall find himself able to stand erect? It has become fashionable to heap blame and ridicule upon those who violently defend an antiquated order of things; and Goetze has received at the hands of posterity his full share of abuse. His wrath contrasted unfavourably with Lessing's calmness; and it was his misfortune to have taken up arms against an opponent who always knew how to keep the laugh upon his own side. For my own part I am constrained to admire the militant pastor, as Lessing himself admired him. From an artistic point of view he is not an uninteresting figure to contemplate. And although his attempts to awaken persecution were reprehensible, yet his ardour in defending what he believed to be vital truth is none the less to be respected. He had the acuteness to see that Lessing's refutation of deism did not make him a Christian, while the new views proposed as a substitute for those of Reimarus were such as Goetze and his age could in no wise comprehend.

Lessing's own views of dogmatic religion are to be found in his work entitled, "The Education of the Human Race." These views have since so far become the veriest commonplaces of criticism, that one can hardly realize that, only ninety years ago, they should have been regarded as dangerous paradoxes. They may be summed up in the statement that all great religions are good in their time and place; that, "as there is a soul of goodness in things evil, so also there is a soul of truth in things erroneous." According to Lessing, the successive phases of religious belief constitute epochs in the mental evolution of the human race. So that the crudest forms of theology, even fetishism, now to all appearance so utterly revolting, and polytheism, so completely inadequate, have once been the best, the natural and inevitable results of man's reasoning powers and appliances for attaining truth. The mere fact that a system of religious thought has received the willing allegiance of large masses of men shows that it must have supplied some consciously felt want, some moral or intellectual craving. And the mere fact that knowledge and morality are progressive implies that each successive system may in due course of time be essentially modified or finally supplanted. The absence of any reference to a future state of retribution, in the Pentateuch and generally in the sacred writings of the Jews, and the continual appeal to hopes and fears of a worldly character, have been pronounced by deists an irremediable defect in the Jewish religion. It is precisely this, however, says Lessing, which constitutes one of its signal excellences. "That thy days may be long in the land which Jehovah thy God giveth thee," was an appeal which the uncivilized Jew could understand, and which could arouse him to action; while the need of a future world, to rectify the injustices of this, not yet being felt, the doctrine would have been of but little service. But in later Hebrew literature, many magnificent passages revealed the despair felt by prophet and thinker over the insoluble problem presented by the evil fate of the good and the triumphant success of the wicked; and a solution was sought in the doctrine of a Messianic kingdom, until Christianity with its proclamation of a future life set the question entirely aside. By its appeal to what has been aptly termed "other-worldliness," Christianity immeasurably intensified human responsibility, besides rendering clearer its nature and limits. But according to Lessing, yet another step remains to be taken; and here we come upon the gulf which separates him from men of the stamp of Theodore Parker. For, says Lessing, the appeal to unearthly rewards and punishments is after all an appeal to our lower feelings; other-worldliness is but a refined selfishness; and we are to cherish virtue for its own sake not because it will lead us to heaven. Here is the grand principle of Stoicism. Lessing believed, with Mr. Mill, that the less we think about getting rewarded either on earth or in heaven the better. He was cast in the same heroic mould as Muhamad Efendi, who when led to the stake exclaimed: "Though I have no hope of recompense hereafter, yet the love of truth constraineth me to die in its defence!"

    With the truth or completeness of these views of Lessing we are not here concerned; our business being not to expound our own opinions, but to indicate as clearly as possible Lessing's position. Those who are familiar with the general philosophical spirit of the present age, as represented by writers otherwise so different as Littre and Sainte-Beuve, will best appreciate the power and originality of these speculations. Coming in the last century, amid the crudities of deism, they made a well-defined epoch. They inaugurated the historical method of criticism, and they robbed the spirit of intolerance of its only philosophical excuse for existing. Hitherto the orthodox had been intolerant toward the philosophers because they considered them heretics; and the philosophers had been intolerant toward the orthodox because they considered them fools. To Voltaire it naturally seemed that a man who could believe in the reality of miracles must be what in French is expressively termed a sot. But henceforth, to the disciple of Lessing, men of all shade of opinion were but the representatives and exponents of different phases in the general evolution of human intelligence, not necessarily to be disliked or despised if they did not happen to represent the maturest phase.

Religion, therefore, from this point of view, becomes clearly demarcated from theology. It consists no longer in the mental assent to certain prescribed formulas, but in the moral obedience to the great rule of life; the great commandment laid down and illustrated by the Founder of the Christian religion, and concerning which the profoundest modern philosophy informs us that the extent to which a society has learned to conform to it is the test and gauge of the progress in civilization which that society has achieved. The command "to love one another," to check the barbarous impulses inherited from the pre-social state, while giving free play to the beneficent impulses needful for the ultimate attainment of social equilibrium,—or as Tennyson phrases it, to "move upward, working out the beast, and letting the ape and tiger die,"—was, in Lessing's view, the task set before us by religion. The true religious feeling was thus, in his opinion, what the author of "Ecce Homo" has finely termed "the enthusiasm of humanity." And we shall find no better language than that of the writer just mentioned, in which to describe Lessing's conception of faith:—

"He who, when goodness is impressively put before him, exhibits an instinctive loyalty to it, starts forward to take its side, trusts himself to it, such a man has faith, and the root of the matter is in such a man. He may have habits of vice, but the loyal and faithful instinct in him will place him above many that practice virtue. He may be rude in thought and character, but he will unconsciously gravitate toward what is right. Other virtues can scarcely thrive without a fine natural organization and a happy training. But the most neglected and ungifted of men may make a beginning with faith. Other virtues want civilization, a certain amount of knowledge, a few books; but in half-brutal countenances faith will light up a glimmer of nobleness. The savage, who can do little else, can wonder and worship and enthusiastically obey. He who cannot know what is right can know that some one else knows; he who has no law may still have a master; he who is incapable of justice may be capable of fidelity; he who understands little may have his sins forgiven because he loves much."

Such was Lessing's religion, so far as it can be ascertained from the fragmentary writings which he has left on the subject. Undoubtedly it lacked completeness. The opinions which we have here set down, though constituting something more than a mere theory of morality, certainly do not constitute a complete theory of religion. Our valiant knight has examined but one side of the shield,—the bright side, turned toward us, whose marvellous inscriptions the human reason can by dint of unwearied effort decipher. But the dark side, looking out upon infinity, and covered with hieroglyphics the meaning of which we can never know, he has quite forgotten to consider. Yet it is this side which genuine religious feeling ever seeks to contemplate. It is the consciousness that there is about us an omnipresent Power, in which we live and move and have our being, eternally manifesting itself throughout the whole range of natural phenomena, which has ever disposed men to be religious, and lured them on in the vain effort to construct adequate theological systems. We may, getting rid of the last traces of fetishism, eliminate arbitrary volition as much as we will or can. But there still remains the consciousness of a divine Life in the universe, of a Power which is beyond and above our comprehension, whose goings out and comings in no man can follow. The more we know, the more we reach out for that which we cannot know. And who can realize this so vividly as the scientific philosopher? For our knowledge being, according to the familiar comparison, like a brilliant sphere, the more we increase it the greater becomes the number of peripheral points at which we are confronted by the impenetrable darkness beyond. I believe that this restless yearning,—vague enough in the description, yet recognizable by all who, communing with themselves or with nature, have felt it,—this constant seeking for what cannot be found, this persistent knocking at gates which, when opened, but reveal others yet to be passed, constitutes an element which no adequate theory of religion can overlook. But of this we find nothing in Lessing. With him all is sunny, serene, and pagan. Not the dim aisle of a vast cathedral, but the symmetrical portico of an antique temple, is the worshipping-place into which he would lead us.

But if Lessing's theology must be considered imperfect, it is none the less admirable as far as it goes. With its peculiar doctrines of love and faith, it teaches a morality far higher than any that Puritanism ever dreamed of. And with its theory of development it cuts away every possible logical basis for intolerance. It is this theology to which Lessing has given concrete expression in his immortal poem of "Nathan."

The central idea of "Nathan" was suggested to Lessing by Boccaccio's story of "The Three Rings," which is supposed to have had a Jewish origin. Saladin, pretending to be inspired by a sudden, imperious whim, such as is "not unbecoming in a Sultan," demands that Nathan shall answer him on the spur of the moment which of the three great religions then known—Judaism, Mohammedanism, Christianity—is adjudged by reason to be the true one. For a moment the philosopher is in a quandary. If he does not pronounce in favour of his own religion, Judaism, he stultifies himself; but if he does not award the precedence to Mohammedanism, he will apparently insult his sovereign. With true Oriental tact he escapes from the dilemma by means of a parable. There was once a man, says Nathan, who possessed a ring of inestimable value. Not only was the stone which it contained incomparably fine, but it possessed the marvellous property of rendering its owner agreeable both to God and to men.

The old man bequeathed this ring to that one of his sons whom he loved the most; and the son, in turn, made a similar disposition of it. So that, passing from hand to hand, the ring finally came into the possession of a father who loved his three sons equally well. Unto which one should he leave it? To get rid of the perplexity, he had two other rings made by a jeweller, exactly like the original, and to each of his three sons he bequeathed one. Each then thinking that he had obtained the true talisman, they began violently to quarrel, and after long contention agreed to carry their dispute before the judge. But the judge said: "Quarrelsome fellows! You are all three of you cheated cheats. Your three rings are alike counterfeit. For the genuine ring is lost, and to conceal the loss, your father had made these three substitutes." At this unexpected denouement the Sultan breaks out in exclamations of delight; and it is interesting to learn that when the play was brought upon the stage at Constantinople a few years ago, the Turkish audience was similarly affected. There is in the story that quiet, stealthy humour which is characteristic of many mediaeval apologues, and in which Lessing himself loved to deal. It is humour of the kind which hits the mark, and reveals the truth. In a note upon this passage, Lessing himself said: "The opinion of Nathan upon all positive religions has for a long time been my own." Let him who has the genuine ring show it by making himself loved of God and man. This is the central idea of the poem. It is wholly unlike the iconoclasm of the deists, and, coming in the eighteenth century, it was like a veritable evangel.

"Nathan" was not brought out until three years after Lessing's death, and it kept possession of the stage for but a short time. In a dramatic point of view, it has hardly any merits. Whatever plot there is in it is weak and improbable. The decisive incidents seem to be brought in like the deus ex machina of the later Greek drama. There is no movement, no action, no development. The characters are poetically but not dramatically conceived. Considered as a tragedy, "Nathan" would be weak; considered as a comedy, it would be heavy. With full knowledge of these circumstances, Lessing called it not a drama, but a dramatic poem; and he might have called it still more accurately a didactic poem, for the only feature which it has in common with the drama is that the personages use the oratio directa.

"Nathan" is a didactic poem: it is not a mere philosophic treatise written in verse, like the fragments of Xenophanes. Its lessons are conveyed concretely and not abstractly; and its characters are not mere lay figures, but living poetical conceptions. Considered as a poem among classic German poems, it must rank next to, though immeasurably below, Goethe's "Faust."

There are two contrasted kinds of genius, the poetical and the philosophical; or, to speak yet more generally, the artistic and the critical. The former is distinguished by a concrete, the latter by an abstract, imagination. The former sees things synthetically, in all their natural complexity; the latter pulls things to pieces analytically, and scrutinizes their relations. The former sees a tree in all its glory, where the latter sees an exogen with a pair of cotyledons. The former sees wholes, where the latter sees aggregates.

Corresponding with these two kinds of genius there are two classes of artistic productions. When the critical genius writes a poem or a novel, he constructs his plot and his characters in conformity to some prearranged theory, or with a view to illustrate some favourite doctrine. When he paints a picture, he first thinks how certain persons would look under certain given circumstances, and paints them accordingly. When he writes a piece of music, he first decides that this phrase expresses joy, and that phrase disappointment, and the other phrase disgust, and he composes accordingly. We therefore say ordinarily that he does not create, but only constructs and combines. It is far different with the artistic genius, who, without stopping to think, sees the picture and hears the symphony with the eyes and ears of imagination, and paints and plays merely what he has seen and heard. When Dante, in imagination, arrived at the lowest circle of hell, where traitors like Judas and Brutus are punished, he came upon a terrible frozen lake, which, he says,—

"Ever makes me shudder at the sight of frozen pools." I have always considered this line a marvellous instance of the intensity of Dante's imagination. It shows, too, how Dante composed his poem. He did not take counsel of himself and say: "Go to, let us describe the traitors frozen up to their necks in a dismal lake, for that will be most terrible." But the picture of the lake, in all its iciness, with the haggard faces staring out from its glassy crust, came unbidden before his mind with such intense reality that, for the rest of his life, he could not look at a frozen pool without a shudder of horror. He described it exactly as he saw it; and his description makes us shudder who read it after all the centuries that have intervened. So Michael Angelo, a kindred genius, did not keep cutting and chipping away, thinking how Moses ought to look, and what sort of a nose he ought to have, and in what position his head might best rest upon his shoulders. But, he looked at the rectangular block of Carrara marble, and beholding Moses grand and lifelike within it, knocked away the environing stone, that others also might see the mighty figure. And so Beethoven, an artist of the same colossal order, wrote out for us those mysterious harmonies which his ear had for the first time heard; and which, in his mournful old age, it heard none the less plainly because of its complete physical deafness. And in this way Shakespeare wrote his "Othello"; spinning out no abstract thoughts about jealousy and its fearful effects upon a proud and ardent nature, but revealing to us the living concrete man, as his imperial imagination had spontaneously fashioned him.

Modern psychology has demonstrated that this is the way in which the creative artistic imagination proceeds. It has proved that a vast portion of all our thinking goes on unconsciously; and that the results may arise into consciousness piecemeal and gradually, checking each other as they come; or that they may come all at once, with all the completeness and definiteness of perceptions presented from without. The former is the case with the critical, and the latter with the artistic intellect. And this we recognize imperfectly when we talk of a genius being "inspired." All of us probably have these two kinds of imagination to a certain extent. It is only given to a few supremely endowed persons like Goethe to possess them both to an eminent degree. Perhaps of no other man can it be said that he was a poet of the first order, and as great a critic as poet.

It is therefore apt to be a barren criticism which studies the works of creative geniuses in order to ascertain what theory lies beneath them. How many systems of philosophy, how many subtle speculations, have we not seen fathered upon Dante, Cervantes, Shakespeare, and Goethe! Yet their works are, in a certain sense, greater than any systems. They partake of the infinite complexity and variety of nature, and no more than nature itself can they be narrowed down to the limits of a precise formula.

Lessing was wont to disclaim the title of poet; but, as Goethe said, his immortal works refute him. He had not only poetical, but dramatic genius; and his "Emilia Galotti" has kept the stage until to-day. Nevertheless, he knew well what he meant when he said that he was more of a critic than a poet. His genius was mainly of the critical order; and his great work, "Nathan the Wise," was certainly constructed rather than created. It was intended to convey a doctrine, and was carefully shaped for the purpose. And when we have pronounced it the greatest of all poems that have been written for a set purpose, and admit of being expressed in a definite formula, we have classified it with sufficient accuracy.

For an analysis of the characters in the poem, nothing can be better than the essay by Kuno Fischer, appended to the present volume. The work of translation has been admirably done; and thanks are due to Miss Frothingham for her reproduction of this beautiful poem.

June, 1868.

VIII.

HISTORICAL DIFFICULTIES.[29]

History, says Sainte-Beuve, is in great part a set of fables which people agree to believe in. And, on reading books like the present, one certainly needs a good deal of that discipline acquired by long familiarity with vexed historical questions, in order to check the disposition to accept the great critic's ironical remark in sober earnest. Much of what is currently accredited as authentic history is in fact a mixture of flattery and calumny, myth and fable. Yet in this set of fables, whatever may have been the case in past times, people will no longer agree to believe. During the present century the criticism of recorded events has gone far toward assuming the developed and systematized aspect of a science, and canons of belief have been established. which it is not safe to disregard. Great occurrences, such as the Trojan War and the Siege of Thebes, not long ago faithfully described by all historians of Greece, have been found to be part of the common mythical heritage of the Aryan nations. Achilleus and Helena, Oidipous and Iokasta, Oinone and Paris, have been discovered in India and again in Scandinavia, and so on, until their nonentity has become the legitimate inference from their very ubiquity. Legislators like Romulus and Numa, inventors like Kadmos, have evaporated into etymologies. Whole legions of heroes, dynasties of kings, and adulteresses as many as Dante saw borne on the whirlwind, have vanished from the face of history, and terrible has been the havoc in the opening pages of our chronological tables. Nor is it primitive history alone which has been thus metamorphosed. Characters unduly exalted or defamed by party spirit are daily being set before us in their true, or at least in a truer, light. What Mr. Froude has done for Henry VIII. we know; and he might have done more if he had not tried to do so much. Humpbacked Richard turns out to have been one of the handsomest kings that ever sat on the throne of England. Edward I., in his dealings with Scotland, is seen to have been scrupulously just; while the dignity of the patriot hero Wallace has been somewhat impaired. Elizabeth is proved to have befriended the false Mary Stuart much longer than was consistent with her personal safety. Eloquent Cicero has been held up as an object of contempt; and even weighty Tacitus has been said to owe much of his reputation to his ability to give false testimony with a grave face. It has lately been suspected that gloomy Tiberius, apart from his gloominess, may have been rather a good fellow; not so licentious as puritanical, not cruel so much as exceptionally merciful,—a rare general, a sagacious statesman, and popular to boot with all his subjects save the malignant oligarchy which he consistently snubbed, and which took revenge on him by writing his life. And, to crown all, even Catiline, abuser of

---

[29] Historical Difficulties and Contested Events. By Octave Delepierre, LL. D., F. S. A., Secretary of Legation to the King of the Belgians. 8vo. London: Murray. 1868.

our patience, seducer of vestal nuns, and drinker of children's blood,—whose very name suggests murder, incest, and robbery,—even Catiline has found an able defender in Professor Beesly. It is claimed that Catiline was a man of great abilities and average good character, a well-calumniated leader of the Marian party which Caesar afterwards led to victory, and that his famous plot for burning Rome never existed save in the unscrupulous Ciceronian fancy. And those who think it easy to refute these conclusions of Professor Beesly had better set to work and try it. Such are a few of the surprising questions opened by recent historical research; and in the face of them the public is quite excusable if it declares itself at a loss what to believe.

These, however, are cases in which criticism has at least made some show of ascertaining the truth and detecting the causes of the prevalent misconception. That men like Catiline and Tiberius should have had their characters blackened is quite easily explicable. President Johnson would have little better chance of obtaining justice at the hands of posterity, if the most widely read history of his administration should happen to be written by a radical member of the Rump Congress. But the cases which Mr. Delepierre invites us to contemplate are of a different character. They come neither under the head of myths nor under that of misrepresentations. Some of them are truly vexed questions which it may perhaps always be impossible satisfactorily to solve. Others may be dealt with more easily, but afford no clew to the origin of the popularly received error. Let us briefly examine a few of Mr. Delepierre's "difficulties." And first, because simplest, we will take the case of the Alexandrian Library.

Every one has heard how Amrou, after his conquest of Egypt, sent to Caliph Omar to know what should be done with the Alexandrian Library. "If the books agree with the Koran," said the Caliph, "they are superfluous; if they contradict it, they are damnable; in either case, destroy them." So the books were taken and used to light the fires which heated water for the baths; and so vast was the number that, used in this way, they lasted six months! All this happened because John the Grammarian was over-anxious enough to request that the books might be preserved, and thus drew Amrou's attention to them. Great has been the obloquy poured upon Omar for this piece of vandalism, and loud has been the mourning over the treasures of ancient science and literature supposed to have been irrecoverably lost in this ignominious conflagration Theologians, Catholic and Protestant, have been fond of quoting it as an instance of the hostility of Mahometanism to knowledge, and we have even heard an edifying sermon preached about it. On seeing the story put to such uses, one feels sometimes like using the ad hominem argument, and quoting the wholesale destruction of pagan libraries under Valens, the burning of books by the Latin stormers of Constantinople, the alleged annihilation of 100,000 volumes by Genoese crusaders at Tripoli, the book-burning exploits of Torquemada, the bonfire of 80,000 valuable Arabic manuscripts, lighted up in the square of Granada by order of Cardinal Ximenes, and the irreparable cremation of Aztec writings by the first Christian bishops of Mexico. These examples, with perhaps others which do not now occur to us, might be applied in just though ungentle retort by Mahometan doctors. Yet the most direct rejoinder would probably not occur to them: the Alexandrian Library was NOT destroyed by the orders of Omar, and the whole story is a figment!

The very pithiness of it, so characteristic of the excellent but bigoted Omar, is enough to cast suspicion upon it. De Quincey tells us that "if a saying has a proverbial fame, the probability is that it was never said." How many amusing stories stand a chance of going down to posterity as the inventions of President Lincoln, of which, nevertheless, he is doubtless wholly innocent! How characteristic was Caesar's reply to the frightened pilot! Yet in all probability Caesar never made it.

Now for the evidence. Alexandria was captured by Amrou in 640. The story of the burning of the library occurs for the first time in the works of Abulpharagius, who flourished in 1264. Six hundred years had elapsed. It is as if a story about the crusades of Louis IX. were to be found for the first time in the writings of Mr. Bancroft. The Byzantine historians were furiously angry with the Saracens; why did they, one and all, neglect to mention such an outrageous piece of vandalism? Their silence must be considered quite conclusive. Moreover we know "that the caliphs had forbidden under severe penalties the destruction" of Jewish and Christian books, a circumstance wholly inconsistent with this famous story. And finally, what a mediaeval recklessness of dates is shown in lugging into the story John the Grammarian, who was dead and in his grave when Alexandria was taken by Amrou!

But the chief item of proof remains to be mentioned. The Saracens did not burn the library, because there was no library there for them to burn! It had been destroyed just two hundred and fifty years before by a rabble of monks, incited by the patriarch Theophilus, who saw in such a vast collection of pagan literature a perpetual insult and menace to religion. In the year 390 this turbulent bigot sacked the temple of Serapis, where the books were kept, and drove out the philosophers who lodged there. Of this violent deed we have contemporary evidence, for Orosius tells us that less than fifteen years afterwards, while passing through Alexandria, he saw the empty shelves. This fact disposes of the story.

Passing from Egypt to France, and from the seventh century to the fifteenth, we meet with a much more difficult problem. That Jeanne d'Arc was burnt at the stake, at Rouen, on the 30th of May, 1431, and her bones and ashes thrown into the Seine, is generally supposed to be as indisputable as any event in modern history. Such is, however, hardly the case. Plausible evidence has been brought to prove that Jeanne d'Arc was never burnt at the stake, but lived to a ripe age, and was even happily married to a nobleman of high rank and reputation. We shall abridge Mr. Delepierre's statement of this curious case.

In the archives of Metz, Father Vignier discovered the following remarkable entry: "In the year 1436, Messire Phlin Marcou was Sheriff of Metz, and on the 20th day of May of the aforesaid year came the maid Jeanne, who had been in France, to La Grange of Ormes, near St. Prive, and was taken there to confer with any one of the sieurs of Metz, and she called herself Claude; and on the same day there came to see her there her two brothers, one of whom was a knight, and was called Messire Pierre, and the other 'petit Jehan,' a squire, and they thought that she had been burnt, but as soon as they saw her they recognized her and she them. And on Monday, the 21st day of the said month, they took their sister with them to Boquelon, and the sieur Nicole, being a knight, gave her a stout stallion of the value of thirty francs, and a pair of saddle-cloths; the sieur Aubert Boulle, a riding-hood, the sieur Nicole Groguet, a sword; and the said maiden mounted the said horse nimbly, and said several things to the sieur Nicole by which he well understood that it was she who had been in France; and she was recognized by many tokens to be the maid Jeanne of France who escorted King Charles to Rheims, and several declared that she had been burnt in Normandy, and she spoke mostly in parables. She afterwards returned to the town of Marnelle for the feast of Pentecost, and remained there about three weeks, and then set off to go to Notre Dame d'Alliance. And when she wished to leave, several of Metz went to see her at the said Marnelle and gave her several jewels, and they knew well that she was the maid Jeanne of France; and she then went to Erlon, in the Duchy of Luxembourg, where she was thronged,.... and there was solemnized the marriage of Monsieur de Hermoise, knight, and the said maid Jeanne, and afterwards the said sieur Hermoise, with his wife, the Maid, came to live at Metz, in the house the said sieur had, opposite St. Seglenne, and remained there until it pleased them to depart."

This is surprising enough; but more remains behind. Dining shortly afterwards with M. des Armoises, member of one of the oldest families in Lorraine, Father Vignier was invited to look over the family archives, that he might satisfy his curiosity regarding certain ancestors of his host. And on looking over the family register, what was his astonishment at finding a contract of marriage between Robert des Armoises, Knight, and Jeanne d'Arcy, the so-called Maid of Orleans!

In 1740, some time after these occurrences, there was found, in the town hall of Orleans, a bill of one Jacques l'Argentier, of the year 1436, in which mention is made of a small sum paid for refreshments furnished to a messenger who had brought letters from the Maid of Orleans, and of twelve livres given to Jean du Lis, brother of Jeanne d'Arc, to help him pay the expenses of his journey back to his sister. Then come two charges which we shall translate literally. "To the sieur de Lis, 18th October, 1436, for a journey which he made through the said city while on his way to the Maid, who was then at Erlon in Luxembourg, and for carrying letters from Jeanne the Maid to the King at Loicher, where he was then staying, six livres." And again: "To Renard

Brune, 25th July, 1435, at evening, for paying the hire of a messenger who was carrying letters from Jeanne the Maid, and was on his way to William Beliers, bailiff of Troyes, two livres."

As no doubt has been thrown upon the genuineness of these documents, it must be considered established that in 1436, five years after the public execution at Rouen, a young woman, believed to be the real Jeanne d'Arc, was alive in Lorraine and was married to a M. Hermoises or Armoises. She may, of course, have been an impostor; but in this case it is difficult to believe that her brothers, Jean and Pierre, and the people of Lorraine, where she was well known, would not have detected the imposture at once. And that Jean du Lis, during a familiar intercourse of at least several months, as indicated in the above extracts, should have continued to mistake a stranger for his own sister, with whom he had lived from childhood, seems a very absurd supposition. Nor is it likely that an impostor would have exposed herself to such a formidable test. If it had been a bold charlatan who, taking advantage of the quite general belief, to which we have ample testimony, that there was something more in the execution at Rouen than was allowed to come to the surface, had resolved to usurp for herself the honours due to the woman who had saved France, she would hardly have gone at the outset to a part of the country where the real Maid had spent nearly all her life. Her instant detection and exposure, perhaps a disgraceful punishment, would have been inevitable. But if this person were the real Jeanne, escaped from prison or returning from an exile dictated by prudence, what should she have done but go straightway to the haunts of her childhood, where she might meet once more her own friends and family?

But the account does not end here. M. Wallon, in his elaborate history of Jeanne d'Arc, states that in 1436 the supposed Maid visited France, and appears to have met some of the men-at-arms with whom she had fought. In 1439 she came to Orleans, for in the accounts of the town we read, "July 28, for ten pints of wine presented to Jeanne des Armoises, 14 sous." And on the day of her departure, the citizens of Orleans, by a special decree of the town-council, presented her with 210 livres, "for the services which she had rendered to the said city during the siege." At the same time the annual ceremonies for the repose of her soul were, quite naturally, suppressed. Now we may ask if it is at all probable that the people of Orleans, who, ten years before, during the siege, must have seen the Maid day after day, and to whom her whole appearance must have been perfectly familiar, would have been likely to show such attentions as these to an impostor? "In 1440," says Mr. Delepierre, "the people so firmly believed that Jeanne d'Arc was still alive, and that another had been sacrificed in her place, that an adventuress who endeavoured to pass herself off as the Maid of Orleans was ordered by the government to be exposed before the public on the marble stone of the palace hall, in order to prove that she was an impostor. Why were not such measures taken against the real Maid of Orleans, who is mentioned in so many public documents, and who took no pains to hide herself?"

There is yet another document bearing on this case, drawn from the accounts of the auditor of the Orleans estate, in the year 1444, which we will here translate. "An island on the River Loire is restored to Pierre du Lis, knight, 'on account of the supplication of the said Pierre, alleging that for the acquittal of his debt of loyalty toward our Lord the King and M. the Duke of Orleans, he left his country to come to the service of the King and M. the Duke, accompanied by his sister, Jeanne the Maid, with whom, down to the time of her departure, and since, unto the present time, he has exposed his body and goods in the said service, and in the King's wars, both in resisting the former enemies of the kingdom who were besieging the town of Orleans, and since then in divers enterprises,' &c., &c." Upon this Mr. Delepierre justly remarks that the brother might have presented his claims in a much stronger light, "if in 1444," instead of saying 'up to the time of her departure,' he had brought forward the martyrdom of his sister, as having been the means of saving France from the yoke of England." The expression here cited and italicized in the above translation, may indeed be held to refer delicately to her death, but the particular French phrase employed, "jusques a son absentement," apparently excludes such an interpretation. The expression, on the other hand, might well refer to Jeanne's departure for Lorraine, and her marriage, after which there is no evidence that she returned to France, except for brief visits. Thus a notable amount of evidence goes to show that Jeanne was not put to death in 1431, as usually supposed, but was alive, married, and flourishing in 1444. Upon this supposition, certain alleged difficulties in the traditional account are easily disposed of. Mr. Delepierre urges upon the testimony of Perceval de Cagny, that at the execution in Rouen "the victim's face was covered when walking to the stake, while at the same time a spot had been chosen for the execution that permitted the populace to have a good view. Why this contradiction? A place is chosen to enable the people to see everything, but the victim is carefully hidden from their sight." Whether otherwise explicable or not, this fact is certainly consistent with the hypothesis that some other victim was secretly substituted for Jeanne by the English authorities.

We have thus far contented ourselves with presenting and re-enforcing Mr. Delepierre's statement of the case. It is now time to interpose a little criticism. We must examine our data somewhat more closely, for vagueness of conception allows a latitude to belief which accuracy of conception considerably restricts.

On the hypothesis of her survival, where was Jeanne, and what was she doing all the time from her capture before Compiegne, May 24, 1430, until her appearance at Metz, May 20, 1436? Mr. Delepierre reminds us that the Duke of Bedford, regent of France for the English king, died in 1435, and "that most probably Jeanne d'Arc was released from prison after this event." Now this supposition lands us in a fatally absurd conclusion. We are, in fact, asked to believe that the English, while holding Jeanne fast in their clutches, gratuitously went through the horrid farce of burning some one else in her stead; and that, after having thus inexplicably behaved, they further stultified themselves by letting her go scot-free, that their foolishness might be duly exposed and confuted. Such a theory is childish. If Jeanne d'Arc ever survived the 30th May, 1431, it was because she escaped from prison and succeeded in hiding herself until safer times. When could she have done this? In a sortie from Compiegne, May 24, 1430, she was thrown from her horse by a Picard archer and taken prisoner by the Bastard of Vendome, who sold her to John of Luxembourg. John kept her in close custody at Beaulieu until August. While there, she made two attempts to escape; first, apparently, by running out through a door, when she was at once caught by the guards; secondly, by jumping from a high window, when the shock of the fall was so great that she lay insensible on the ground until discovered. She was then removed to Beaurevoir, where she remained until the beginning of November. By this time, Philip "the Good," Duke of Burgundy, had made up his mind to sell her to the English for 10,000 francs; and Jeanne was accordingly taken to Arras, and thence to Cotoy, where she was delivered to the English by Philip's officers. So far, all is clear; but here it may be asked, WAS she really delivered to the English, or did Philip, pocketing his 10,000 francs, cheat and defraud his allies with a counterfeit Jeanne? Such crooked dealing would have been in perfect keeping with his character. Though a far more agreeable and gentlemanly person, he was almost as consummate and artistic a rascal as his great-great-great-grandson and namesake, Philip II. of Spain. His duplicity was so unfathomable and his policy so obscure, that it would be hardly safe to affirm a priori that he might not, for reasons best known to himself, have played a double game with his friend the Duke of Bedford. On this hypothesis, he would of course keep Jeanne in close custody so long as there was any reason for keeping his treachery secret. But in 1436, after the death of Bedford and the final expulsion of the English from France, no harm could come from setting her at liberty.

But as soon as we cease to reason a priori, this is seen to be, after all, a lame hypothesis. No one can read the trial of Jeanne at Rouen, the questions that were put to her and the answers which she made, without being convinced that we are here dealing with the genuine Maid and not with a substitute. The first step of a counterfeit Jeanne would have naturally been to save herself from the flames by revealing her true character. Moreover, among the multitudes who saw her during her cruel trial, it is not likely that none were acquainted with the true Jeanne's voice and features. We must therefore conclude that Jeanne d'Arc was really consigned to the tender mercies of the English. About the 21st of November she was taken on horseback, strongly guarded, from Cotoy to Rouen, where the trial began January 9, 1431. On the 21st of February she appeared before the court; on the 13th of March she was examined in the prison by an inquisitor; and on May 24, the Thursday after Pentecost, upon a scaffold conspicuously placed in the Cemetery of St. Ouen, she publicly recanted, abjuring her "heresies" and asking the Church's pardon for her "witchcraft." We may be sure that the Church dignitaries would not knowingly have made such public display of a counterfeit Jeanne; nor could they well have been deceived themselves under such circumstances. It may indeed be said, to exhaust all possible suppositions, that a young girl wonderfully similar in feature and voice to Jeanne d'Arc was palmed off upon the English by Duke Philip, and afterwards, on her trial, comported herself like the Maid, trusting in this recantation to effect her release. But we consider such an hypothesis extremely far-fetched, nor does it accord with the events which immediately followed. It seems hardly questionable that it was the real Jeanne who publicly recanted on the 24th of May. This was only six days before the execution. Four days after, on Monday the 28th, it was reported that Jeanne had relapsed, that she had, in defiance of the Church's prohibition, clothed herself in male attire, which had been left in a convenient place by the authorities, expressly to test her sincerity. On the next day but one, the woman purporting to be the Maid of Orleans was led out, with her face carefully covered, and burnt at the stake.

Here is the first combination of circumstances which bears a suspicious look. It disposes of our Burgundy hypothesis, for a false Jeanne, after recanting to secure her safety, would never have stultified herself by such a barefaced relapse. But the true Jeanne, after recanting, might certainly have escaped. Some compassionate guard, who before would have scrupled to assist her while under the ban of the Church, might have deemed himself excusable for lending her his aid after she had been absolved. Postulating, then, that Jeanne escaped from Rouen between the 24th and the 28th, how shall we explain what happened immediately afterward?

The English feared Jeanne d'Arc as much as they hated her. She had, by her mere presence at the head of the French army, turned their apparent triumph into ignominious defeat. In those days the true psychological explanation of such an event was by no means obvious. While the French attributed the result to celestial interposition in their behalf, the English, equally ready to admit its supernatural character, considered the powers of hell rather than those of heaven to have been the prime instigators. In their eyes Jeanne was a witch, and it was at least their cue to exhibit her as such. They might have put her to death when she first reached Rouen. Some persons, indeed, went so far as to advise that she should be sewed up in a sack and thrown at once into the Seine; but this was not what the authorities wanted. The whole elaborate trial, and the extorted recantation, were devised for the purpose of demonstrating her to be a witch, and thus destroying her credit with the common people. That they intended afterwards to burn her cannot for an instant be doubted; that was the only fit consummation for their evil work.

Now when, at the end of the week after Pentecost, the bishops and inquisitors at Rouen learned, to their dismay, that their victim had escaped, what were they to do? Confess that they had been foiled, and create a panic in the army by the news that their dreaded enemy was at liberty? Or boldly carry out their purposes by a fictitious execution, trusting in the authority which official statements always carry, and shrewdly foreseeing that, after her recantation, the disgraced Maid would no more venture to claim for herself the leadership of the French forces? Clearly, the latter would have been the wiser course. We may assume, then, that, by the afternoon of the 28th, the story of the relapse was promulgated, as a suitable preparation for what was to come; and that on the 30th the poor creature who had been hastily chosen to figure as the condemned Maid was led out, with face closely veiled, to perish by a slow fire in the old market-place. Meanwhile the true Jeanne would have made her way, doubtless, in what to her was the effectual disguise of a woman's apparel, to some obscure place of safety, outside of doubtful France and treacherous Burgundy, perhaps in Alsace or the Vosges. Here she would remain, until the final expulsion of the English and the conclusion of a treaty of peace in 1436 made it safe for her to show herself; when she would naturally return to Lorraine to seek her family.

The comparative obscurity in which she must have remained for the rest of her life, otherwise quite inexplicable on any hypothesis of her survival, is in harmony with the above-given explanation. The ingratitude of King Charles towards the heroine who had won him his crown is the subject of common historical remark. M. Wallon insists upon the circumstance that, after her capture at Compiegne, no attempts were made by the French Court to ransom her or to liberate her by a bold coup de main. And when, at Rouen, she appealed in the name of the Church to the Pope to grant her a fair trial, not a single letter was written by the Archbishop of Rheims, High Chancellor of France, to his suffragan, the Bishop of Beauvais, demanding cognizance of the proceedings. Nor did the King make any appeal to the Pope, to prevent the consummation of the judicial murder. The Maid was deliberately left to her fate. It is upon her enemies at court, La Tremouille and Regnault de Chartres, that we must lay part of the blame for this wicked negligence. But it is also probable that the King, and especially his clerical advisers, were at times almost disposed to acquiesce in the theory of Jeanne's witchcraft. Admire her as they might, they could not help feeling that in her whole behaviour there was something uncanny; and, after having reaped the benefits of her assistance, they were content to let her shift for herself. This affords the clew to the King's inconsistencies. It may be thought sufficient to explain the fact that Jeanne is said to have received public testimonials at Orleans, while we have no reason to suppose that she visited Paris. It may help to dispose of the objection that she virtually disappears from history after the date of the tragedy at Rouen.

Nevertheless, this last objection is a weighty one, and cannot easily be got rid of. It appears to me utterly incredible that, if Jeanne d'Arc had really survived, we should find no further mention of her than such as haply occurs in one or two town-records and dilapidated account-books. If she was alive in

1436, and corresponding with the King, some of her friends at court must have got an inkling of the true state of things. Why did they not parade their knowledge, to the manifest discomfiture of La Tremouille and his company? Or why did not Pierre du Lis cause it to be proclaimed that the English were liars, his sister being safely housed in Metz?

In the mere interests of historical criticism, we have said all that we could in behalf of Mr. Delepierre's hypothesis. But as to the facts upon which it rests, we may remark, in the first place, that the surname Arc or "Bow" was not uncommon in those days, while the Christian name Jeanne was and now is the very commonest of French names. There might have been a hundred Jeanne d'Arcs, all definable as pucelle or maid, just as we say "spinster": we even read of one in the time of the Revolution. We have, therefore, no doubt that Robert des Hermoises married a Jeanne d'Arc, who may also have been a maid of Orleans; but this does not prove her to have been the historic Jeanne. Secondly, as to the covering of the face, we may mention the fact, hitherto withheld, that it was by no means an uncommon circumstance: the victims of the Spanish Inquisition were usually led to the stake with veiled faces. Thirdly, the phrase "jusques a son absentement" is hopelessly ambiguous, and may as well refer to Pierre du Lis himself as to his sister.

These brief considerations seem to knock away all the main props of Mr. Delepierre's hypothesis, save that furnished by the apparent testimony of Jeanne's brothers, given at second hand in the Metz archives. And those who are familiar with the phenomena of mediaeval delusions will be unwilling to draw too hasty an inference from this alone. From the Emperor Nero to Don Sebastian of Portugal, there have been many instances of the supposed reappearance of persons generally believed to be dead. For my own part, therefore, I am by no means inclined to adopt the hypothesis of Jeanne's survival, although I have endeavoured to give it tangible shape and plausible consistency. But the fact that so much can be said in behalf of a theory running counter not only to universal tradition, but also to such a vast body of contemporaneous testimony, should teach us to be circumspect in holding our opinions, and charitable in our treatment of those who dissent from them. For those who can discover in the historian Renan and the critic Strauss nothing but the malevolence of incredulity, the case of Jeanne d'Arc, duly contemplated, may serve as a wholesome lesson.

We have devoted so much space to this problem, by far the most considerable of those treated in Mr. Delepierre's book, that we have hardly room for any of the others. But a false legend concerning Solomon de Caus, the supposed original inventor of the steam-engine, is so instructive that we must give a brief account of it.

In 1834 "there appeared in the Musee des Familles a letter from the celebrated Marion Delorme, supposed to have been written on the 3d February, 1641, to her lover Cinq-Mars." In this letter it is stated that De Caus came four years ago [1637] from Normandy, to inform the King concerning a marvellous invention which he had made, being nothing less than the application of steam to the propulsion of carriages. "The Cardinal [Richelieu] dismissed this fool without giving him a hearing." But De Caus, nowise discouraged, followed close upon the autocrat's heels wherever he went, and so teased him, that the Cardinal, out of patience, sent him off to a madhouse, where he passed the remainder of his days behind a grated window, proclaiming his invention to the passengers in the street, and calling upon them to release him. Marion gives a graphic account of her visit, accompanied by the famous Lord Worcester, to the asylum at Bicetre, where they saw De Caus at his window; and Worcester, in whose mind the conception of the steam-engine was already taking shape, informed her that the raving prisoner was not a madman, but a genius. A great stir was made by this letter. The anecdote was copied into standard works, and represented in engravings. Yet it was a complete hoax. De Caus was not only never confined in a madhouse, but he was architect to Louis XIII. up to the time of his death, in 1630, just eleven years BEFORE Marion Delorme was said to have seen him at his grated window!

"On tracing this hoax to its source," says Mr. Delepierre, "we find that M. Henri Berthoud, a literary man of some repute, and a constant contributor to the Musee des Familles, confesses that the letter attributed to Marion was in fact written by himself. The editor of this journal had requested Gavarni to furnish him with a drawing for a tale in which a madman was introduced looking through the bars of his cell. The drawing was executed and engraved, but arrived too late; and the tale, which could not wait, appeared without the illustration. However, as the wood-engraving was effective, and, moreover, was paid for, the editor was unwilling that it should be useless. Berthoud was, therefore, commissioned to look for a subject and to invent a story to which the engraving might be applied. Strangely enough, the world refused to believe in M. Berthoud's confession, so great a hold had the anecdote taken on the public mind; and a Paris newspaper went so far even as to declare that the original autograph of this letter was to be seen in a library in Normandy! M. Berthoud wrote again, denying its existence, and offered a million francs to any one who would produce the said letter."

From this we may learn two lessons, the first being that utterly baseless but plausible stories may arise in queer ways. In the above case, the most far-fetched hypothesis to account for the origin of the legend could hardly have been as apparently improbable as the reality. Secondly, we may learn that if a myth once gets into the popular mind, it is next to impossible to get it out again. In the Castle of Heidelberg there is a portrait of De Caus, and a folio volume of his works, accompanied by a note, in which this letter of Marion Delorme is unsuspectingly cited as genuine. And only three years ago, at a public banquet at Limoges, a well-known French Senator and man of letters made a speech, in which he retailed the story of the madhouse for the edification of his hearers. Truly a popular error has as many lives as a cat; it comes walking in long after you have imagined it effectually strangled.

In conclusion, we may remark that Mr. Delepierre does very scant justice to many of the interesting questions which he discusses. It is to be regretted that he has not thought it worth while to argue his points more thoroughly, and that he has not been more careful in making statements of fact. He sometimes makes strange blunders, the worst of which, perhaps, is contained in his article on Petrarch and Laura. He thinks Laura was merely a poetical allegory, and such was the case, he goes on to say, "with Dante himself, whose Beatrice was a child who died at nine years of age." Dante's Beatrice died on the 9th of June, 1290, at the age of twenty-four, having been the wife of Simone dei Bardi rather more than three years.

October, 1868.

IX.

THE FAMINE OF 1770 IN BENGAL.[30]

No intelligent reader can advance fifty pages in this volume without becoming aware that he has got hold of a very remarkable book. Mr. Hunter's style, to begin with, is such as is written only by men of large calibre and high culture. No words are wasted. The narrative flows calmly and powerfully along, like a geometrical demonstration, omitting nothing which is significant, admitting nothing which is irrelevant, glowing with all the warmth of rich imagination and sympathetic genius, yet never allowing any overt manifestation of feeling, ever concealing the author's personality beneath the unswerving exposition of the subject-matter. That highest art, which conceals art, Mr. Hunter appears to have learned well. With him, the curtain is the picture.

Such a style as this would suffice to make any book interesting, in spite of the remoteness of the subject. But the "Annals of Rural Bengal" do not concern us so remotely as one might at first imagine. The phenomena of the moral and industrial growth or stagnation of a highly-endowed people must ever possess the interest of fascination for those who take heed of the maxim that "history is philosophy teaching by example." National prosperity depends upon circumstances sufficiently general to make the experience of one country of great value to another, though ignorant Bourbon dynasties and Rump Congresses refuse to learn the lesson. It is of the intimate every-day life of rural Bengal that Mr. Hunter treats. He does not, like old historians, try our patience with a bead-roll of names that have earned no just title to remembrance, or dazzle us with a bountiful display of "barbaric pearls and gold," or lead us in the gondolas of Buddhist kings down sacred rivers, amid "a summer fanned with spice"; but he describes the labours and the sufferings, the mishaps and the good fortune, of thirty millions of people, who, however dusky may be their hue, tanned by the tropical suns of fifty centuries, are nevertheless members of the imperial Aryan race, descended from the cool highlands eastward of the Caspian, where, long before the beginning of recorded history, their ancestors and those of the Anglo-American were indistinguishably united in the same primitive community.

The narrative portion of the present volume is concerned mainly with the social and economical disorganization wrought by the great famine of 1770, and with the attempts of the English government to remedy the same. The remainder of the book is occupied with inquiries into the ethnic character of the population of Bengal, and particularly with an exposition of the peculiarities of the language, religion, customs, and institutions of the Santals,

---

[30] The Annals of Rural Bengal. By W. W. Hunter. Vol. I. The Ethnical Frontier of Lower Bengal, with the Ancient Principalities of Beerbhoom and Bishenpore. Second Edition. New York: Leypoldt and Holt. 1868. 8vo., pp. xvi., 475.

or hill-tribes of Beerbhoom. A few remarks on the first of these topics may not be uninteresting.

Throughout the entire course of recorded European history, from the remote times of which the Homeric poems preserve the dim tradition down to the present moment, there has occurred no calamity at once so sudden and of such appalling magnitude as the famine which in the spring and summer of 1770 nearly exterminated the ancient civilization of Bengal. It presents that aspect of preternatural vastness which characterizes the continent of Asia and all that concerns it. The Black Death of the fourteenth century was, perhaps, the most fearful visitation which has ever afflicted the Western world. But in the concentrated misery which it occasioned the Bengal famine surpassed it, even as the Himalayas dwarf by comparison the highest peaks of Switzerland. It is, moreover, the key to the history of Bengal during the next forty years; and as such, merits, from an economical point of view, closer attention than it has hitherto received.

Lower Bengal gathers in three harvests each year; in the spring, in the early autumn, and in December, the last being the great rice-crop, the harvest on which the sustenance of the people depends. Through the year 1769 there was great scarcity, owing to the partial failure of the crops of 1768, but the spring rains appeared to promise relief, and in spite of the warning appeals of provincial officers, the government was slow to take alarm, and continued rigorously to enforce the land-tax. But in September the rains suddenly ceased. Throughout the autumn there ruled a parching drought; and the rice-fields, according to the description of a native superintendent of Bishenpore, "became like fields of dried straw." Nevertheless, the government at Calcutta made—with one lamentable exception, hereafter to be noticed—no legislative attempt to meet the consequences of this dangerous condition of things. The administration of local affairs was still, at that date, intrusted to native officials. The whole internal regulation was in the hands of the famous Muhamad Reza Ehan. Hindu or Mussulman assessors pried into every barn and shrewdly estimated the probable dimensions of the crops on every field; and the courts, as well as the police, were still in native hands. "These men," says our author, "knew the country, its capabilities, its average yield, and its average requirements, with an accuracy that the most painstaking English official can seldom hope to attain to. They had a strong interest in representing things to be worse than they were; for the more intense the scarcity, the greater the merit in collecting the land-tax. Every consultation is filled with their apprehensions and highly-coloured accounts of the public distress; but it does not appear that the conviction entered the minds of the Council during the previous winter months, that the question was not so much one of revenue as of depopulation." In fact, the local officers had cried "Wolf!" too often. Government was slow to believe them, and announced that nothing better could be expected than the adoption of a generous policy toward those landholders whom the loss of harvest had rendered unable to pay their land-tax.

But very few indulgences were granted, and the tax was not diminished, but on the contrary was, in the month of April, 1770, increased by ten per cent for the following year. The character of the Bengali people must also be taken into the account in explaining this strange action on the part of the government.

"From the first appearance of Lower Bengal in history, its inhabitants have been reticent, self-contained, distrustful of foreign observation, in a degree without parallel among other equally civilized nations. The cause of this taciturnity will afterwards be clearly explained; but no one who is acquainted either with the past experiences or the present condition of the people can be ignorant of its results. Local officials may write alarming reports, but their apprehensions seem to be contradicted by the apparent quiet that prevails. Outward, palpable proofs of suffering are often wholly wanting; and even when, as in 1770, such proofs abound, there is generally no lack of evidence on the other side. The Bengali bears existence with a composure that neither accident nor chance can ruffle. He becomes silently rich or uncomplainingly poor. The emotional part of his nature is in strict subjection, his resentment enduring but unspoken, his gratitude of the sort that silently descends from generation to generation. The. passion for privacy reaches its climax in the domestic relations. An outer apartment, in even the humblest households, is set apart for strangers and the transaction of business, but everything behind it is a mystery. The most intimate friend does not venture to make those commonplace kindly inquiries about a neighbour's wife or daughter which European courtesy demands from mere acquaintances. This family privacy is maintained at any price. During the famine of 1866 it was found impossible to render public charity available to the female members of the respectable classes, and many a rural household starved slowly to death without uttering a complaint or making a sign.

"All through the stifling summer of 1770 the people went on dying. The husbandmen sold their cattle; they sold their implements of agriculture; they devoured their seed-grain; they sold their sons and daughters, till at length no buyer of children could be found; they ate the leaves of trees and the grass of the field; and in June, 1770, the Resident at the Durbar affirmed that the living were feeding on the dead. Day and night a torrent of famished and disease-stricken wretches poured into the great cities. At an early period of the year pestilence had broken out. In March we find small-pox at Moorshedabad, where it glided through the vice-regal mutes, and cut off the Prince Syfut in his palace. The streets were blocked up with promiscuous heaps of the dying and dead. Interment could not do its work quick enough; even the dogs and jackals, the public scavengers of the East, became unable to accomplish their revolting work, and the multitude of mangled and festering corpses at length threatened the existence of the citizens..... In 1770, the rainy season brought relief, and before the end of September the province reaped an abundant harvest. But the relief came too late to avert depopulation. Starving and shelterless crowds crawled despairingly from one deserted village to another in a vain search for food, or a resting-place in which to hide themselves from the rain. The epidemics incident to the season were thus spread over the whole country; and, until the close of the year, disease continued so prevalent as to form a subject of communication from the government in Bengal to the Court of Directors. Millions of famished wretches died in the struggle to live through the few intervening weeks that separated them from the harvest, their last gaze being probably fixed on the densely-covered fields that would ripen only a little too late for them..... Three months later, another bountiful harvest, the great rice-crop of the year, was gathered in. Abundance returned to Bengal as suddenly as famine had swooped down upon it, and in reading some of the manuscript records of December it is difficult to realize that the scenes of the preceding ten months have not been hideous phantasmagoria or a long, troubled dream. On Christmas eve, the Council in Calcutta wrote home to the Court of Directors that the scarcity had entirely ceased, and, incredible as it may seem, that unusual plenty had returned..... So generous had been the harvest that the government proposed at once to lay in its military stores for the ensuing year, and expected to obtain them at a very cheap rate."

Such sudden transitions from the depths of misery to the most exuberant plenty are by no means rare in the history of Asia, where the various centres of civilization are, in an economical sense, so isolated from each other that the welfare of the population is nearly always absolutely dependent on the irregular and apparently capricious bounty of nature. For the three years following the dreadful misery above described, harvests of unprecedented abundance were gathered in. Yet how inadequate they were to repair the fearful damage wrought by six months of starvation, the history of the next quarter of a century too plainly reveals. "Plenty had indeed returned," says our annalist, "but it had returned to a silent and deserted province." The extent of the depopulation is to our Western imaginations almost incredible. During those six months of horror, more than TEN MILLIONS of people had perished! It was as if the entire population of our three or four largest States—man, woman, and child—were to be utterly swept away between now and next August, leaving the region between the Hudson and Lake Michigan as quiet and deathlike as the buried streets of Pompeii. Yet the estimate is based upon most accurate and trustworthy official returns; and Mr. Hunter may well say that "it represents an aggregate of individual suffering which no European nation has been called upon to contemplate within historic times."

This unparalleled calamity struck down impartially the rich and the poor. The old, aristocratic families of Lower Bengal were irretrievably ruined. The Rajah of Burdwan, whose possessions were so vast that, travel as far as he would, he always slept under a roof of his own and within his own jurisdiction, died in such indigence that his son had to melt down the family plate and beg a loan from the government in order to discharge his father's funeral expenses. And our author gives other similar instances. The wealthy natives who were appointed to assess and collect the internal revenue, being unable to raise the sums required by the government, were in many cases imprisoned, or their estates were confiscated and re-let in order to discharge the debt.

For fifteen years the depopulation went on increasing. The children in a community, requiring most nourishment to sustain their activity, are those who soonest succumb to famine. "Until 1785," says our author, "the old died off without there being any rising generation to step into their places." From lack of cultivators, one third of the surface of Bengal fell out of tillage and became waste land. The landed proprietors began each "to entice away the tenants of his neighbour, by offering protection against judicial proceedings, and farms at very low rents." The disputes and deadly feuds which arose from this practice were, perhaps, the least fatal of the evil results which flowed from it. For the competition went on until, the tenants obtaining their holdings at half-rates, the resident cultivators—who had once been the wealthiest farmers in the country—were no longer able to complete on such terms. They began to sell, lease, or desert their property, migrating to less afflicted regions, or flying to the hills on the frontier to adopt a savage life. But, in a climate like that of Northeastern India, it takes but little time to transform a tract of untilled land into formidable wilderness. When the functions of society are impeded, nature is swift to assert its claims. And accordingly, in 1789, "Lord Cornwallis after three years' vigilant inquiry, pronounced one third of the company's territories in Bengal to be a jungle, inhabited only by wild beasts."

On the Western frontier of Beerbhoom the state of affairs was, perhaps, most calamitous. In 1776, four acres out of every seven remained untilled. Though in earlier times this district had been a favourite highway for armies, by the year 1780 it had become an almost impassable jungle. A small company of Sepoys, which in that year by heroic exertions forced its way through, was obliged to traverse 120 miles of trackless forest, swarming with tigers and black shaggy bears. In 1789 this jungle "continued so dense as to shut off all communication between the two most important towns, and to cause the mails to be carried by a circuit of fifty miles through another district."

Such a state of things it is difficult for us to realize; but the monotonous tale of disaster and suffering is not yet complete. Beerbhoom was, to all intents and purposes, given over to tigers. "A belt of jungle, filled with wild beasts, formed round each village." At nightfall the hungry animals made their dreaded incursions carrying away cattle, and even women and children, and devouring them. "The official records frequently speak of the mail-bag being carried off by wild beasts." So great was the damage done by these depredations, that "the company offered a reward for each tiger's head, sufficient to maintain a peasant's family in comfort for three months; an item of expenditure it deemed so necessary, that, when under extraordinary pressure it had to suspend all payments, the tiger-money and diet allowance for prisoners were the sole exceptions to the rule." Still more formidable foes were found in the herds of wild elephants, which came trooping along in the rear of the devastation caused by the famine. In the course of a few years fifty-six villages were reported as destroyed by elephants, and as having lapsed into jungle in consequence; "and an official return states that forty market-towns throughout the district had been deserted from the same cause. In many parts of the country the peasantry did not dare to sleep in their houses, lest they should be buried beneath them during the night." These terrible beasts continued to infest the province as late as 1810.

But society during these dark days had even worse enemies than tigers and elephants. The barbarous highlanders, of a lower type of mankind, nourishing for forty centuries a hatred of their Hindu supplanters, like that which the Apache bears against the white frontiersman, seized the occasion to renew their inroads upon the lowland country. Year by year they descended from their mountain fastnesses, plundering and burning. Many noble Hindu families, ousted by the tax-collectors from their estates, began to seek subsistence from robbery. Others, consulting their selfish interests amid the general distress, "found it more profitable to shelter banditti on their estates, levying blackmail from the surrounding villages as the price of immunity from depredation, and sharing in the plunder of such as would not come to terms. Their country houses were robber strongholds, and the early English administrators of Bengal have left it on record that a gang-robbery never occurred without a landed proprietor being at the bottom of it." The peasants were not slow to follow suit, and those who were robbed of their winter's store had no alternative left but to become robbers themselves. The thieveries of the Fakeers, or religious mendicants, and the bold, though stealthy attacks of Thugs and Dacoits—members of Masonic brotherhoods, which at all times have lived by robbery and assassination—added to the general turmoil. In the cold weather of 1772 the province was ravaged far and wide by bands of armed freebooters, fifty thousand strong; and to such a pass did things arrive that the regular forces sent by Warren Hastings to preserve order were twice disastrously routed; while, in Mr. Hunter's graphic language, "villages high up the Ganges lived by housebreaking in Calcutta." In English mansions "it was the invariable practice for the porter to shut the outer door at the commencement of each meal, and not to open it till the butler brought him word that the plate was safely locked up." And for a long time nearly all traffic ceased upon the imperial roads.

This state of things, which amounted to chronic civil war, induced Lord Cornwallis in 1788 to place the province under the direct military control of an English officer. The administration of Mr. Keating—the first hardy gentleman to whom this arduous office was assigned—is minutely described by our author. For our present purpose it is enough to note that two years of severe campaigning, attended and followed by relentless punishment of all transgressors, was required to put an end to the disorders.

Such was the appalling misery, throughout a community of thirty million persons, occasioned by the failure of the winter rice-crop in 1769. In abridging Mr. Hunter's account we have adhered as closely to our original as possible, but he who would obtain adequate knowledge of this tale of woe must seek it in the ever memorable description of the historian himself. The first question which naturally occurs to the reader—though, as Mr. Hunter observes, it would have been one of the last to occur to the Oriental mind—is, Who was to blame? To what culpable negligence was it due that such a dire calamity was not foreseen, and at least partially warded off? We shall find reason to believe that it could not have been adequately foreseen, and that no legislative measures could in that state of society have entirely prevented it. Yet it will appear that the government, with the best of intentions, did all in its power to make matters worse; and that to its blundering ignorance the distress which followed is largely due.

The first duty incumbent upon the government in a case like that of the failure of the winter rice-crop of 1769, was to do away with all hindrance to the importation of food into the province. One chief cause of the far-reaching distress wrought by great Asiatic famines has been the almost complete commercial isolation of Asiatic communities. In the Middle Ages the European communities were also, though to a far less extent, isolated from each other, and in those days periods of famine were comparatively frequent and severe. And one of the chief causes which now render the occurrence of a famine on a great scale almost impossible in any part of the civilized world is the increased commercial solidarity of civilized nations. Increased facility of distribution has operated no less effectively than improved methods of production.

Now, in 1770 the province of Lower Bengal was in a state of almost complete commercial isolation from other communities. Importation of food on an adequate scale was hardly possible. "A single fact speaks volumes as to the isolation of each district. An abundant harvest, we are repeatedly told, was as disastrous to the revenues as a bad one; for, when a large quantity of grain had to be carried to market, the cost of carriage swallowed up the price obtained. Indeed, even if the means of intercommunication and transport had rendered importation practicable, the province had at that time no money to give in exchange for food. Not only had its various divisions a separate currency which would pass nowhere else except at a ruinous exchange, but in that unfortunate year Bengal seems to have been utterly drained of its specie..... The absence of the means of importation was the more to be deplored, as the neighbouring districts could easily have supplied grain. In the southeast a fair harvest had been reaped, except, in circumscribed spots; and we are assured that, during the famine, this part of Bengal was enabled to export without having to complain of any deficiency in consequence..... INDEED, NO MATTER HOW LOCAL A FAMINE MIGHT BE IN THE LAST CENTURY, THE EFFECTS WERE EQUALLY DISASTROUS. Sylhet, a district in the northeast of Bengal, had reaped unusually plentiful harvests in 1780 and 1781, but the next crop was destroyed by a local inundation, and, notwithstanding the facilities for importation afforded by water-carriage, one third of the people died."

Here we have a vivid representation of the economic condition of a society which, however highly civilized in many important respects, still retained, at the epoch treated of, its aboriginal type of organization. Here we see each community brought face to face with the impossible task of supplying, unaided, the deficiencies of nature. We see one petty district a prey to the most frightful destitution, even while profuse plenty reigns in the districts round about it. We find an almost complete absence of the commercial machinery which, by enabling the starving region to be fed out of the surplus of more favoured localities, has in the most advanced countries rendered a great famine practically impossible.

Now this state of things the government of 1770 was indeed powerless to remedy. Legislative power and wisdom could not anticipate the invention of railroads; nor could it introduce throughout the length and breadth of Bengal a system of coaches, canals, and caravans; nor could it all at once do away with the time-honoured brigandage, which increased the cost of transport by decreasing the security of it; nor could it in a trice remove the curse of a heterogeneous coinage. None, save those uninstructed agitators who believe that governments can make water run up-hill, would be disposed to find fault with the authorities in Bengal for failing to cope with these difficulties. But what we are to blame them for—though it was an error of the judgment and not of the intentions—is their mischievous interference with the natural course of trade, by which, instead of helping matters, they but added another to the many powerful causes which were conspiring to bring about the economic ruin of Bengal. We refer to the act which in 1770 prohibited under penalties all speculation in rice.

This disastrous piece of legislation was due to the universal prevalence of a prejudice from which so-called enlightened communities are not yet wholly free. It is even now customary to heap abuse upon those persons who in a season of scarcity, when prices are rapidly rising, buy up the "necessaries of life," thereby still increasing for a time the cost of living. Such persons are commonly assailed with specious generalities to the effect that they are enemies of society. People whose only ideas are "moral ideas" regard them as heartless sharpers who fatten upon the misery of their fellow-creatures. And it is sometimes hinted that such "practices" ought to be stopped by legislation.

Now, so far is this prejudice, which is a very old one, from being justified by facts, that, instead of being an evil, speculation in breadstuffs and other necessaries is one of the chief agencies by which in modern times and civilized countries a real famine is rendered almost impossible. This natural monopoly operates in two ways. In the first place, by raising prices, it checks consumption, putting every one on shorter allowance until the season of scarcity is over, and thus prevents the scarcity from growing into famine. In the second place, by raising prices, it stimulates importation from those localities where abundance reigns and prices are low. It thus in the long run does much to equalize the pressure of a time of dearth and diminish those extreme oscillations of prices which interfere with the even, healthy course of trade. A government which, in a season of high prices, does anything to check such speculation, acts about as sagely as the skipper of a wrecked vessel who should refuse to put his crew upon half rations.

The turning-point of the great Dutch Revolution, so far as it concerned the provinces which now constitute Belgium, was the famous siege and capture of Antwerp by Alexander Farnese, Duke of Parma. The siege was a long one, and the resistance obstinate, and the city would probably not have been captured if famine had not come to the assistance of the besiegers. It is interesting, therefore, to inquire what steps the civic authorities had taken to prevent such a calamity. They knew that the struggle before them was likely to be the life-and-death struggle of the Southern Netherlands; they knew that there was risk of their being surrounded so that relief from without would be impossible; they knew that their assailant was one of the most astute and unconquerable of men, by far the greatest general of the sixteenth century. Therefore they proceeded to do just what our Republican Congress, under such circumstances, would probably have done, and just what the New York Tribune, if it had existed in those days, would have advised them to do. Finding that sundry speculators were accumulating and hoarding up provisions in anticipation of a season of high prices, they hastily decided, first of all to put a stop to such "selfish iniquity." In their eyes the great thing to be done was to make things cheap. They therefore affixed a very low maximum price to everything which could be eaten, and prescribed severe penalties for all who should attempt to take more than the sum by law decreed. If a baker refused to sell his bread for a price which would have been adequate only in a time of great plenty, his shop was to be broken open, and his loaves distributed among the populace. The consequences of this idiotic policy were twofold.

In the first place, the enforced lowness of prices prevented any breadstuffs or other provisions from being brought into the city. It was a long time before Farnese succeeded in so blockading the Scheldt as to prevent ships laden with eatables from coming in below. Corn and preserved meats might have been hurried by thousands of tons into the beleaguered city. Friendly Dutch vessels, freighted with abundance, were waiting at the mouth of the river. But all to no purpose. No merchant would expose his valuable ship, with its cargo, to the risk of being sunk by Farnese's batteries, merely for the sake of finding a market no better than a hundred others which could be entered without incurring danger. No doubt if the merchants of Holland had followed out the maxim Vivre pour autrui, they would have braved ruin and destruction rather than behold their neighbours of Antwerp enslaved. No doubt if they could have risen to a broad philosophic view of the future interests of the Netherlands, they would have seen that Antwerp must be saved, no matter if some of them were to lose money by it. But men do not yet sacrifice themselves for their fellows, nor do they as a rule look far beyond the present moment and its emergencies. And the business of government is to legislate for men as they are, not as it is supposed they ought to be. If provisions had brought a high price in Antwerp, they would have been carried thither. As it was, the city, by its own stupidity, blockaded itself far more effectually than Farnese could have done it.

In the second place, the enforced lowness of prices prevented any general retrenchment on the part of the citizens. Nobody felt it necessary to economize. Every one bought as much bread, and ate it as freely, as if the government by insuring its cheapness had insured its abundance. So the city lived in high spirits and in gleeful defiance of its besiegers, until all at once provisions gave out, and the government had to step in again to palliate the distress which it had wrought. It constituted itself quartermaster-general to the community, and doled out stinted rations alike to rich and poor, with that stern democratic impartiality peculiar to times of mortal peril. But this served only, like most artificial palliatives, to lengthen out the misery. At the time of the surrender, not a loaf of bread could be obtained for love or money.

In this way a bungling act of legislation helped to decide for the worse a campaign which involved the territorial integrity and future welfare of what might have become a great nation performing a valuable function in the system of European communities.

The striking character of this instructive example must be our excuse for presenting it at such length. At the beginning of the famine in Bengal the authorities legislated in very much the same spirit as the burghers who had to defend Antwerp against Parma.

"By interdicting what it was pleased to term the monopoly of grain, it prevented prices from rising at once to their natural rates. The Province had a certain amount of food in it, and this food had to last about nine months. Private enterprise if left to itself would have stored up the general supply at the harvest, with a view to realizing a larger profit at a later period in the scarcity. Prices would in consequence have immediately risen, compelling the population to reduce their consumption from the very beginning of the dearth. The general stock would thus have been husbanded, and the pressure equally spread over the whole nine months, instead of being concentrated upon the last six. The price of grain, in place of promptly rising to three half-pence a pound as in 1865-66, continued at three farthings during the earlier months of the famine. During the latter ones it advanced to twopence, and in certain localities reached fourpence."

The course taken by the great famine of 1866 well illustrates the above views. This famine, also, was caused by the total failure of the December rice-crop, and it was brought to a close by an abundant harvest in the succeeding year.

"Even as regards the maximum price reached, the analogy holds good, in each case rice having risen in general to nearly twopence, and in particular places to fourpence, a pound; and in each the quoted rates being for a brief period in several isolated localities merely nominal, no food existing in the market, and money altogether losing its interchangeable value. In both the people endured silently to the end, with a fortitude that casual observers of a different temperament and widely dissimilar race may easily mistake for apathy, but which those who lived among the sufferers are unable to distinguish from qualities that generally pass under a more honourable name. During 1866, when the famine was severest, I superintended public instruction throughout the southwestern division of Lower Bengal, including Orissa. The subordinate native officers, about eight hundred in number, behaved with a steadiness, and when called upon, with a self-abnegation, beyond praise. Many of them ruined their health. The touching scenes of self-sacrifice and humble heroism which I witnessed among the poor villagers on my tours of inspection will remain in my memory till my latest day."

But to meet the famine of 1866 Bengal was equipped with railroads and canals, and better than all, with an intelligent government. Far from trying to check speculation, as in 1770, the government did all in its power to stimulate it. In the earlier famine one could hardly engage in the grain trade without becoming amenable to the law. "In 1866 respectable men in vast numbers went into the trade; for government, by publishing weekly returns of the rates in every district, rendered the traffic both easy and safe. Every one knew where to buy grain cheapest, and where to sell it dearest, and food was accordingly brought from the districts that could best spare it, and carried to those which most urgently needed it. Not only were prices equalized so far as possible throughout the stricken parts, but the publicity given to the high rates in Lower Bengal induced large shipments from the upper provinces, and the chief seat of the trade became unable to afford accommodation for landing the vast stores of grain brought down the river. Rice poured into the affected districts from all parts,—railways, canals, and roads vigorously doing their duty."

The result of this wise policy was that scarcity was heightened into famine only in one remote corner of Bengal. Orissa was commercially isolated in 1866, as the whole country had been in 1770. "As far back as the records extend, Orissa has produced more grain than it can use. It is an exporting, not an importing province, sending away its surplus grain by sea, and neither requiring nor seeking any communication with Lower Bengal by land." Long after the rest of the province had begun to prepare for a year of famine, Orissa kept on exporting. In March, when the alarm was first raised, the southwest monsoon had set in, rendering the harbours inaccessible. Thus the district was isolated. It was no longer possible to apply the wholesome policy which was operating throughout the rest of the country. The doomed population of Orissa, like passengers in a ship without provisions, were called upon to suffer the extremities of famine; and in the course of the spring and summer of 1866, some seven hundred thousand people perished.

January, 1869.

X.

SPAIN AND THE NETHERLANDS.[31]

Tandem fit surculus arbor: the twig which Mr. Motley in his earlier volumes has described as slowly putting forth its leaves and rootless, while painfully struggling for existence in a hostile soil, has at last grown into a mighty tree of liberty, drawing sustenance from all lands, and protecting all civilized peoples with its pleasant shade. We congratulate Mr. Motley upon the successful completion of the second portion of his great work; and we think that the Netherlanders of our time have reason to be grateful to the writer who has so faithfully and eloquently told the story of their country's fearful struggle against civil and ecclesiastical tyranny, and its manifold contributions to the advancement of European civilization.

Mr. Motley has been fortunate in his selection of a subject upon which to write. Probably no century of modern times lends itself to the purposes of the descriptive historian so well as the sixteenth. While on the one hand the problems which it presents are sufficiently near for us to understand them without too great an effort of the imagination, on the other hand they are sufficiently remote for us to study them without passionate and warping prejudice. The contest between Catholicism and the reformed religion—between ecclesiastical autocracy and the right of private investigation—has become a thing of the past, and constitutes a closed chapter in human history. The epoch which begins where Mr. Motley's history is designed to close—at the peace of Westphalia—is far more complicated. Since the middle of the seventeenth century a double movement has been going on in religion and philosophy, society and politics,—a movement of destruction typified by Voltaire and Rousseau, and a constructive movement represented by Diderot and Lessing. We are still living in the midst of this great epoch: the questions which it presents are liable to disturb our prejudices as well as to stimulate our reason; the results to which it must sooner or later attain can now be only partially foreseen; and even its present tendencies are generally misunderstood, and in many quarters wholly ignored. With the sixteenth century, as we have said, the case is far different. The historical problem is far less complex. The issues at stake are comparatively simple, and the historian has before him a straightforward story.

From the dramatic, or rather from the epic, point of view, the sixteenth century is pre-eminent. The essentially transitional character of modern history since the breaking up of the papal and feudal systems is at no period more distinctly marked. In traversing the sixteenth century we realize that we have

---

[31] History of the United Netherlands: from the Death of William the Silent to the Twelve Years' Truce, 1609. By John Lothrop Motley, D. C. L. In four volumes. Vols. III. and IV. New York. 1868.

fairly got out of one state of things and into another. At the outset, events like the challenge of Barletta may make us doubt whether we have yet quite left behind the Middle Ages. The belief in the central position of the earth is still universal, and the belief in its rotundity not yet, until the voyage of Magellan, generally accepted. We find England—owing partly to the introduction of gunpowder and the consequent disuse of archery, partly to the results of the recent integration of France under Louis XI.—fallen back from the high relative position which it had occupied under the rule of the Plantagenets; and its policy still directed in accordance with reminiscences of Agincourt, and garnet, and Burgundian alliances. We find France just beginning her ill-fated career of intervention in the affairs of Italy; and Spain, with her Moors finally vanquished and a new world beyond the ocean just added to her domain, rapidly developing into the greatest empire which had been seen since the days of the first Caesars. But at the close of the century we find feudal life in castles changed into modern life in towns; chivalric defiances exchanged for over-subtle diplomacy; Maurices instead of Bayards; a Henry IV. instead of a Gaston de Foix. We find the old theory of man's central position in the universe—the foundation of the doctrine of final causes and of the whole theological method of interpreting nature—finally overthrown by Copernicus. Instead of the circumnavigability of the earth, the discovery of a Northwest passage—as instanced by the heroic voyage of Barendz, so nobly described by Mr. Motley—is now the chief geographical problem. East India Companies, in place of petty guilds of weavers and bakers, bear witness to the vast commercial progress. We find England, fresh from her stupendous victory over the whole power of Spain, again in the front rank of nations; France, under the most astute of modern sovereigns, taking her place for a time as the political leader of the civilized world; Spain, with her evil schemes baffled in every quarter, sinking into that terrible death-like lethargy, from which she has hardly yet awakened, and which must needs call forth our pity, though it is but the deserved retribution for her past behaviour. While the little realm of the Netherlands, filched and cozened from the unfortunate Jacqueline by the "good" Duke of Burgundy, carried over to Austria as the marriage-portion of Lady Mary, sent down to Spain as the personal inheritance of the "prudent" Philip, and by him intolerably tormented with an Inquisition, a Blood-Council, and a Duke of Alva, has after a forty years' war of independence taken its position for a time as the greatest of commercial nations, with the most formidable navy and one of the best disciplined armies yet seen upon the earth.

    But the central phenomenon of the sixteenth century is the culmination of the Protestant movement in its decisive proclamation by Luther. For nearly three hundred years already the power of the Church had been declining, and its function as a civilizing agency had been growing more and more obsolete. The first great blow at its supremacy had been directed with partial success in the thirteenth century by the Emperor Frederick II. Coincident with this attack from without, we find a reformation begun within, as exemplified in the

Dominican and Franciscan movements. The second great blow was aimed by Philip IV. of France, and this time it struck with terrible force. The removal of the Papacy to Avignon, in 1305, was the virtual though unrecognized abdication of its beneficent supremacy. Bereft of its dignity and independence, from that time forth it ceased to be the defender of national unity against baronial anarchy, of popular rights against monarchical usurpation, and became a formidable instrument of despotism and oppression. Through the vicissitudes of the great schism in the fourteenth century, and the refractory councils in the fifteenth, its position became rapidly more and more retrograde and demoralized. And when, in 1530, it joined its forces with those of Charles V., in crushing the liberties of the worthiest of mediaeval republics, it became evident that the cause of freedom and progress must henceforth be intrusted to some more faithful champion. The revolt of Northern Europe, led by Luther and Henry VIII. was but the articulate announcement of this altered state of affairs. So long as the Roman Church had been felt to be the enemy of tyrannical monarchs and the steadfast friend of the people, its encroachments, as represented by men like Dunstan and Becket, were regarded with popular favour. The strength of the Church lay ever in its democratic instincts; and when these were found to have abandoned it, the indignant protest of Luther sufficed to tear away half of Europe from its allegiance.

By the end of the sixteenth century, we find the territorial struggle between the Church and the reformed religion substantially decided. Protestantism and Catholicism occupied then the same respective areas which they now occupy. Since 1600 there has been no instance of a nation passing from one form of worship to the other; and in all probability there never will be. Since the wholesale dissolution of religious beliefs wrought in the last century, the whole issue between Romanism and Protestantism, regarded as dogmatic systems, is practically dead. M. Renan is giving expression to an almost self-evident truth, when he says that religious development is no longer to proceed by way of sectarian proselytism, but by way of harmonious internal development. The contest is no longer between one theology and another, but it is between the theological and the scientific methods of interpreting natural phenomena. The sixteenth century has to us therefore the interest belonging to a rounded and completed tale. It contains within itself substantially the entire history of the final stage of the theological reformation.

This great period falls naturally into two divisions, the first corresponding very nearly with the reigns of Charles V. and Henry VIII., and the second with the age of Philip II. and Elizabeth. The first of these periods was filled with the skirmishes which were to open the great battle of the Reformation. At first the strength and extent of the new revolution were not altogether apparent. While the Inquisition was vigorously crushing out the first symptoms of disaffection in Spain, it at one time seemed as if the Reformers were about to gain the whole of the Empire, besides acquiring an excellent foothold in France. Again, while England was wavering between the old and the new faith, the last hopes of the Reform in Germany seemed likely to be destroyed by the military genius of Charles. But in Maurice, the red-bearded hero of Saxony, Charles found more than his match. The picture of the rapid and desperate march of Maurice upon Innspruck, and of the great Emperor flying for his life at the very hour of his imagined triumph, has still for us an intenser interest than almost any other scene of that age; for it was the event which proved that Protestantism was not a mere local insurrection which a monarch like Charles could easily put down, but a gigantic revolution against which all the powers in the world might well strive in vain.

With the abdication of Charles in 1556 the new period may be said to begin, and it is here that Mr. Motley's history commences. Events crowded thick and fast. In 1556 Philip II., a prince bred and educated for the distinct purpose of suppressing heresy, succeeded to the rule of the most powerful empire which had been seen since the days of the Antonines. In the previous year a new era had begun at the court of Rome. The old race of pagan pontiffs, the Borgias, the Farneses, and the Medicis, had come to an end, and the papal throne was occupied by the puritanical Caraffa, as violent a fanatic as Robespierre, and a foe of freedom as uncompromising as Philip II. himself. Under his auspices took place the great reform in the Church signalized by the rise of the Jesuits, as the reform in the thirteenth century had been attended by the rise of the Cordeliers and Dominicans. His name should not be forgotten, for it is mainly owing to the policy inaugurated by him that Catholicism was enabled to hold its ground as well as it did. In 1557 the next year, the strength of France was broken at St. Quentin, and Spain was left with her hands free to deal with the Protestant powers. In 1558, by the accession of Elizabeth, England became committed to the cause of Reform. In 1559 the stormy administration of Margaret began in the Netherlands. In 1560 the Scotch nobles achieved the destruction of Catholicism in North Britain. By this time every nation except France, had taken sides in the conflict which was to last, with hardly any cessation, during two generations.

Mr. Motley, therefore, in describing the rise and progress of the united republic of the Netherlands, is writing not Dutch but European history. On his pages France, Spain, and England make almost as large a figure as Holland itself. He is writing the history of the Reformation during its concluding epoch, and he chooses the Netherlands as his main subject, because during that period the Netherlands were the centre of the movement. They constituted the great bulwark of freedom, and upon the success or failure of their cause the future prospect of Europe and of mankind depended. Spain and the Netherlands, Philip II. and William the Silent, were the two leading antagonists and were felt to be such by the other nations and rulers that came to mingle in the strife. It is therefore a stupid criticism which we have seen made upon Mr. Motley, that, having brought his narrative down to the truce of 1609, he ought, instead of describing the Thirty Years' War, to keep on with Dutch history, and pourtray the wars against Cromwell and Charles II., and the struggle of the second William of Orange against Louis XIV. By so doing he would only violate the unity of his narrative. The wars of the Dutch against England and France belong to an entirely different epoch in European history,—a modern epoch, in which political and commercial interests were of prime importance, and theological interests distinctly subsidiary. The natural terminus of Mr. Motley's work is the Peace of Westphalia. After bringing down his history to the time when the independence of the Netherlands was virtually acknowledged, after describing the principal stages of the struggle against Catholicism and universal monarchy, as carried on in the first generation by Elizabeth and William, and in the second by Maurice and Henry, he will naturally go on to treat of the epilogue as conducted by Richelieu and Gustavus, ending in the final cessation of religious wars throughout Europe.

The conflict in the Netherlands was indeed far more than a mere religious struggle. In its course was distinctly brought into prominence the fact which we have above signalized, that since the Roman Church had abandoned the liberties of the people they had found a new defender in the reformed religion. The Dutch rebellion is peculiarly interesting, because it was a revolt not merely against the Inquisition, but also against the temporal sovereignty of Philip. Besides changing their religion, the sturdy Netherlanders saw fit to throw off the sway of their legitimate ruler, and to proclaim the thrice heretical doctrine of the sovereignty of the people. In this one respect their views were decidedly more modern than those of Elizabeth and Henry IV. These great monarchs apparently neither understood nor relished the republican theories of the Hollanders; though it is hardly necessary for Mr. Motley to sneer at them quite so often because they were not to an impossible degree in advance of their age. The proclamation of a republic in the Netherlands marked of itself the beginning of a new era,—an era when flourishing communities of men were no longer to be bought and sold, transferred and bequeathed like real estate and chattels, but were to have and maintain the right of choosing with whom and under whom they should transact their affairs. The interminable negotiations for a truce, which fill nearly one third of Mr. Motley's concluding volume, exhibit with striking distinctness the difference between the old and new points of view. Here again we think Mr. Motley errs slightly, in calling too much attention to the prevaricating diplomacy of the Spanish court, and too little to its manifest inability to comprehend the demands of the Netherlanders. How should statesmen brought up under Philip II. and kept under the eye of the Inquisition be expected to understand a claim for liberty originating in the rights of the common people and not in the gracious benevolence or intelligent policy of the King? The very idea must have been practically inconceivable by them. Accordingly, they strove by every available device of chicanery to wheedle the Netherlanders into accepting their independence as a gift from the King of Spain. But to such a piece of self-stultification the clear-sighted Dutchmen could by no persuasion be brought to consent. Their independence, they argued, was not the King's to give. They had won it from him and his father, in a war of forty years, during which they had suffered atrocious miseries, and all that the King of Spain could do was to acknowledge it as their right, and cease to molest them in future. Over this point, so simple to us but knotty enough in those days, the commissioners wrangled for nearly two years. And when the Spanish government, unable to carry on the war any longer without risk of utter bankruptcy, and daily crippled in its resources by the attacks of the Dutch navy, grudgingly a reed to a truce upon the Netherlanders' terms, it virtually acknowledged its own defeat and the downfall of the principles for which it had so obstinately fought. By the truce of 1609 the republican principle was admitted by the most despotic of governments.

Here was the first great triumph of republicanism over monarchy; and it was not long in bearing fruits. For the Dutch revolution, the settlement of America by English Puritans, the great rebellion of the Commons, the Revolution of 1688, the revolt of the American Colonies, and the general overthrow of feudalism in 1789, are but successive acts in the same drama William the Silent was the worthy forerunner of Cromwell and Washington; and but for the victory which he won, during his life and after his untimely death, the subsequent triumphs of civil liberty might have been long, postponed.

Over the sublime figure of William—saevis tranquillus in undis—we should be glad to dwell, but we are not reviewing the "Rise of the Dutch Republic," and in Mr. Motley's present volumes the hero of toleration appears no longer. His antagonist, however,—the Philip whom God for some inscrutable purpose permitted to afflict Europe during a reign of forty-two years,—accompanies us nearly to the end of the present work, dying just in time for the historian to sum up the case against him, and pronounce final judgment. For the memory of Philip II. Mr. Motley cherishes no weak pity. He rarely alludes to him without commenting upon his total depravity, and he dismisses him with the remark that "if there are vices—as possibly there are—from which he was exempt, it is because it is not permitted to human nature to attain perfection in evil." The verdict is none the less just because of its conciseness. If there ever was a strife between Hercules and Cacus, between Ormuzd and Ahriman, between the Power of Light and the Power of Darkness, it was certainly the strife between the Prince of Orange and the Spanish Monarch. They are contrasted like the light and shade in one of Dore's pictures. And yet it is perhaps unnecessary for Mr. Motley to say that if Philip had been alive when Spinola won for him the great victory of Ostend, "he would have felt it his duty to make immediate arrangements for poisoning him." Doubtless the imputation is sufficiently justified by what we know of Philip; but it is uncalled for. We do not care to hear about what the despot might have done. We know what he did do, and the record is sufficiently damning. There is no harm in our giving the Devil his due, or as Llorente wittily says, "Il ne faut pas calomnier meme l'Inquisition."

Philip inherited all his father's bad qualities, without any of his good ones; and so it is much easier to judge him than his father. Charles, indeed, is one of those characters whom one hardly knows whether to love or hate, to admire or despise. He had much bad blood in him. Charles the Bold and Ferdinand of Aragon were not grandparents to be proud of. Yet with all this he inherited from his grandmother Isabella much that one can like, and his face, as preserved by Titian, in spite of its frowning brow and thick Burgundian lip, is rather prepossessing, while the face of Philip is simply odious. In intellect he must probably be called great, though his policy often betrayed the pettiness of selfishness. If, in comparison with the mediaeval emperor whose fame he envied, he may justly be called Charles the Little, he may still, when compared to a more modern emulator of Charlemagne,—the first of the Bonapartes,—be considered great and enlightened. If he could lie and cheat more consummately than any contemporary monarch, not excepting his rival, Francis, he could still be grandly magnanimous, while the generosity of Francis flowed only from the shallow surface of a maudlin good-nature. He spoke many languages and had the tastes of a scholar, while his son had only the inclinations of an unfeeling pedagogue. He had an inkling of urbanity, and could in a measure become all things to all men, while Philip could never show himself except as a gloomy, impracticable bigot. It is for some such reasons as these, I suppose, that Mr. Buckle—no friend to despots—speaks well of Charles, and that Mr. Froude is moved to tell the following anecdote: While standing by the grave of Luther, and musing over the strange career of the giant monk whose teachings had gone so far to wreck his most cherished schemes and render his life a failure, some fanatical bystander advised the Emperor to have the body taken up and burned in the market-place. "There was nothing," says Mr. Froude, "unusual in the proposal; it was the common practice of the Catholic Church with the remains of heretics, who were held unworthy to be left in repose in hallowed ground. There was scarcely, perhaps another Catholic prince who would have hesitated to comply. But Charles was one of nature's gentlemen. He answered, 'I war not with the dead.' " Mr. Motley takes a less charitable view of the great Emperor. His generous indignation against all persecutors makes him severe; and in one of his earlier volumes, while speaking of the famous edicts for the suppression of heresy in the Netherlands, he somewhere uses the word "murder." Without attempting to palliate the crime of persecution, I doubt if it is quite fair to Charles to call him a murderer. We must not forget that persecution, now rightly deemed an atrocious crime, was once really considered by some people a sacred duty; that it was none other than the compassionate Isabella who established the Spanish Inquisition; and that the "bloody" Mary Tudor was a woman who would not wilfully have done wrong. With the progress of civilization the time will doubtless come when warfare, having ceased to be necessary, will be thought highly criminal; yet it will not then be fair to hold Marlborough or Wellington accountable for the lives lost in their great battles. We still live in an age when war is, to the imagination of some persons, surrounded with false glories; and the greatest of modern generals[32] has still many undiscriminating admirers. Yet the day is no less certainly at hand when the edicts of Charles V. will be deemed a more pardonable offence against humanity than the wanton march to Moscow.

Philip II. was different from his father in capacity as a drudging clerk, like Boutwell, is different from a brilliant financier like Gladstone. In organization he differed from him as a boor differs from a gentleman. He seemed made of a coarser clay. The difference between them is well indicated by their tastes at the table. Both were terrible gluttons, a fact which puritanic criticism might set down as equally to the discredit of each of them. But even in intemperance there are degrees of refinement, and the impartial critic of life and manners will no doubt say that if one must get drunk, let it be on Chateau Margaux rather than on commissary whiskey. Pickled partridges, plump capons, syrups of fruits, delicate pastry, and rare fish went to make up the diet of Charles in his last days at Yuste. But the beastly Philip would make himself sick with a surfeit of underdone pork.

Whatever may be said of the father, we can hardly go far wrong in ascribing the instincts of a murderer to the son. He not only burned heretics, but he burned them with an air of enjoyment and self-complacency. His nuptials with Elizabeth of France were celebrated by a vast auto-da-fe. He studied murder as a fine art, and was as skilful in private assassinations as Cellini was in engraving on gems. The secret execution of Montigny, never brought to light until the present century, was a veritable chef d'oeuvre of this sort. The cases of Escobedo and Antonio Perez may also be cited in point. Dark suspicions hung around the premature death of Don John of Austria, his too brilliant and popular half-brother. He planned the murder of William the Silent, and rewarded the assassin with an annuity furnished by the revenues of the victim's confiscated estates. He kept a staff of ruffians constantly in service for the purpose of taking off Elizabeth, Henry IV., Prince Maurice, Olden-Barneveldt, and St. Aldegonde. He instructed Alva to execute sentence of death upon the whole population of the Netherlands. He is partly responsible for the martyrdoms of Ridley and Latimer, and the judicial murder of Cranmer. He first conceived the idea of the wholesale massacre of St. Bartholomew, many years before Catharine de' Medici carried it into operation. His ingratitude was as dangerous as his revengeful fanaticism. Those who had best served his interests were the least likely to escape the consequences of his jealousy. He destroyed Egmont, who had won for him the splendid victories of St. Quentin and Gravelines; and "with minute and artistic treachery" he plotted "the disgrace and ruin" of Farnese, "the man who was his near blood-relation, and who had served him most faithfully from earliest youth." Contemporary opinion even held him accountable for the obscure deaths of his wife Elizabeth and his son Carlos; but M. Gachard has shown that this suspicion is

---

[32] This was written before the deeds of Moltke had eclipsed those of Napoleon.

unfounded. Philip appears perhaps to better advantage in his domestic than in his political relations. Yet he was addicted to vulgar and miscellaneous incontinence; toward the close of his life he seriously contemplated marrying his own daughter Isabella; and he ended by taking for his fourth wife his niece, Anne of Austria, who became the mother of his half-idiotic son and successor. We know of no royal family, unless it may be the Claudians of Rome, in which the transmission of moral and intellectual qualities is more thoroughly illustrated than in this Burgundian race which for two centuries held the sceptre of Spain. The son Philip and the grandmother Isabella are both needful in order to comprehend the strange mixture of good and evil in Charles. But the descendants of Philip—two generations of idiocy, and a third of utter impotence—are a sufficient commentary upon the organization and character of their progenitor.

Such was the man who for two generations had been considered the bulwark of the Catholic Church; who, having been at the bottom of nearly all the villany that had been wrought in Europe for half a century, was yet able to declare upon his death-bed that "in all his life he had never consciously done wrong to any one." At a ripe old age he died of a fearful disease. Under the influence of a typhus fever, supervening upon gout, he had begun to decompose while yet alive. "His sufferings," says Mr. Motley, "were horrible, but no saint could have manifested in them more gentle resignation or angelic patience. He moralized on the condition to which the greatest princes might thus be brought at last by the hand of God, and bade the Prince observe well his father's present condition, in order that when he too should be laid thus low, he might likewise be sustained by a conscience void of offence." What more is needed to complete the disgusting picture? Philip was fanatical up to the point where fanaticism borders upon hypocrisy. He was possessed with a "great moral idea," the idea of making Catholicism the ruler of the world, that he might be the ruler of Catholicism. Why, it may be said, shall the charge of fanaticism be allowed to absolve Isabella and extenuate the guilt of Charles, while it only strengthens the case against Philip? Because Isabella persecuted heretics in order to save their souls from a worse fate, while Philip burnt them in order to get them out of his way. Isabella would perhaps have gone to the stake herself, if thereby she might have put an end to heresy. Philip would have seen every soul in Europe consigned to eternal perdition before he would have yielded up an iota of his claims to universal dominion. He could send Alva to browbeat the Pope, as well as to oppress the Netherlanders. He could compass the destruction of the orthodox Egmont and Farnese, as well as of the heretical William. His unctuous piety only adds to the abhorrence with which we regard him; and his humility in face of death is neither better nor worse than the assumed humility which had become second nature to Uriah Heep. In short, take him for all in all, he was probably the most loathsome character in all European history. He has frequently been called, by Protestant historians, an incarnate devil; but we do not think that Mephistopheles would acknowledge him. He should rather be classed among those creatures described by Dante as "a Dio spiacenti ed ai nemici sui."

    The abdication of Charles V. left Philip ruler over wider dominions than had ever before been brought together under the sway of one man. In his own right Philip was master not only of Spain, but of the Netherlands, Franche Comte, Lombardy, Naples, and Sicily, with the whole of North and South America; besides which he was married to the Queen of England. In the course of his reign he became possessed of Portugal, with all its vast domains in the East Indies. His revenues were greater than those of any other contemporary monarch; his navy was considered invincible, and his army was the best disciplined in Europe. All these great advantages he was destined to throw to the winds. In the strife for universal monarchy, in the mad endeavour to subject England, Scotland, and France to his own dominion and the tyranny of the Inquisition, besides re-conquering the Netherlands, all his vast resources were wasted. The Dutch war alone, like a bottomless pit, absorbed all that he could pour into it. Long before the war was over, or showed signs of drawing to an end, his revenues were wasted, and his troops in Flanders were mutinous for want of pay. He had to rely upon energetic viceroys like Farnese and the Spinolas to furnish funds out of their own pockets. Finally, he was obliged to repudiate all his debts; and when he died the Spanish empire was in such a beggarly condition that it quaked at every approach of a hostile Dutch fleet. Such a result is not evidence of a statesmanlike ability; but Philip's fanatical selfishness was incompatible with statesmanship. He never could be made to believe that his projects had suffered defeat. No sooner had the Invincible Armada been sent to the bottom by the guns of the English fleet and the gales of the German Ocean, than he sent orders to Farnese to invade England at once with the land force under his command! He thought to obtain Scotland, when, after the death of Mary, it had passed under the undisputed control of the Protestant noblemen. He dreamed of securing for his family the crown of France, even after Henry, with free consent of the Pope, had made his triumphal entry into Paris. He asserted complete and entire sovereignty over the Netherlands, even after Prince Maurice had won back from him the last square foot of Dutch territory. Such obstinacy as this can only be called fatuity. If Philip had lived in Pagan times, he would doubtless, like Caligula, have demanded recognition of his own divinity.

    The miserable condition of the Spanish people under this terrible reign, and the causes of their subsequent degeneracy, have been well treated by Mr. Motley. The causes of the failure of Spanish civilization are partly social and partly economical; and they had been operating for eight hundred years when Philip succeeded to the throne. The Moorish conquest in 711 had practically isolated Spain from the rest of Europe. In the Crusades she took no part, and reaped none of the signal advantages resulting from that great movement. Her whole energies were directed toward throwing off the yoke of her civilized but "unbelieving" oppressors. For a longer time than has now elapsed since the

Norman Conquest of England, the entire Gothic population of Spain was engaged in unceasing religious and patriotic warfare. The unlimited power thus acquired by an unscrupulous clergy, and the spirit of uncompromising bigotry thus imparted to the whole nation, are in this way readily accounted for. But in spite of this, the affairs of Spain at the accession of Charles V. were not in an unpromising condition. The Spanish Visigoths had been the least barbarous of the Teutonic settlers within the limits of the Empire; their civil institutions were excellent; their cities had obtained municipal liberties at an earlier date than those of England; and their Parliaments indulged in a liberty of speech which would have seemed extravagant even to De Montfort. So late as the time of Ferdinand, the Spaniards were still justly proud of their freedom; and the chivalrous ambition which inspired the marvellous expedition of Cortes to Mexico, and covered the soil of Italy with Spanish armies, was probably in the main a healthy one. But the forces of Spanish freedom were united at too late an epoch; in 1492, the power of despotism was already in the ascendant. In England the case was different. The barons were enabled to combine and wrest permanent privileges from the crown, at a time when feudalism was strong. But the Spanish communes waited for combined action until feudalism had become weak, and modern despotism, with its standing armies and its control of the spiritual power, was arrayed in the ranks against them. The War of the Communes, early in the reign of Charles V., irrevocably decided the case in favour of despotism, and from that date the internal decline of Spain may be said to have begun.

But the triumphant consolidation of the spiritual and temporal powers of despotism, and the abnormal development of loyalty and bigotry, were not the only evil results of the chronic struggle in which Spain had been engaged. For many centuries, while Christian Spain had been but a fringe of debatable border-land on the skirts of the Moorish kingdom, perpetual guerilla warfare had rendered consecutive labour difficult or impracticable; and the physical configuration of the country contributed in bringing about this result. To plunder the Moors across the border was easier than to till the ground at home. Then as the Spaniards, exemplifying the military superiority of the feudal over the sultanic form of social organization, proceeded steadily to recover dominion over the land, the industrious Moors, instead of migrating backward before the advance of their conquerors, remained at home and submitted to them. Thus Spanish society became compounded of two distinct castes,—the Moorish Spaniards, who were skilled labourers, and the Gothic Spaniards, by whom all labour, crude or skilful, was deemed the stigma of a conquered race, and unworthy the attention of respectable people. As Mr. Motley concisely says:—

"The highest industrial and scientific civilization that had been exhibited upon Spanish territory was that of Moors and Jews. When in the course of time those races had been subjugated, massacred, or driven into exile, not only was Spain deprived of its highest intellectual culture and its most productive labour, but intelligence, science, and industry were accounted degrading, because the mark of inferior and detested peoples."

This is the key to the whole subsequent history of Spain. Bigotry, loyalty, and consecrated idleness are the three factors which have made that great country what it is to-day,—the most backward region in Europe. In view of the circumstances just narrated, it is not surprising to learn that in Philip II.'s time a vast portion of the real estate of the country was held by the Church in mortmain; that forty-nine noble families owned all the rest; that all great estates were held in tail; and that the property of the aristocracy and the clergy was completely exempt from taxation. Thus the accumulation and the diffusion of capital were alike prevented; and the few possessors of property wasted it in unproductive expenditure. Hence the fundamental error of Spanish political economy, that wealth is represented solely by the precious metals; an error which well enough explains the total failure, in spite of her magnificent opportunities, of Spain's attempts to colonize the New World. Such was the frightful condition of Spanish society under Philip II.; and as if this state of things were not bad enough, the next king, Philip III., at the instigation of the clergy, decided to drive into banishment the only class of productive labourers yet remaining in the country. In 1610, this stupendous crime and blunder—unparalleled even in Spanish history—was perpetrated. The entire Moorish population were expelled from their homes and driven into the deserts of Africa. For the awful consequences of this mad action no remedy was possible. No system of native industry could be created on demand, to take the place of that which had been thus wantonly crushed forever. From this epoch dates the social ruin of Spain. In less than a century her people were riotous with famine; and every sequestered glen and mountain pathway throughout the country had become a lurking-place for robbers. Whoever would duly realize to what a lamentable condition this beautiful peninsula had in the seventeenth century been reduced, let him study the immortal pages of Lesage. He will learn afresh the lesson, not yet sufficiently regarded in the discussion of social problems, that the laws of nature cannot be violated without entailing a penalty fearful in proportion to the extent of the violation. But let him carefully remember also that the Spaniards are not and never have been a despicable people. If Spain has produced one of the lowest characters in history, she has also produced one of the highest. That man was every inch a Spaniard who, maimed, diseased, and poor, broken down by long captivity, and harassed by malignant persecution, lived nevertheless a life of grandeur and beauty fit to be a pattern for coming generations,—the author of a book which has had a wider fame than any other in the whole range of secular literature, and which for delicate humour, exquisite pathos, and deep ethical sentiment, remains to-day without a peer or a rival. If Philip II. was a Spaniard, so, too, was Cervantes.

Spain could not be free, for she violated every condition by which freedom is secured to a people. "Acuteness of intellect, wealth of imagination, heroic qualities of heart and hand and brain, rarely surpassed in any race and manifested on a thousand battle-fields, and in the triumphs of a magnificent and most original literature, had not been able to save a whole nation from the disasters and the degradation which the mere words Philip II. and the Holy Inquisition suggest to every educated mind." Nor could Spain possibly become rich, for, as Mr. Motley continues, "nearly every law, according to which the prosperity of a country becomes progressive, was habitually violated." On turning to the Netherlands we find the most complete contrast, both in historical conditions and in social results; and the success of the Netherlands in their long struggle becomes easily intelligible. The Dutch and Flemish provinces had formed a part of the renovated Roman Empire of Charles the Great and the Othos. Taking advantage of the perennial contest for supremacy between the popes and the Roman emperors, the constituent baronies and municipalities of the Empire succeeded in acquiring and maintaining a practical though unrecognized independence; and this is the original reason why Italy and Germany, unlike the three western European communities, have remained fragmentary until our own time. By reason of the practical freedom of action thus secured, the Italian civic republics, the Hanse towns, and the cities of Holland and Flanders, were enabled gradually to develop a vast commerce. The outlying position of the Netherlands, remote from the imperial authorities, and on the direct line of commerce between Italy and England, was another and a peculiar advantage. Throughout the Middle Ages the Flemish and Dutch cities were of considerable political importance, and in the fifteenth century the Netherland provinces were the most highly civilized portion of Europe north of the Alps. For several generations they had enjoyed, and had known how to maintain, civic liberties, and when Charles and Philip attempted to fasten upon them their "peculiar institution," the Spanish Inquisition, they were ripe for political as well as theological revolt. Natural laws were found to operate on the Rhine as well as on the Tagus, and at the end of the great war of independence, Holland was not only better equipped than Spain for a European conflict, but was rapidly ousting her from the East Indian countries which she had in vain attempted to colonize.

But if we were to take up all the interesting and instructive themes suggested by Mr. Motley's work, we should never come to an end. We must pass over the exciting events narrated in these last volumes; the victory of Nieuport, the siege of Ostend, the marvellous career of Maurice, the surprising exploits of Spinola. We have attempted not so much to describe Mr. Motley's book as to indulge in sundry reflections suggested by the perusal of it. But we cannot close without some remarks upon a great man, whose character Mr. Motley seems to have somewhat misconceived.

If Mr. Motley exhibits any serious fault, it is perhaps the natural tendency to TAKE SIDES in the events which he is describing, which sometimes operates as a drawback to complete and thoroughgoing criticism. With every intention to do justice to the Catholics, Mr. Motley still writes as a Protestant, viewing all questions from the Protestant side. He praises and condemns like a very fair-minded Huguenot, but still like a Huguenot. It is for this reason that he fails to interpret correctly the very complex character of Henry IV., regarding him as a sort of selfish renegade whom he cannot quite forgive for accepting the crown of France at the hands of the Pope. Now this very action of Henry, in the eye of an impartial criticism, must seem to be one of his chief claims to the admiration and gratitude of posterity. Henry was more than a mere Huguenot: he was a far-seeing statesman. He saw clearly what no ruler before him, save William the Silent, had even dimly discerned, that not Catholicism and not Protestantism, but absolute spiritual freedom was the true end to be aimed at by a righteous leader of opinion. It was as a Catholic sovereign that he could be most useful even to his Huguenot subjects; and he shaped his course accordingly. It was as an orthodox sovereign, holding his position by the general consent of Europe, that he could best subserve the interests of universal toleration. This principle he embodied in his admirable edict of Nantes. What a Huguenot prince might have done, may be seen from the shameful way in which the French Calvinists abused the favour which Henry—and Richelieu afterwards—accorded to them. Remembering how Calvin himself "dragooned" Geneva, let us be thankful for the fortune which, in one of the most critical periods of history, raised to the highest position in Christendom a man who was something more than a sectarian.

  With this brief criticism, we must regretfully take leave of Mr. Motley's work. Much more remains to be said about a historical treatise which is, on the whole, the most valuable and important one yet produced by an American; but we have already exceeded our limits. We trust that our author will be as successful in the future as he has been in the past; and that we shall soon have an opportunity of welcoming the first instalment of his "History of the Thirty Years' War."

March, 1868.

XI.

LONGFELLOW'S DANTE.[33]

THE task of a translator is a thankless one at best. Be he never so skilful and accurate, be he never so amply endowed with the divine qualifications of the poet, it is still questionable if he can ever succeed in saying satisfactorily with new words that which has once been inimitably said—said for all time—with the old words. Psychologically, there is perhaps nothing more complex than an elaborate poem. The sources of its effect upon our minds may be likened to a system of forces which is in the highest degree unstable; and the slightest displacement of phrases, by disturbing the delicate rhythmical equilibrium of the whole, must inevitably awaken a jarring sensation." Matthew Arnold has given us an excellent series of lectures upon translating Homer, in which he doubtless succeeds in showing that some methods of translation are preferable to others, but in which he proves nothing so forcibly as that the simplicity and grace, the rapidity, dignity, and fire, of Homer are quite incommunicable, save by the very words in which they first found expression. And what is thus said of Homer will apply to Dante with perhaps even greater force. With nearly all of Homer's grandeur and rapidity, though not with nearly all his simplicity, the poem of Dante manifests a peculiar intensity of subjective feeling which was foreign to the age of Homer, as indeed to all pre-Christian antiquity. But concerning this we need not dilate, as it has often been duly remarked upon, and notably by Carlyle, in his "Lectures on Hero-Worship." Who that has once heard the wail of unutterable despair sounding in the line

"Ahi, dura terra, perche non t' apristi?"can rest satisfied with the interpretation

"Ah, obdurate earth, wherefore didst thou not open?"yet this rendering is literally exact.[34]

A second obstacle, hardly less formidable, hardly less fatal to a satisfactory translation, is presented by the highly complicated system of triple rhyme upon which Dante's poem is constructed. This, which must ever be a stumbling-block to the translator, seems rarely to interfere with the free and graceful movement of the original work. The mighty thought of the master felt

---

[33] The Divine Comedy of Dante Alighieri. Translated by Henry Wadsworth Longfellow. 3 vols. Boston: Ticknor & Fields, 1867.

[34] As Dante himself observes, "E pero sappia ciascuno, che nulla cosa per legame musaico armonizzata si puo della sue loquela in altra trasmutare sanza rompere tutta sue dolcezza e armonia. E questa e la ragione per che Omero non si muto di greco in latino, come l'altre scritture che avemo da loro: e questa e la ragione per che i versi del Psaltero sono sanza dolcezza di musica e d'armonia; che essi furono trasmutati d' ebreo in greco, e di greco in latino, e nella prima trasmutazione tutta quella dolcezza venne meno." Convito, I. 7, Opere Minori, Tom. III. p. 80. The noble English version of the Psalms possesses a beauty which is all its own.

no impediment from the elaborate artistic panoply which must needs obstruct and harass the interpretation of the disciple. Dante's terza rima is a bow of Odysseus which weaker mortals cannot bend with any amount of tugging, and which Mr. Longfellow has judiciously refrained from trying to bend. Yet no one can fail to remark the prodigious loss entailed by this necessary sacrifice of one of the most striking characteristics of the original poem. Let any one who has duly reflected upon the strange and subtle effect produced on him by the peculiar rhyme of Tennyson's "In Memoriam," endeavour to realize the very different effect which would be produced if the verses were to be alternated or coupled in successive pairs, or if rhyme were to be abandoned for blank verse. The exquisite melody of the poem would be silenced. The rhyme-system of the "Divine Comedy" refuses equally to be tampered with or ignored. Its effect upon the ear and the mind is quite as remarkable as that of the rhyme-system of "In Memoriam"; and the impossibility of reproducing it is one good reason why Dante must always suffer even more from translation than most poets.

Something, too, must be said of the difficulties inevitably arising from the diverse structure and genius of the Italian and English languages. None will deny that many of them are insurmountable. Take the third line of the first canto,—

"Che la diritta via era smarrita," which Mr. Longfellow translates

"For the straightforward pathway had been lost." Perhaps there is no better word than "lost" by which to translate smarrita in this place; yet the two words are far from equivalent in force. About the word smarrita there is thrown a wide penumbra of meaning which does not belong to the word lost.[35] By its diffuse connotations the word smarrita calls up in our minds an adequate picture of the bewilderment and perplexity of one who is lost in a trackless forest. The high-road with out, beaten hard by incessant overpassing of men and beasts and wheeled vehicles, gradually becomes metamorphosed into the shady lane, where grass sprouts up rankly between the ruts, where bushes encroach upon the roadside, where fallen trunks now and then intercept the traveller; and this in turn is lost in crooked by-ways, amid brambles and underbrush and tangled vines, growing fantastically athwart the path, shooting up on all sides of tile bewildered wanderer, and rendering advance and retreat alike hopeless. No one who in childhood has wandered alone in the woods can help feeling all this suggested by the word smarrita in this passage. How bald in comparison is the word lost, which might equally be applied to a pathway, a reputation, and a pocket-book![36] The English is no doubt the most copious and variously expressive of all living languages, yet I doubt if it can furnish any word capable by itself of calling up the complex images here suggested by

---

[35] See Diez, Romance Dictionary, s. v. "Marrir."
[36] On literally retranslating lost into Italian, we should get the quite different word perduta.

smarrita.[37] And this is but one example, out of many that might be cited, in which the lack of exact parallelism between the two languages employed causes every translation to suffer.

All these, however, are difficulties which lie in the nature of things,—difficulties for which the translator is not responsible; of which he must try to make the best that can be made, but which he can never expect wholly to surmount. We have now to inquire whether there are not other difficulties, avoidable by one method of translation, though not by another; and in criticizing Mr. Longfellow, we have chiefly to ask whether he has chosen the best method of translation,—that which most surely and readily awakens in the reader's mind the ideas and feelings awakened by the original.

The translator of a poem may proceed upon either of two distinct principles. In the first case, he may render the text of his original into English, line for line and word for word, preserving as far as possible its exact verbal sequences, and translating each individual word into an English word as nearly as possible equivalent in its etymological force. In the second case, disregarding mere syntactic and etymologic equivalence, his aim will be to reproduce the inner meaning and power of the original, so far as the constitutional difference of the two languages will permit him.

It is the first of these methods that Mr. Longfellow has followed in his translation of Dante. Fidelity to the text of the original has been his guiding principle; and every one must admit that, in carrying out that principle, he has achieved a degree of success alike delightful and surprising. The method of literal translation is not likely to receive any more splendid illustration. It is indeed put to the test in such a way that the shortcomings now to be noticed bear not upon Mr. Longfellow's own style of work so much as upon the method itself with which they are necessarily implicated. These defects are, first, the too frequent use of syntactic inversion, and secondly, the too manifest preference extended to words of Romanic over words of Saxon origin.

To illustrate the first point, let me give a few examples. In Canto I. we have:—

"So bitter is it, death is little more;
But of the good to treat which there I found,
Speak will I of the other things I saw there";which is thus rendered by Mr. Cary,—

"Which to remember only, my dismay
Renews, in bitterness not far from death.
Yet to discourse of what there good befell,
All else will I relate discovered there";and by Dr. Parsons,—

---

[37] The more flexible method of Dr. Parsons leads to a more satisfactory but still inadequate result:—
"Half-way on our life's Journey, in a wood, From the right path I found myself astray."

"Its very thought is almost death to me;
Yet, having found some good there, I will tell
Of other things which there I chanced to see."[38]

Again in Canto X. we find:—

"Their cemetery have upon this side
With Epicurus all his followers,
Who with the body mortal make the soul";—an inversion which is perhaps not more unidiomatic than Mr. Cary's,—

"The cemetery on this part obtain
With Epicurus all his followers,
Who with the body make the spirit die";but which is advantageously avoided by Mr. Wright,—

"Here Epicurus hath his fiery tomb,
And with him all his followers, who maintain
That soul and body share one common doom";and is still better rendered by Dr. Parsons,—

"Here in their cemetery on this side,
With his whole sect, is Epicurus pent,
Who thought the spirit with its body died."[39]

And here my eyes, reverting to the end of Canto IX.,
fall upon a similar contrast between Mr. Longfellow's lines,—

"For flames between the sepulchres were scattered,
By which they so intensely heated were,
That iron more so asks not any art,"—and those of Dr. Parsons,—

"For here mid sepulchres were sprinkled fires,
Wherewith the enkindled tombs all-burning gleamed;
Metal more fiercely hot no art requires."[40]

Does it not seem that in all these cases Mr. Longfellow, and to a slightly less extent Mr. Cary, by their strict adherence to the letter, transgress the ordinary rules of English construction; and that Dr. Parsons, by his comparative freedom of movement, produces better poetry as well as better English? In the last example especially, Mr. Longfellow's inversions are so

---

[38] "Tanto e amara, che poco e piu morte:
Ma per trattar del teen ch' i' vi trovai,
Diro dell' altre Bose, ch' io v' ho scorte."Inferno, I. 7-10.

[39] "Suo cimitero da questa parte hanno
Con Epieuro tutti i suoi seguaci,
Che l'anima col corpo morta fanno."
Inferno, X. 13-15.

[40] "Che tra gli avelli flamme erano sparte,
Per le quali eran si del tutto accesi,
Che ferro piu non chiede verun' arte."
Inferno, IX. 118-120.

violent that to a reader ignorant of the original Italian, his sentence might be hardly intelligible. In Italian such inversions are permissible; in English they are not; and Mr. Longfellow, by transplanting them into English, sacrifices the spirit to the letter, and creates an obscurity in the translation where all is lucidity in the original. Does not this show that the theory of absolute literality, in the case of two languages so widely different as English and Italian, is not the true one?

Secondly, Mr. Longfellow's theory of translation leads him in most cases to choose words of Romanic origin in preference to those of Saxon descent, and in many cases to choose an unfamiliar instead of a familiar Romanic word, because the former happens to be etymologically identical with the word in the original. Let me cite as an example the opening of Canto III.:—

"Per me si va nella eitti dolente,
Per me si va nell' eterno dolore,
Per me si va tra la perduta gente."Here are three lines which, in their matchless simplicity and grandeur, might well excite despair in the breast of any translator. Let us contrast Mr. Longfellow's version.—

"Through me the way is to the city dolent;
Through me the way is to eternal dole;
Through me the way among the people lost,"—with that of Dr. Parsons,—,

"Through me you reach the city of despair;
Through me eternal wretchedness ye find;
Through me among perdition's race ye fare."I do not think any one will deny that Dr. Parsons's version, while far more remote than Mr. Longfellow's from the diction of the original, is somewhat nearer its spirit. It remains to seek the explanation of this phenomenon. It remains to be seen why words the exact counterpart of Dante's are unfit to call up in our minds the feelings which Dante's own words call up in the mind of an Italian. And this inquiry leads to some general considerations respecting the relation of English to other European languages.

Every one is aware that French poetry, as compared with German poetry, seems to the English reader very tame and insipid; but the cause of this fact is by no means so apparent as the fact itself. That the poetry of Germany is actually and intrinsically superior to that of France, may readily be admitted; but this is not enough to account for all the circumstances of the case. It does not explain why some of the very passages in Corneille and Racine, which to us appear dull and prosaic, are to the Frenchman's apprehension instinct with poetic fervour. It does not explain the undoubted fact that we, who speak English, are prone to underrate French poetry, while we are equally disposed to render to German poetry even more than its due share of merit. The reason is to be sought in the verbal associations established in our minds by the peculiar composition of the English language. Our vocabulary is chiefly made up on the one hand of indigenous Saxon words, and on the other hand of words derived from Latin or French. It is mostly words of the first class that we learn in childhood, and that are associated with our homeliest and deepest emotions; while words of the second class—usually acquired somewhat later in life and employed in sedate abstract discourse—have an intellectual rather than an emotional function to fulfil. Their original significations, the physical metaphors involved in them, which are perhaps still somewhat apparent to the Frenchman, are to us wholly non-existent. Nothing but the derivative or metaphysical signification remains. No physical image of a man stepping over a boundary is presented to our minds by the word transgress, nor in using the word comprehension do we picture to ourselves any manual act of grasping. It is to this double structure of the English language that it owes its superiority over every other tongue, ancient or modern, for philosophical and scientific purposes. Albeit there are numerous exceptions, it may still be safely said, in a general way, that we possess and habitually use two kinds of language,—one that is physical, for our ordinary purposes, and one that is metaphysical, for purposes of abstract reasoning and discussion. We do not say like the Germans, that we "begripe" (begreifen) an idea, but we say that we "conceive" it. We use a word which once had the very same material meaning as begreifen, but which has in our language utterly lost it. We are accordingly able to carry on philosophical inquiries by means of words which are nearly or quite free from those shadows of original concrete meaning which, in German, too often obscure the acquired abstract signification. Whoever has dealt in English and German metaphysics will not fail to recognize the prodigious superiority of English in force and perspicuity, arising mainly from the causes here stated. But while this homogeneity of structure in German injures it for philosophical purposes, it is the very thing which makes it so excellent as an organ for poetical expression, in the opinion of those who speak English. German being nearly allied to Anglo-Saxon, not only do its simple words strike us with all the force of our own homely Saxon terms, but its compounds also, preserving their physical significations almost unimpaired, call up in our minds concrete images of the greatest definiteness and liveliness. It is thus that German seems to us pre-eminently a poetical language, and it is thus that we are naturally inclined to overrate rather than to depreciate the poetry that is written in it.

With regard to French, the case is just the reverse. The Frenchman has no Saxon words, but he has, on the other hand, an indigenous stock of Latin words, which he learns in early childhood, which give outlet to his most intimate feelings, and which retain to some extent their primitive concrete picturesqueness. They are to him just as good as our Saxon words are to us. Though cold and merely intellectual to us, they are to him warm with emotion; and this is one reason why we cannot do justice to his poetry, or appreciate it as he appreciates it. To make this perfectly clear, let us take two or three lines from Shakespeare:—

"Blow, blow, thou winter wind!
Thou art not so unkind

As man's ingratitude,
Thy tooth is not so keen," etc., etc.;which I have somewhere seen thus rendered into French:
"Souffle, souffle, vent d'hiver!
Tu n'es pas si cruel
Que l'ingratitude de l'homme.
Ta dent n'est pas si penetrante," etc., etc.Why are we inclined to laugh as we read this? Because it excites in us an undercurrent of consciousness which, if put into words, might run something like this:—
"Insufflate, insufflate, wind hibernal!
Thou art not so cruel
As human ingratitude.
Thy dentition is not so penetrating," etc., etc.No such effect would be produced upon a Frenchman. The translation would strike him as excellent, which it really is. The last line in particular would seem poetical to us, did we not happen to have in our language words closely akin to dent and penetrante, and familiarly employed in senses that are not poetical.

Applying these considerations to Mr. Longfellow's choice of words in his translation of Dante, we see at once the unsoundness of the principle that Italian words should be rendered by their Romanic equivalents in English. Words that are etymologically identical with those in the original are often, for that very reason, the worst words that could be used. They are harsh and foreign to the English ear, however homelike and musical they may be to the ear of an Italian. Their connotations are unlike in the two languages; and the translation which is made literally exact by using them is at the same time made actually inaccurate, or at least inadequate. Dole and dolent are doubtless the exact counterparts of dolore and dolente, so far as mere etymology can go. But when we consider the effect that is to be produced upon the mind of the reader, wretchedness and despairing are fat better equivalents. The former may compel our intellectual assent, but the latter awaken our emotional sympathy.

Doubtless by long familiarity with the Romanic languages, the scholar becomes to a great degree emancipated from the conditions imposed upon him by the peculiar composition of his native English. The concrete significance of the Romanic words becomes apparent to him, and they acquire energy and vitality. The expression dolent may thus satisfy the student familiar with Italian, because it calls up in his mind, through the medium of its equivalent dolente, the same associations which the latter calls up in the mind of the Italian himself.[41] But this power of appreciating thoroughly the beauties of a foreign tongue is in the last degree an acquired taste,—as much so as the taste for olives and kirschenwasser to the carnal palate. It is only by long and profound

---

[41] A consummate Italian scholar, the delicacy of whose taste is questioned by no one, and whose knowledge of Dante's diction is probably not inferior to Mr. Longfellow's, has told me that he regards the expression as a noble and effective one, full of dignity and solemnity.

study that we can thus temporarily vest ourselves, so to speak, with a French or Italian consciousness in exchange for our English one. The literary epicure may keenly relish such epithets as dolent; but the common English reader, who loves plain fare, can hardly fail to be startled by it. To him it savours of the grotesque; and if there is any one thing especially to be avoided in the interpretation of Dante, it is grotesqueness.

Those who have read over Dante without reading into him, and those who have derived their impressions of his poem from M. Dore's memorable illustrations, will here probably demur. What! Dante not grotesque! That tunnel-shaped structure of the infernal pit; Minos passing sentence on the damned by coiling his tail; Charon beating the lagging shades with his oar; Antaios picking up the poets with his fingers and lowering them in the hollow of his hand into the Ninth Circle; Satan crunching in his monstrous jaws the arch-traitors, Judas, Brutus and Cassius; Ugolino appeasing his famine upon the tough nape of Ruggieri; Bertrand de Born looking (if I may be allowed the expression) at his own dissevered head; the robbers exchanging form with serpents; the whole demoniac troop of Malebolge,—are not all these things grotesque beyond everything else in poetry? To us, nurtured in this scientific nineteenth century, they doubtless seem so; and by Leigh Hunt, who had the eighteenth-century way of appreciating other ages than his own, they were uniformly treated as such. To us they are at first sight grotesque, because they are no longer real to us. We have ceased to believe in such things, and they no longer awaken any feeling akin to terror. But in the thirteenth century, in the minds of Dante and his readers, they were living, terrible realities. That Dante believed literally in all this unearthly world, and described it with such wonderful minuteness because he believed in it, admits of little doubt. As he walked the streets of Verona the people whispered, "See, there is the man who has been in hell!" Truly, he had been in hell, and described it as he had seen it, with the keen eyes of imagination and faith. With all its weird unearthliness, there is hardly another book in the whole range of human literature which is marked with such unswerving veracity as the "Divine Comedy." Nothing is there set down arbitrarily, out of wanton caprice or for the sake of poetic effect, but because to Dante's imagination it had so imposingly shown itself that he could not but describe it as he saw it. In reading his cantos we forget the poet, and have before us only the veracious traveller in strange realms, from whom the shrewdest cross-examination can elicit but one consistent account. To his mind, and to the mediaeval mind generally, this outer kingdom, with its wards of Despair, Expiation, and Beatitude, was as real as the Holy Roman Empire itself. Its extraordinary phenomena were not to be looked on with critical eyes and called grotesque, but were to be seen with eyes of faith, and to be worshipped, loved, or shuddered at. Rightly viewed, therefore, the poem of Dante is not grotesque, but unspeakably awful and solemn; and the statement is justified that all grotesqueness and bizarrerie in its interpretation is to be sedulously avoided.

Therefore, while acknowledging the accuracy with which Mr. Longfellow has kept pace with his original through line after line, following the "footing of its feet," according to the motto quoted on his title-page, I cannot but think that his accuracy would have been of a somewhat higher kind if he had now and then allowed himself a little more liberty of choice between English and Romanic words and idioms.

A few examples will perhaps serve to strengthen as well as to elucidate still further this position.

"Inferno," Canto III., line 22, according to Longfellow:—

"There sighs, complaints, and ululations loud
Resounded through the air without a star,
Whence I at the beginning wept thereat." According to Cary:—

"Here sighs, with lamentations and loud moans
Resounded through the air pierced by no star,
That e'en I wept at entering." According to Parsons:—

"Mid sighs, laments, and hollow howls of woe,
Which, loud resounding through the starless air,
Forced tears of pity from mine eyes at first."[42]

Canto V., line 84:—

LONGFELLOW.—"Fly through the air by their volition borne." CARY.—"Cleave the air, wafted by their will along." PARSONS.—"Sped ever onward by their wish alone."[43]

Canto XVII., line 42:—

LONGFELLOW.—"That he concede to us his stalwart shoulders."
CARY—"That to us he may vouchsafe
  The aid of his strong shoulders."
PARSONS.—"And ask for us his shoulders' strong support."[44]

Canto XVII., line 25:—

LONGFELLOW.—

"His tail was wholly quivering in the void,
    Contorting upwards the envenomed fork
    That in the guise of scorpion armed its point."

CARY.—

"In the void
Glancing, his tail upturned its venomous fork,
With sting like scorpions armed." PARSONS.—"In the void chasm his trembling tail he showed,
    As up the envenomed, forked point he swung,   Which, as in scorpions, armed its tapering end."[45]

---

[42] "Quivi sospiri, pianti ed alti guai Risonavan per l' ner senza stelle, Perch' io al cominciar ne lagrimai."
[43] "Volan per l' aer dal voler portate."
[44] "Che ne conceda i suoi omeri forti."

Canto V., line 51:—
LONGFELLOW.—"People whom the black air so castigates."
CARY.—"By the black air so scourged."[46]
Line 136:—
LONGFELLOW.—"Kissed me upon the mouth all palpitating."
CARY.—"My lips all trembling kissed."[47]
"Purgatorio," Canto XV., line 139:—
LONGFELLOW.—

"We passed along, athwart the twilight peering
 Forward as far as ever eye could stretch
 Against the sunbeams serotine and lucent."[48]

Mr. Cary's "bright vespertine ray" is only a trifle better; but Mr. Wright's "splendour of the evening ray" is, in its simplicity, far preferable.

Canto XXXI., line 131:—
LONGFELLOW.—"Did the other three advance Singing to their
angelic saraband."CARY.—"To their own carol on they came Dancing, in festive ring
angelical "WRIGHT.—"And songs accompanied their angel dance."Here Mr. Longfellow has apparently followed the authority of the Crusca, reading

"Cantando al loro angelico carribo,"and translating carribo by saraband, a kind of Moorish dance. The best manuscripts, however, sanction M. Witte's reading:—

"Danzando al loro angelico carribo."If this be correct, carribo cannot signify "a dance," but rather "the song which accompanies the dance"; and the true sense of the passage will have been best rendered by Mr. Cary.[49]

Whenever Mr. Longfellow's translation is kept free from oddities of diction and construction, it is very animated and vigorous. Nothing can be finer than his rendering of "Purgatorio," Canto VI., lines 97-117:—

"O German Albert! who abandonest
 Her that has grown recalcitrant and savage,
 And oughtest to bestride her saddle-bow,

 May a just judgment from the stars down fall

---

[45] "Nel vano tutta sue coda guizzava,
Torcendo in su la venenosa forca,
Che, a guisa di scorpion, la punta armava."
[46] "Genti che l' aura nera si gastiga."
[47] "La bocca mi bacio tutto tremante."
[48] "Noi andavam per lo vespero attenti
Oltre, quanto potean gli occhi allungarsi,
Contra i raggi serotini e lucenti."

[49] See Blanc, Vocabolario Dantesco, s. v. "caribo."

    Upon thy blood, and be it new and open,
      That thy successor may have fear thereof:

Because thy father and thyself have suffered,
    By greed of those transalpine lands distrained,
    The garden of the empire to be waste.

Come and behold Montecchi and Cappelletti,
    Monaldi and Filippeschi, careless man!
    Those sad already, and these doubt-depressed!

Come, cruel one! come and behold the oppression
    Of thy nobility, and cure their wounds,
    And thou shalt see how safe is Santafiore.

Come and behold thy Rome that is lamenting,
    Widowed, alone, and day and night exclaims
    'My Caesar, why hast thou forsaken me?'

Come and behold how loving are the people;
    And if for us no pity moveth thee,
    Come and be made ashamed of thy renown."[50]
So, too, Canto III., lines 79-84:—

---

[50] "O Alberto Tedesco, che abbandoni
  Costei ch' e fatta indomita e selvaggia,
  E dovresti inforcar li suoi arcioni,

Giusto gindizio dalle stelle caggia
  Sopra il tuo sangue, e sia nuovo ed aperto,
  Tal che il tuo successor temenza n' aggia:
Cheavete tu e il tuo padre sofferto,
  Per cupidigia di costa distretti,
  Che il giardin dell' imperio sia diserto.

Vieni a veder Montecchi e Cappelletti,
  Monaldi e Filippeschi, uom senza cura:
  Color gia tristi, e questi con sospetti.
Vien, crudel, vieni, e vedi la pressura
  De' tuoi gentili, e cure lor magagne,
  E vedrai Santafior com' e oscura [secura?].
Vieni a veder la tua Roma che piagne,
  Vedova e sola, e di e notte chiama:
  Cesare mio, perche non m' accompagne?
Vieni a veder la gente quanto s' ama;
  E se nulla di noi pieta ti move,
  A vergognar ti vien della tua fama."

"As sheep come issuing forth from out the fold
  By ones, and twos, and threes, and the others stand
Timidly holding down their eyes and nostrils,

 And what the foremost does the others do
   Huddling themselves against her if she stop,
   Simple and quiet, and the wherefore know not."[51]
Francesca's exclamation to Dante is thus rendered by Mr. Longfellow:—
  "And she to me: There is no greater sorrow
   Than to be mindful of the happy time
   In misery."[52]

This is admirable,—full of the true poetic glow, which would have been utterly quenched if some Romanic equivalent of dolore had been used instead of our good Saxon sorrow.[53] So, too, the "Paradiso," Canto I., line 100:—
  "Whereupon she, after a pitying sigh,
   Her eyes directed toward me with that look
   A mother casts on a delirious child."[54]

And, finally, the beginning of the eighth canto of the "Purgatorio":—
  "'T was now the hour that turneth back desire
   In those who sail the sea, and melts the heart,
   The day they've said to their sweet friends farewell;
  And the new pilgrim penetrates with love,
   If he doth hear from far away a bell
   That seemeth to deplore the dying day."[55]

---

[51] "Come le pecorelle escon del chiuso
  Ad una, a due, a tre, e l' altre stanno
  Timidette atterrando l' occhio e il muso;

E cio che fa la prima, e l' altre sanno,
  Addossandosi a lei s' ella s' arresta,
  Semplici e quete, e lo 'mperche non sanno."

[52] "Ed ella a me: Nessun maggior dolore
Che ricordarsi del tempo felice Nella miseria."
Inferno, V. 121-123.
[53] Yet admirable as it is, I am not quite sure that Dr. Parsons, by taking further liberty with the original, has not surpassed it:—
  "And she to me: The mightiest of all woes
  Is in the midst of misery to be cursed
  With bliss remembered."
[54] "Ond' ella, appresso d'un pio sospiro , Gli occhi drizzo ver me con quel sembiante, Che madre fa sopra figlinol deliro."
[55] "Era gia l' ora che volge il disio
  Ai naviganti, e intenerisce il core
  Lo di ch' hen detto ai dolci amici addio;

This passage affords an excellent example of what the method of literal translation can do at its best. Except in the second line, where "those who sail the sea" is wisely preferred to any Romanic equivalent of naviganti the version is utterly literal; as literal as the one the school-boy makes, when he opens his Virgil at the Fourth Eclogue, and lumberingly reads, "Sicilian Muses, let us sing things a little greater." But there is nothing clumsy, nothing which smacks of the recitation-room, in these lines of Mr. Longfellow. For easy grace and exquisite beauty it would be difficult to surpass them. They may well bear comparison with the beautiful lines into which Lord Byron has rendered the same thought:—

"Soft hour which wakes the wish, and melts the heart,
  Of those who sail the seas, on the first day
When they from their sweet friends are torn apart;
  Or fills with love the pilgrim on his way,
As the far bell of vesper makes him start,
  Seeming to weep the dying day's decay.
Is this a fancy which our reason scorns?
Ah, surely nothing dies but something mourns!"[56]

Setting aside the concluding sentimental generalization,—which is much more Byronic than Dantesque,—one hardly knows which version to call more truly poetical; but for a faithful rendering of the original conception one can hardly hesitate to give the palm to Mr. Longfellow.

Thus we see what may be achieved by the most highly gifted of translators who contents himself with passively reproducing the diction of his original, who constitutes himself, as it were, a conduit through which the meaning of the original may flow. Where the differences inherent in the languages employed do not intervene to alloy the result, the stream of the original may, as in the verses just cited, come out pure and unweakened. Too often, however, such is the subtle chemistry of thought, it will come out diminished in its integrity, or will appear, bereft of its primitive properties as a mere element in some new combination. Our channel is a trifle too alkaline perhaps; and that the transferred material may preserve its pleasant sharpness, we may need to throw in a little extra acid. Too often the mere differences between English and Italian prevent Dante's expressions from coming out in Mr. Longfellow's version so pure and unimpaired as in the instance just cited. But these differences cannot be ignored. They lie deep in the very structure of human speech, and are narrowly implicated with equally profound nuances in the composition of human thought. The causes which make dolente a solemn

---

E che lo nuovo peregrin d' amore
  Punge, se ode squilla di lontano,
  Che paia il giorno pianger che si more."

[56] Don Juan, III. 108.

word to the Italian ear, and dolent a queer word to the English ear, are causes which have been slowly operating ever since the Italican and the Teuton parted company on their way from Central Asia. They have brought about a state of things which no cunning of the translator can essentially alter, but to the emergencies of which he must graciously conform his proceedings. Here, then, is the sole point on which we disagree with Mr. Longfellow, the sole reason we have for thinking that he has not attained the fullest possible measure of success. Not that he has made a "realistic" translation,—so far we conceive him to be entirely right; but that, by dint of pushing sheer literalism beyond its proper limits, he has too often failed to be truly realistic. Let us here explain what is meant by realistic translation.

Every thoroughly conceived and adequately executed translation of an ancient author must be founded upon some conscious theory or some unconscious instinct of literary criticism. As is the critical spirit of an age, so among other things will be its translations. Now the critical spirit of every age previous to our own has been characterized by its inability to appreciate sympathetically the spirit of past and bygone times. In the seventeenth century criticism made idols of its ancient models; it acknowledged no serious imperfections in them; it set them up as exemplars for the present and all future times to copy. Let the genial Epicurean henceforth write like Horace, let the epic narrator imitate the supreme elegance of Virgil,—that was the conspicuous idea, the conspicuous error, of seventeenth-century criticism. It overlooked the differences between one age and another. Conversely, when it brought Roman patricians and Greek oligarchs on to the stage, it made them behave like French courtiers or Castilian grandees or English peers. When it had to deal with ancient heroes, it clothed them in the garb and imputed to them the sentiments of knights-errant. Then came the revolutionary criticism of the eighteenth century, which assumed that everything old was wrong, while everything new was right. It recognized crudely the differences between one age and another, but it had a way of looking down upon all ages except the present. This intolerance shown toward the past was indeed a measure of the crudeness with which it was comprehended. Because Mohammed, if he had done what he did, in France and in the eighteenth century, would have been called an impostor, Voltaire, the great mouthpiece and representative of this style of criticism, portrays him as an impostor. Recognition of the fact that different ages are different, together with inability to perceive that they ought to be different, that their differences lie in the nature of progress,—this was the prominent characteristic of eighteenth-century criticism. Of all the great men of that century, Lessing was perhaps the only one who outgrew this narrow critical habit.

Now nineteenth-century criticism not only knows that in no preceding age have men thought and behaved as they now think and behave, but it also understands that old-fashioned thinking and behaviour was in its way just as natural and sensible as that which is now new-fashioned. It does not flippantly sneer at an ancient custom because we no longer cherish it; but with an enlightened regard for everything human, it inquires into its origin, traces its effects, and endeavours to explain its decay. It is slow to characterize Mohammed as an impostor, because it has come to feel that Arabia in the seventh century is one thing and Europe in the nineteenth another. It is scrupulous about branding Caesar as an usurper, because it has discovered that what Mr. Mill calls republican liberty and what Cicero called republican liberty are widely different notions. It does not tell us to bow down before Lucretius and Virgil as unapproachable models, while lamenting our own hopeless inferiority; nor does it tell us to set them down as half-skilled apprentices, while congratulating ourselves on our own comfortable superiority; but it tells us to study them as the exponents of an age forever gone, from which we have still many lessons to learn, though we no longer think as it thought or feel as it felt. The eighteenth century, as represented by the characteristic passage from Voltaire, cited by Mr. Longfellow, failed utterly to understand Dante. To the minds of Voltaire and his contemporaries the great mediaeval poet was little else than a Titanic monstrosity,—a maniac, whose ravings found rhythmical expression; his poem a grotesque medley, wherein a few beautiful verses were buried under the weight of whole cantos of nonsensical scholastic quibbling. This view, somewhat softened, we find also in Leigh Hunt, whose whole account of Dante is an excellent specimen of this sort of criticism. Mr. Hunt's fine moral nature was shocked and horrified by the terrible punishments described in the "Inferno." He did not duly consider that in Dante's time these fearful things were an indispensable part of every man's theory of the world; and, blinded by his kindly prejudices, he does not seem to have perceived that Dante, in accepting eternal torments as part and parcel of the system of nature, was nevertheless, in describing them, inspired with that ineffable tenderness of pity which, in the episodes of Francesca and of Brunetto Latini, has melted the hearts of men in past times, and will continue to do so in times to come. "Infinite pity, yet infinite rigour of law! It is so Nature is made: it is so Dante discerned that she was made."[57] This remark of the great seer of our time is what the eighteenth century could in no wise comprehend. The men of that day failed to appreciate Dante, just as they were oppressed or disgusted at the sight of Gothic architecture; just as they pronounced the scholastic philosophy an unmeaning jargon; just as they considered mediaeval Christianity a gigantic system of charlatanry, and were wont unreservedly to characterize the Papacy as a blighting despotism. In our time cultivated men think differently. We have learned that the interminable hair-splitting of Aquinas and Abelard has added precision to modern thinking.[58] We do not curse Gregory VII. and Innocent III. as enemies of the human race, but revere them as benefactors. We can spare a morsel of hearty admiration for Becket, however strongly we may sympathize

---

[57] Carlyle, Heroes and Hero-Worship, p. 84.
[58] See my Outlines of Cosmic Philosophy, Vol. I. p. 123.

with the stalwart king who did penance for his foul murder; and we can appreciate Dante's poor opinion of Philip the Fair no less than his denunciation of Boniface VIII. The contemplation of Gothic architecture, as we stand entranced in the sublime cathedrals of York or Rouen, awakens in our breasts a genuine response to the mighty aspirations which thus became incarnate in enduring stone. And the poem of Dante—which has been well likened to a great cathedral—we reverently accept, with all its quaint carvings and hieroglyphic symbols, as the authentic utterance of feelings which still exist, though they no longer choose the same form of expression.

A century ago, therefore, a translation of Dante such as Mr. Longfellow's would have been impossible. The criticism of that time was in no mood for realistic reproductions of the antique. It either superciliously neglected the antique, or else dressed it up to suit its own notions of propriety. It was not like a seven-league boot which could fit everybody, but it was like a Procrustes-bed which everybody must be made to fit. Its great exponent was not a Sainte-Beuve, but a Boileau. Its typical sample of a reproduction of the antique was Pope's translation of the Iliad. That book, we presume, everybody has read; and many of those who have read it know that, though an excellent and spirited poem, it is no more Homer than the age of Queen Anne was the age of Peisistratos. Of the translations of Dante made during this period, the chief was unquestionably Mr. Cary's.[59] For a man born and brought up in the most unpoetical of centuries, Mr. Cary certainly made a very good poem, though not so good as Pope's. But it fell far short of being a reproduction of Dante. The eighteenth-century note rings out loudly on every page of it. Like much other poetry of the time, it is laboured and artificial. Its sentences are often involved and occasionally obscure. Take, for instance, Canto IV. 25-36 of the "Paradiso":

> "These are the questions which they will
> Urge equally; and therefore I the first
> Of that will treat which hath the more of gall.
> Of seraphim he who is most enskied,
> Moses, and Samuel, and either John,
> Choose which thou wilt, nor even Mary's self,
> Have not in any other heaven their seats,
> Than have those spirits which so late thou saw'st;
> Nor more or fewer years exist; but all
> Make the first circle beauteous, diversely
> Partaking of sweet life, as more or less
> Afflation of eternal bliss pervades them."

Here Mr. Cary not only fails to catch Dante's grand style; he does not even write a style at all. It is too constrained and awkward to be dignified, and dignity is an indispensable

---

[59] This work comes at the end of the eighteenth-century period, as Pope's translation of Homer comes at the beginning.

element of style. Without dignity we may write clearly, or nervously, or racily, but we have not attained to a style. This is the second shortcoming of Mr. Cary's translation. Like Pope's, it fails to catch the grand style of its original. Unlike Pope's, it frequently fails to exhibit any style.

It is hardly necessary to spend much time in proving that Mr. Longfellow's version is far superior to Mr. Cary's. It is usually easy and flowing, and save in the occasional use of violent inversions, always dignified. Sometimes, as in the episode of Ugolino, it even rises to something like the grandeur of the original:

"When he had said this, with his eyes distorted,
The wretched skull resumed he with his teeth,
Which, as a dog's, upon the bone were strong."[60]

That is in the grand style, and so is the following, which describes those sinners locked in the frozen lake below Malebolge:—

"Weeping itself there does not let them weep,
And grief that finds a barrier in the eyes
Turns itself inward to increase the anguish.[61]

And the exclamation of one of these poor "wretches of the frozen crust" is an exclamation that Shakespeare might have written:—

"Lift from mine eyes the rigid veils, that I
May vent the sorrow which impregns my heart."[62]

There is nothing in Mr. Cary's translation which can stand a comparison with that. The eighteenth century could not translate like that. For here at last we have a real reproduction of the antique. In the Shakespearian ring of these lines we recognize the authentic rendering of the tones of the only man since the Christian era who could speak like Shakespeare.

In this way Mr. Longfellow's translation is, to an eminent degree, realistic. It is a work conceived and executed in entire accordance with the spirit of our time. Mr. Longfellow has set about making a reconstructive translation, and he has succeeded in the attempt. In view of what he has done, no one can ever wish to see the old methods of Pope and Cary again resorted to. It is only where he fails to be truly realistic that he comes short of success. And, as already hinted, it is oftenest through sheer excess of LITERALISM

---

[60] "Quand' ebbe detto cio, eon gli occhi torti
Riprese il teschio misero coi denti,
Che furo all' osso, come d'un can, forti."
Inferno, XXXIII. 76.
[61] "Lo pianto stesso li pianger non lascia,
E il duol, che trova in sugli occhi rintoppo,
Si volve in entro a far crescer l' ambascia."
Inferno, XXXIII. 94.
[62] "Levatemi dal viso i duri veli,
Si ch' io sfoghi il dolor che il cor m' impregna."
Ib. 112.

that he ceases to be realistic, and departs from the spirit of his author instead of coming nearer to it. In the "Paradiso," Canto X. 1-6, his method leads him into awkwardness:—

"Looking into His Son with all the love
Which each of them eternally breathes forth,
The primal and unutterable Power
Whate'er before the mind or eye revolves
With so much order made, there can be none
Who this beholds without enjoying Him."

This seems clumsy and halting, yet it is an extremely literal paraphrase of a graceful and flowing original:—

"Guardando nel suo figlio con l' amore
 Che l' uno e l' altro eternalmente spire,
 Lo primo ed ineffabile Valore,
Quanto per mente o per loco si gira
 Con tanto ordine fe', ch' esser non puote
 Senza gustar di lui ehi cio rimira

"Now to turn a graceful and flowing sentence into one that is clumsy and halting is certainly not to reproduce it, no matter how exactly the separate words are rendered, or how closely the syntactic constructions match each other. And this consideration seems conclusive as against the adequacy of the literalist method. That method is inadequate, not because it is too REALISTIC, but because it runs continual risk of being too VERBALISTIC. It has recently been applied to the translation of Dante by Mr. Rossetti, and it has sometimes led him to write curious verses. For instance, he makes Francesca say to Dante,—

"O gracious and benignant ANIMAL!" for

"O animal grazioso e benigno!" Mr. Longfellow's good taste has prevented his doing anything like this, yet Mr. Rossetti's extravagance is due to an unswerving adherence to the very rules by which Mr. Longfellow has been guided.

Good taste and poetic genius are, however, better than the best of rules, and so, after all said and done, we can only conclude that Mr. Longfellow has given us a great and noble work not likely soon to be equalled. Leopardi somewhere, in speaking of the early Italian translators of the classics and their well-earned popularity, says, who knows but Caro will live in men's remembrance as long as Virgil? "La belie destinee," adds Sainte-Beuve, "de ne pouvoir plus mourir, sinon avec un immortel!" Apart from Mr. Longfellow's other titles to undying fame, such a destiny is surely marked out for him, and throughout the English portions of the world his name will always be associated with that of the great Florentine.

June, 1867.

XII.

PAINE'S "ST. PETER."

For music-lovers in America the great event of the season has been the performance of Mr. Paine's oratorio, "St. Peter," at Portland, June 3. This event is important, not only as the first appearance of an American oratorio, but also as the first direct proof we have had of the existence of creative musical genius in this country. For Mr. Paine's Mass in D—a work which was brought out with great success several years ago in Berlin—has, for some reason or other, never been performed here. And, with the exception of Mr. Paine, we know of no American hitherto who has shown either the genius or the culture requisite for writing music in the grand style, although there is some of the Kapellmeister music, written by our leading organists and choristers, which deserves honourable mention. Concerning the rank likely to be assigned by posterity to "St. Peter," it would be foolish now to speculate; and it would be equally unwise to bring it into direct comparison with masterpieces like the "Messiah," "Elijah," and "St. Paul," the greatness of which has been so long acknowledged. Longer familiarity with the work is needed before such comparisons, always of somewhat doubtful value, can be profitably undertaken. But it must at least be said, as the net result of our impressions derived both from previous study of the score and from hearing, the performance at Portland, that Mr. Paine's oratorio has fairly earned for itself the right to be judged by the same high standard which we apply to these noble works of Mendelssohn and Handel.

In our limited space we can give only the briefest description of the general structure of the work. The founding of Christianity, as illustrated in four principal scenes of the life of St. Peter, supplies the material for the dramatic development of the subject. The overture, beginning with an adagio movement in B-flat minor, gives expression to the vague yearnings of that time of doubt and hesitancy when the "oracles were dumb," and the dawning of a new era of stronger and diviner faith was matter of presentiment rather than of definite hope or expectation. Though the tonality is at first firmly established, yet as the movement becomes more agitated, the final tendency of the modulations also becomes uncertain, and for a few bars it would seem as if the key of F-sharp minor might be the point of destination. But after a short melody by the wind instruments, accompanied by a rapid upward movement of strings, the dominant chord of C major asserts itself, being repeated, with sundry inversions, through a dozen bars, and leading directly into the triumphant and majestic chorus, " The time is fulfilled, and the kingdom of heaven is at hand." The second subject, introduced by the word "repent" descending through the interval of a diminished seventh and contrasted with the florid counterpoint of the phrase, "and believe the glad tidings of God," is a masterpiece of contrapuntal writing, and, if performed by a choir of three or four hundred voices, would produce an overpowering effect. The divine call of Simon Peter and his brethren is next described in a tenor recitative; and the acceptance of the glad tidings is expressed in an aria, "The spirit of the Lord is upon me," which, by an original but appropriate conception, is given to the soprano voice. In the next number, the disciples are dramatically represented by twelve basses and tenors, singing in four-part harmony, and alternating or combining with the full chorus in description of the aims of the new religion. The poem ends with the choral, "How lovely shines the Morning Star!" Then follows the sublime scene from Matthew xvi. 14-18, where Peter declares his master to be "the Christ, the Son of the living God,"—one of the most impressive scenes, we have always thought, in the gospel history, and here not inadequately treated. The feeling of mysterious and awful grandeur awakened by Peter's bold exclamation, "Thou art the Christ," is powerfully rendered by the entrance of the trombones upon the inverted subdominant triad of C-sharp minor, and their pause upon the dominant of the same key. Throughout this scene the characteristic contrast between the ardent vigour of Peter and the sweet serenity of Jesus is well delineated in the music. After Peter's stirring aria, "My heart is glad," the dramatic climax is reached in the C-major chorus, "The Church is built upon the foundation of the apostles and prophets."

The second scene is carried out to somewhat greater length, corresponding nearly to the last half of the first part of "Elijah," from the point where the challenge is given to the prophets of Baal. In the opening passages of mingled recitative and arioso, Peter is forewarned that he shall deny his Master, and his half-indignant remonstrance is sustained, with added emphasis, by the voices of the twelve disciples, pitched a fourth higher. Then Judas comes, with a great multitude, and Jesus is carried before the high-priest. The beautiful F-minor chorus, "We hid our faces from him," furnishes the musical comment upon the statement that "the disciples all forsook him and fled." We hardly dare to give full expression to our feelings about this chorus (which during the past month has been continually singing itself over and over again in our recollection), lest it should be supposed that our enthusiasm has got the better of our sober judgment. The second theme, "He was brought as a lamb to the slaughter, yet he opened not his mouth," is quite Handel-like in the simplicity and massiveness of its magnificent harmonic progressions. With the scene of the denial, for which we are thus prepared, the dramatic movement becomes exceedingly rapid, and the rendering of the events in the high-priest's hall—Peter's bass recitative alternating its craven protestations with the clamorous agitato chorus of the servants—is stirring in the extreme. The contralto aria describing the Lord's turning and looking upon Peter is followed by the orchestra with a lament in B-flat minor, introducing the bass aria of the repentant and remorse-stricken disciple, "O God, my God, forsake me not." As the last strains of the lamentation die away, a choir of angels is heard, of sopranos and contraltos divided, singing, "Remember from whence thou art fallen," to an accompaniment of harps. The second theme, "He that overcometh shall receive a crown of life," is introduced in full chorus, in a cheering allegro movement, preparing the way for a climax higher than any yet reached in the course of the work. This climax—delayed for a few moments by an andante aria for a contralto voice, "The Lord is faithful and righteous"—at last bursts upon us with a superb crescendo of strings, and the words, "Awake, thou that sleepest, arise from the dead, and Christ shall give thee light." This chorus, which for reasons presently to be given was heard at considerable disadvantage at Portland, contains some of the best fugue-writing in the work, and is especially rich and powerful in its instrumentation.

The second part of the oratorio begins with the crucifixion and ascension of Jesus. Here we must note especially the deeply pathetic opening chorus, "The Son of Man was delivered into the hands of sinful men," the joyous allegro, "And on the third day he rose again," the choral, "Jesus, my Redeemer, lives," and the quartet, "Feed the flock of God," commenting upon the command of Jesus, "Feed my lambs." This quartet has all the heavenly sweetness of Handel's "He shall feed his flock," which it suggests by similarity of subject, though not by similarity of treatment; but in a certain quality of inwardness, or religious meditativeness, it reminds one more of Mr. Paine's favourite master, Bach. The choral, like the one in the first part and the one which follows the scene of Pentecost, is taken from the Lutheran Choral Book, and arranged with original harmony and instrumentation, in accordance with the custom of Bach, Mendelssohn, and other composers, "of introducing into their sacred compositions the old popular choral melodies which are the peculiar offspring of a religious age." Thus the noblest choral ever written, the "Sleepers, wake," in "St. Paul," was composed in 1604 by Praetorius, the harmonization and accompaniment only being the work of Mendelssohn.

In "St. Peter," as in "Elijah," the second part, while forming the true musical climax of the oratorio, admits of a briefer description than the first part. The wave of emotion answering to the sensuously dramatic element having partly spent itself, the wave of lyric emotion gathers fresh strength, and one feels that one has reached the height of spiritual exaltation, while, nevertheless, there is not so much which one can describe to others who may not happen to have gone through with the same experience. Something of the same feeling one gets in studying Dante's "Paradiso," after finishing the preceding divisions of his poem: there is less which can be pictured to the eye of sense, or left to be supplied by the concrete imagination. Nevertheless, in the scene of Pentecost, which follows that of the Ascension, there is no lack of dramatic vividness. Indeed, there is nothing in the work more striking than the orchestration of the introductory tenor recitative, the mysterious chorus, "The voice of the Lord divideth the flames of fire," or the amazed query which follows, "Behold, are not all these who speak Galileans? and how is it that we every one hear them in our own tongue wherein we were born?" We have heard the opinion expressed that Mr. Paine's oratorio must be lacking in originality, since it suggests such strong reminiscences of "St. Paul." Now, this suggestion, it seems to us, is due partly to the similarity of the subjects, independently of any likeness in the modes of treatment, and partly, perhaps, to the fact that Mr. Paine, as well as Mendelssohn, has been a devoted student of Bach, whose characteristics are so strong that they may well have left their mark upon the works of both composers. But especially it would seem that there is some real, though very general resemblance between this colloquial chorus, "Behold," etc., and some choruses in "St. Paul," as, for example Nos. 29 and 36-38. In the same way the scene in the high-priest's hall might distantly suggest either of these passages, or others in "Elijah;" These resemblances, however, are very superficial, pertaining not to the musical but to the dramatic treatment of situations which are generically similar in so far, and only in so far, as they represent conversational passages between an apostle or prophet and an ignorant multitude, whether amazed or hostile, under the sway of violent excitement. As regards the musical elaboration of these terse and striking alternations of chorus and recitative, its originality can be questioned only after we have decided to refer all originality on such matters to Bach, or, indeed, even behind him, into the Middle Ages.

After the preaching of Peter, and the sweet contralto aria, "As for man, his days are as grass," the culmination of this scene comes in the D-major chorus, "This is the witness of God." What follows, beginning with the choral, "Praise to the Father," is to be regarded as an epilogue or peroration to the whole work. It is in accordance with a sound tradition that the grand sacred drama of an oratorio should conclude with a lyric outburst of thanksgiving, a psalm of praise to the Giver of every good and perfect gift. Thus, after Peter's labours are ended in the aria, "Now as ye were redeemed," in which the twelve disciples and the full chorus join, a duet for tenor and soprano, "Sing unto God," brings us to the grand final chorus in C major, "Great and marvellous are thy works, Lord God Almighty."

The cadence of this concluding chorus reminds us that one of the noteworthy points in the oratorio is the character of its cadences. The cadence prepared by the 6/4 chord, now become so hackneyed from its perpetual and wearisome repetition in popular church music, seems to be especially disliked by Mr. Paine, as it occurs but once or twice in the course of the work. In the great choruses the cadence is usually reached either by a pedal on the tonic, as in the chorus, "Awake, thou that sleepest," or by a pedal on the dominant culminating in a chord of the major ninth, as in the final chorus; or there is a plagal cadence, as in the first chorus of the second part; or, if the 6/4 chord is introduced, as it is in the chorus, "He that overcometh," its ordinary effect is covered and obscured by the movement of the divided sopranos. We do not remember noticing anywhere such a decided use of the 6/4 chord as is made, for example, by Mendelssohn, in "Thanks be to God," or in the final chorus of "St. Paul." Perhaps if we were to confess our lingering fondness for the cadence prepared by the 6/4 chord, when not too frequently introduced, it might only show that we retain a liking for New England "psalm-tunes"; but it does seem to us that a sense of final repose, of entire cessation of movement, is more effectually secured by this cadence than by any other. Yet while the 6/4 cadence most completely expresses finality and rest, it would seem that the plagal and other cadences above enumerated as preferred by Mr. Paine have a certain sort of superiority by reason of the very incompleteness with which they express finality. There is no sense of finality whatever about the Phrygian cadence; it leaves the mind occupied with the feeling of a boundless region beyond, into which one would fain penetrate; and for this reason it has, in sacred music, a great value. Something of the same feeling, too, attaches to those cadences in which an unexpected major third usurps the place of the minor which the ear was expecting, as in the "Incarnatus" of Mozart's "Twelfth Mass," or in Bach's sublime "Prelude," Part I., No. 22 of the "Well-tempered Clavichord." In a less degree, an analogous effect was produced upon us by the cadence with a pedal on the tonic in the choruses, "The Church is built," and "Awake, thou that sleepest." On these considerations it may become intelligible that to some hearers Mr. Paine's cadences have seemed unsatisfactory, their ears having missed the positive categorical assertion of finality which the 6/4 cadence alone can give. To go further into this subject would take us far beyond our limits.

The pleasant little town of Portland has reason to congratulate itself, first, on being the birthplace of such a composer as Mr. Paine; secondly, on having been the place where the first great work of America in the domain of music was brought out; and thirdly, on possessing what is probably the most thoroughly disciplined choral society in this country. Our New York friends, after their recent experiences, will perhaps be slow to believe us when we say that the Portland choir sang this new work even better, in many respects, than the Handel and Haydn Society sing the old and familiar "Elijah"; but it is true. In their command of the pianissimo and the gradual crescendo, and in the precision of their attack, the Portland singers can easily teach the Handel and Haydn a quarter's lessons. And, besides all this, they know how to preserve their equanimity under the gravest persecutions of the orchestra; keeping the even tenour of their way where a less disciplined choir, incited by the excessive blare of the trombones and the undue scraping of the second violins, would be likely to lose its presence of mind and break out into an untimely fortissimo.

No doubt it is easier to achieve perfect chorus-singing with a choir of one hundred and twenty-five voices than with a choir of six hundred. But this diminutive size, which was an advantage so far as concerned the technical excellence of the Portland choir, was decidedly a disadvantage so far as concerned the proper rendering of the more massive choruses in "St. Peter." All the greatest choruses—such as Nos. 1, 8, 19, 20, 28, 35, and 39—were seriously impaired in the rendering by the lack of massiveness in the voices. For example, the grand chorus, "Awake, thou that sleepest," begins with a rapid crescendo of strings, introducing the full chorus on the word "Awake," upon the dominant triad of D major; and after a couple of beats the voices are reinforced by the trombones, producing the most tremendous effect possible in such a crescendo. Unfortunately, however, the brass asserted itself at this point so much more emphatically than the voices that the effect was almost to disjoin the latter portion of the chord from its beginning, and thus to dwarf the utterance of the word "Awake." To us this effect was very disagreeable; and it was obviously contrary to the effect intended by the composer. But with a weight of four or five hundred voices, the effect would be entirely different. Instead of entering upon the scene as intruders, the mighty trombones would only serve to swell and enrich the ponderous chord which opens this noble chorus. Given greater weight only, and the performance of the admirable Portland choir would have left nothing to be desired.

We cannot speak with so much satisfaction of the performance of the orchestra. The instrumentation of "St. Peter" is remarkably fine. But this instrumentation was rather clumsily rendered by the orchestra, whose doings constituted the least enjoyable part of the performance. There was too much blare of brass, whine of hautboy, and scraping of strings. But in condonation of this serious defect, one must admit that the requisite amount of rehearsal is out of the question when one's choir is in Portland and one's orchestra in Boston; besides which the parts had been inaccurately copied. For a moment, at the beginning of the orchestral lament, there was risk of disaster, the wind instruments failing to come in at the right time, when Mr. Paine, with fortunate presence of mind, stopped the players, and the movement was begun over again,—the whole occurring so quickly and quietly as hardly to attract attention.

In conclusion we would say a few words suggested by a recent critical notice of Mr. Paine's work in the "Nation." While acknowledging the importance of the publication of this oratorio, as an event in the art-history of America, the writer betrays manifest disappointment that this work should not rather have been a symphony,[63] and thus have belonged to what he calls the "domain of absolute music." Now with regard to the assumption that the oratorio is not so high a form of music as the symphony, or, in other words, that vocal music in general is artistically inferior to instrumental music, we may observe, first, that Ambros and Dommer—two of the most profound musical critics now living—do not sustain it. It is Beanquier, we think, who suggests that instrumental music should rank above vocal, because it is "pure music," bereft of the fictitious aids of language and of the emotional associations which are grouped about the peculiar timbre of the human voice.[64] At first the suggestion seems plausible; but on analogous grounds we might set the piano

---

[63] Now within two years, Mr. Paine's C-minor symphony has followed the completion of his oratorio.
[64] These peculiar associations are no doubt what is chiefly enjoyed in music, antecedent to a properly musical culture. Persons of slight acquaintance with music invariably prefer the voice to the piano.

above the orchestra, because the piano gives us pure harmony and counterpoint, without the adventitious aid of variety in timbre. And it is indeed true that, for some such reason as this, musicians delight in piano-sonatas, which are above all things tedious and unintelligible to the mind untrained in music. Nevertheless, in spite of its great and peculiar prerogatives, it would be absurd to prefer the piano to the orchestra; and there is a kindred absurdity involved in setting the orchestra above that mighty union of orchestra, organ, and voices which we get in the oratorio. When the reason alleged for ranking the symphony above the oratorio leads us likewise to rank the sonata above the symphony, we seem to have reached a reductio ad absurdum.

Rightly considered, the question between vocal and instrumental music amounts to this, What does music express? This is a great psychological question, and we have not now the space or the leisure requisite for discussing it, even in the most summary way. We will say, however, that we do not see how music can in any way express ideas, or anything but moods or emotional states to which the ideas given in language may add determination and precision. The pure symphony gives utterance to moods, and will be a satisfactory work of art or not, according as the composer has been actuated by a legitimate sequence of emotional states, like Beethoven, or by a desire to produce novel and startling effects, like Liszt. But the danger in purely instrumental music is that it may run riot in the extravagant utterance of emotional states which are not properly concatenated by any normal sequence of ideas associated with them. This is sometimes exemplified in the most modern instrumental music.

Now, as in real life our sequent clusters of emotional states are in general determined by their association with our sequent groups of intellectual ideas, it would seem that music, regarded as an exponent of psychical life, reaches its fullest expressiveness when the sequence of the moods which it incarnates in sound is determined by some sequence of ideas, such as is furnished by the words of a libretto. Not that the words should have predominance over the music, or even coequal sway with it, but that they should serve to give direction to the succession of feelings expressed by the music. "Lift up your heads" and "Hallelujah" do not owe their glory to the text, but to that tremendous energy of rhythmic and contrapuntal progression which the text serves to concentrate and justify. When precision and definiteness of direction are thus added to the powerful physical means of expression which we get in the combination of chorus, orchestra, and organ, we have attained the greatest sureness as well as the greatest wealth of musical expressiveness. And thus we may see the reasonableness of Dommer's opinion that in order to restrain instrumental music from ruining itself by meaningless extravagance, it is desirable that there should be a renaissance of vocal music, such as it was in the golden age of Palestrina and Orlando Lasso.

We are not inclined to deny that in structural beauty—in the symmetrical disposition and elaboration of musical themes—the symphony has the advantage. The words, which in the oratorio serve to give definite direction to the currents of emotion, may also sometimes hamper the free development of the pure musical conception, just as in psychical life the obtrusive entrance of ideas linked by association may hinder the full fruition of some emotional state. Nevertheless, in spite of this possible drawback, it may be doubted if the higher forms of polyphonic composition fall so very far short of the symphony in capability of giving full elaboration to the musical idea. The practical testimony of Beethoven, in his Ninth Symphony, is decidedly adverse to any such supposition.

But to pursue this interesting question would carry us far beyond our limits. Whatever may be the decision as to the respective claims of vocal and instrumental music, we have every reason for welcoming the appearance, in our own country, of an original work in the highest form of vocal music. It is to be hoped that we shall often have the opportunity to "hear with our ears" this interesting work; for as a rule great musical compositions are peculiarly unfortunate among works of art, in being known at first hand by comparatively few persons. In this way is rendered possible that pretentious kind of dilettante criticism which is so common in musical matters, and which is often positively injurious, as substituting a factitious public opinion for one that is genuine. We hope that the favour with which the new oratorio has already been received will encourage the author to pursue the enviable career upon which he has entered. Even restricting ourselves to vocal music, there is still a broad field left open for original work. The secular cantata—attempted in recent times by Schumann, as well as by English composers of smaller calibre—is a very high form of vocal music; and if founded on an adequate libretto, dealing with some supremely grand or tragical situation, is capable of being carried to an unprecedented height of musical elaboration. Here is an opportunity for original achievement, of which it is to be hoped that some gifted and well-trained composer, like the author of "St. Peter," may find it worth while to avail himself.

June, 1873.

XIII. A PHILOSOPHY OF ART.[65]

We are glad of a chance to introduce to our readers one of the works of a great writer. Though not yet[66] widely known in this country, M. Taine has obtained a very high reputation in Europe. He is still quite a young man, but is nevertheless the author of nineteen goodly volumes, witty, acute, and learned; and already he is often ranked with Renan, Littre, and Sainte-Beuve, the greatest living French writers.

Hippolyte Adolphe Taine was born at Vouziers, among the grand forests of Ardennes, in 1828, and is therefore about forty years old. His family was simple in habits and tastes, and entertained a steadfast belief in culture, along with the possession of a fair amount of it. His grandfather was sub-prefect at Rocroi, in 1814 and 1815, under the first restoration of the Bourbons. His father, a lawyer by profession, was the first instructor of his son, and taught him Latin, and from an uncle, who had been in America, he learned English, while still a mere child. Having gone to Paris with his mother in 1842, he began his studies at the College Bourbon and in 1848 was promoted to the ecole Normale. Weiss, About, and Prevost-Paradol were his contemporaries at this institution. At that time great liberty was enjoyed in regard to the order and the details of the exercises; so that Taine, with his surprising rapidity, would do in one week the work laid out for a month, and would spend the remainder of the time in private reading. In 1851 he left college, and after two or three unsatisfactory attempts at teaching, in Paris and in the provinces, he settled down at Paris as a private student. He gave himself the very best elementary preparation which a literary man can have,—a thorough course in mathematics and the physical sciences. His studies in anatomy and physiology were especially elaborate and minute. He attended the School of Medicine as regularly as if he expected to make his daily bread in the profession. In this way, when at the age of twenty-five he began to write books, M. Taine was a really educated man; and his books show it. The day is past when a man could write securely, with a knowledge of the classics alone. We doubt if a philosophical critic is perfectly educated for his task, unless he can read, for instance, Donaldson's "New Cratylus" on the one hand, and Rokitansky's "Pathological Anatomy" on the other, for the sheer pleasure of the thing. At any rate, it was an education of this sort which M. Taine, at the outset of his literary career, had secured. By this solid discipline of mathematics, chemistry, and medicine, M. Taine became that which above all things he now is,—a man possessed of a central philosophy, of an exact, categorical, well-defined system, which accompanies and supports him in his most distant literary excursions. He does not keep throwing out ideas at random, like too many literary critics, but

---

[65] The Philosophy of Art. By H. Taine. New York: Leypoldt &; Holt. 1867.
[66] That is, in 1868.

attaches all his criticisms to a common fundamental principle; in short, he is not a dilettante, but a savant.

His treatise on La Fontaine, in 1853, attracted much attention, both the style and the matter being singularly fresh and original. He has since republished it, with alterations which serve to show that he can be docile toward intelligent criticisms. About the same time he prepared for the French Academy his work upon the historian Livy, which was crowned in 1855. Suffering then from overwork, he was obliged to make a short journey to the Pyrenees, which he has since described in a charming little volume, illustrated by Dore.

His subsequent works are a treatise on the French philosophers of the present century, in which the vapid charlatanism of M. Cousin is satisfactorily dealt with; a history of English literature in five volumes; a humorous book on Paris; three volumes upon the general theory of art; and two volumes of travels in Italy; besides a considerable collection of historical and critical essays. We think that several of these works would be interesting to the American public, and might profitably be translated.

Some three or four years ago, M. Taine was appointed Professor in the ecole des Beaux Arts, and we suppose his journey to Italy must have been undertaken partly with a view to qualify himself for his new position. He visited the four cities which may be considered the artistic centres of Italy,—Rome, Naples, Florence, and Venice,—and a large part of his account of his journey is taken up with descriptions and criticisms of pictures, statues, and buildings.

This is a department of criticism which, we may as well frankly acknowledge, is far better appreciated on the continent of Europe than in England or America. Over the English race there passed, about two centuries ago, a deluge of Puritanism, which for a time almost drowned out its artistic tastes and propensities. The Puritan movement, in proportion to its success, was nearly as destructive to art in the West, as Mohammedanism had long before been in the East. In its intense and one-sided regard for morality, Puritanism not only relegated the love for beauty to an inferior place, but contemned and spat upon it, as something sinful and degrading. Hence, the utter architectural impotence which characterizes the Americans and the modern English; and hence the bewildered ignorant way in which we ordinarily contemplate pictures and statues. For two centuries we have been removed from an artistic environment, and consequently can with difficulty enter into the feelings of those who have all this time been nurtured in love for art, and belief in art for its own sake. These peculiarities, as Mr. Mill has ably pointed out, have entered deep into our ethnic character. Even in pure morals there is a radical difference between the Englishman and the inhabitant of the continent of Europe. The Englishman follows virtue from a sense of duty, the Frenchman from an emotional aspiration toward the beautiful The one admires a noble action because it is right, the other because it is attractive. And this difference underlies the moral judgments upon men and events which are to be found respectively in English and in continental literature. By keeping it constantly in view, we shall be enabled to understand many things which might otherwise surprise us in the writings of French authors.

We are now slowly outgrowing the extravagances of Puritanism. It has given us an earnestness and sobriety of character, to which much of our real greatness is owing, both here and in the mother country. It has made us stronger and steadier, but it has at the same time narrowed us in many respects, and rendered our lives incomplete. This incompleteness, entailed by Puritanism, we are gradually getting rid of; and we are learning to admire and respect many things upon which Puritanism set its mark of contempt. We are beginning, for instance, to recognize the transcendent merits of that great civilizing agency, the drama; we no longer think it necessary that our temples for worshipping God should be constructed like hideous barracks; we are gradually permitting our choirs to discard the droning and sentimental modern "psalm-tune" for the inspiring harmonies of Beethoven and Mozart; and we admit the classical picture and the undraped statue to a high place in our esteem. Yet with all this it will probably be some time before genuine art ceases to be an exotic among us, and becomes a plant of unhindered native growth. It will be some time before we cease to regard pictures and statues as a higher species of upholstery, and place them in the same category with poems and dramas, duly reverencing them as authentic revelations of the beauty which is to be found in nature. It will be some time before we realize that art is a thing to be studied, as well as literature, and before we can be quite reconciled to the familiar way in which a Frenchman quotes a picture as we would quote a poem or novel.

Artistic genius, as M. Taine has shown, is something which will develop itself only under peculiar social circumstances; and, therefore, if we have not art, we can perhaps only wait for it, trusting that when the time comes it will arise among us. But without originating, we may at least intelligently appreciate. The nature of a work of art, and the mode in which it is produced, are subjects well worthy of careful study. Architecture and music, poetry, painting and sculpture, have in times past constituted a vast portion of human activity; and without knowing something of the philosophy of art, we need not hope to understand thoroughly the philosophy of history.

In entering upon the study of art in general, one may find many suggestive hints in the little books of M. Taine, reprinted from the lectures which he has been delivering at the ecole des Beaux Arts. The first, on the Philosophy of Art, designated at the head of this paper, is already accessible to the American reader; and translations of the others are probably soon to follow. We shall for the present give a mere synopsis of M. Taine's general views.

And first it must be determined what a work of art is. Leaving for a while music and architecture out of consideration, it will be admitted that poetry, painting, and sculpture have one obvious character in common: they are arts of IMITATION. This, says Taine, appears at first sight to be their essential character. It would appear that their great object is to IMITATE as closely as possible. It is obvious that a statue is intended to imitate a living man, that a picture is designed to represent real persons in real attitudes, or the interior of a house, or a landscape, such as it exists in nature. And it is no less clear that a novel or drama endeavours to represent with accuracy real characters, actions, and words, giving as precise and faithful an image of them as possible. And when the imitation is incomplete, we say to the painter, "Your people are too largely proportioned, and the colour of your trees is false"; we tell the sculptor that his leg or arm is incorrectly modelled; and we say to the dramatist, "Never has a man felt or thought as your hero is supposed to have felt and thought."

This truth, moreover, is seen. both in the careers of individual artists, and in the general history of art. According to Taine, the life of an artist may generally be divided into two parts. In the first period, that of natural growth, he studies nature anxiously and minutely, he keeps the objects themselves before his eyes, and strives to represent them with scrupulous fidelity. But when the time for mental growth ends, as it does with every man, and the crystallization of ideas and impressions commences, then the mind of the artist is no longer so susceptible to new impressions from without. He begins to nourish himself from his own substance. He abandons the living model, and with recipes which he has gathered in the course of his experience, he proceeds to construct a drama or novel, a picture or statue. Now, the first period, says Taine, is that of genuine art; the second is that of mannerism. Our author cites the case of Michael Angelo, a man who was one of the most colossal embodiments of physical and mental energy that the world has ever seen. In Michael Angelo's case, the period of growth, of genuine art, may be said to have lasted until after his sixtieth year. But look, says Taine, at the works which he executed in his old age; consider the Conversion of St. Paul, and the Last Judgment, painted when he was nearly seventy. Even those who are not connoisseurs can see that these frescos are painted by rule, that the artist, having stocked his memory with a certain set of forms, is making use of them to fill out his tableau; that he wantonly multiplies queer attitudes and ingenious foreshortenings; that the lively invention, the grand outburst of feeling, the perfect truth, by which his earlier works are distinguished, have disappeared; and that, if he is still superior to all others, he is nevertheless inferior to himself. The careers of Scott, of Goethe, and of Voltaire will furnish parallel examples. In every school of art, too, the flourishing period is followed by one of decline; and in every case the decline is due to a failure to imitate the living models. In painting, we have the exaggerated foreshorteners and muscle-makers who copied Michael Angelo; the lovers of theatrical decorations who succeeded Titian and Giorgione and the degenerate boudoir-painters who followed Claucle and Poussin. In literature, we have the versifiers, epigrammatists, and rhetors of the Latin decadence; the sensual and declamatory dramatists who represent the last stages of old English comedy;

and the makers of sonnets and madrigals, or conceited euphemists of the Gongora school, in the decline of Italian and Spanish poetry. Briefly it may be said, that the masters copy nature and the pupils copy the masters. In this way are explained the constantly recurring phenomena of decline in art, and thus, also, it is seen that art is perfect in proportion as it successfully imitates nature.

But we are not to conclude that absolute imitation is the sole and entire object of art. Were this the case, the finest works would be those which most minutely correspond to their external prototypes. In sculpture, a mould taken from the living features is that which gives the most faithful representation of the model; but a well-moulded bust is far from being equal to a good statue. Photography is in many respects more accurate than painting; but no one would rank a photograph, however exquisitely executed, with an original picture. And finally, if exact imitation were the supreme object of art, the best tragedy, the best comedy, and the best drama would be a stenographic report of the proceedings in a court of justice, in a family gathering, in a popular meeting, in the Rump Congress. Even the works of artists are not rated in proportion to their minute exactness. Neither in painting nor in any other art do we give the precedence to that which deceives the eye simply. Every one remembers how Zeuxis was said to have painted grapes so faithfully that the birds came and pecked at them; and how, Parrhasios, his rival, surpassed even this feat by painting a curtain so natural in its appearance that Zeuxis asked him to pull it aside and show the picture behind it. All this is not art, but mere knack and trickery. Perhaps no painter was ever so minute as Denner. It used to take him four years to make one portrait. He would omit nothing,—neither the bluish lines made by the veins under the skin, nor the little black points scattered over the nose, nor the bright spots in the eye where neighbouring objects are reflected; the head seems to start out from the canvas, it is so like flesh and blood. Yet who cares for Denner's portraits? And who would not give ten times as much for one which Van Dyck or Tintoretto might have painted in a few hours? So in the churches of Naples and Spain we find statues coloured and draped, saints clothed in real coats, with their skin yellow and bloodless, their hands bleeding, and their feet bruised; and beside them Madonnas in royal habiliments, in gala dresses of lustrous silk, adorned with diadems, precious necklaces, bright ribbons, and elegant laces, with their cheeks rosy, their eyes brilliant, their eyelashes sweeping. And by this excess of literal imitation, there is awakened a feeling, not of pleasure, but always of repugnance, often of disgust, and sometimes of horror So in literature, the ancient Greek theatre, and the best Spanish and English dramatists, alter on purpose the natural current of human speech, and make their characters talk under all the restraints of rhyme and rhythm. But we pronounce this departure from literal truth a merit and not a defect. We consider Goethe's second "Iphigenie," written in verse, far preferable to the first one written in prose; nay, it is the rhythm or metre itself which communicates to the work its incomparable beauty. In a review of Longfellow's "Dante," published last year, we argued this very point in one of its special applications; the artist must copy his original, but he must not copy it too literally.

What then must he copy? He must copy, says Taine, the mutual relations and interdependences of the parts of his model. And more than this, he must render the essential characteristic of the object—that characteristic upon which all the minor qualities depend—as salient and conspicuous as possible. He must put into the background the traits which conceal it, and bring into the foreground the traits which manifest it. If he is sculpturing a group like the Laocoon, he must strike upon the supreme moment, that in which the whole tragedy reveals itself, and he must pass over those insignificant details of position and movement which serve only to distract our attention and weaken our emotions by dividing them. If he is writing a drama, he must not attempt to give us the complete biography of his character; he must depict only those situations which stand in direct subordination to the grand climax or denouement. As a final result, therefore. Taine concludes that a work of art is a concrete representation of the relations existing between the parts of an object, with the intent to bring the essential or dominating character thereof into prominence.

We should overrun our limits if we were to follow out the admirable discussion in which M. Taine extends this definition to architecture and music. These closely allied arts are distinguished from poetry, painting, and sculpture, by appealing far less directly to the intelligence, and far more exclusively to the emotions. Yet these arts likewise aim, by bringing into prominence certain relations of symmetry in form as perceived by the eye, or in aerial vibrations as perceived by the ear, to excite in us the states of feeling with which these species of symmetry are by subtle laws of association connected. They, too, imitate, not literally, but under the guidance of a predominating sentiment or emotion, relations which really exist among the phenomena of nature. And here, too, we estimate excellence, not in proportion to the direct, but to the indirect imitation. A Gothic cathedral is not, as has been supposed, directly imitated from the towering vegetation of Northern forests; but it may well be the expression of the dim sentiment of an unseen, all-pervading Power, generated by centuries of primeval life amid such forests. So the sounds which in a symphony of Beethoven are woven into a web of such amazing complexity may exist in different combinations in nature; but when a musician steps out of his way to imitate the crowing of cocks or the roar of the tempest, we regard his achievement merely as a graceful conceit. Art is, therefore, an imitation of nature; but it is an intellectual and not a mechanical imitation; and the performances of the camera and the music-box are not to be classed with those of the violinist's bow or the sculptor's chisel.

And lastly, in distinguishing art from science, Taine remarks, that in disengaging from their complexity the, causes which are at work in nature, and the fundamental laws according to which they work, science describes them in abstract formulas conveyed in technical language. But art reveals these operative causes and these dominant laws, not in arid definitions, inaccessible to most people, intelligible only to specially instructed men, but in a concrete symbol, addressing itself not only to the understanding, but still more to the sentiments of the ordinary man. Art has, therefore, this peculiarity, that it is at once elevated and popular, that it manifests that which is often most recondite, and that it manifests it to all.

Having determined what a work of art is, our author goes on to study the social conditions under which works of art are produced; and he concludes that the general character of a work of art is determined by the state of intellect and morals in the society in which it is executed. There is, in fact, a sort of moral temperature which acts upon mental development much as physical temperature acts upon organic development. The condition of society does not produce the artist's talent; but it assists or checks its efforts to display itself; it decides whether or not it shall be successful And it exerts a "natural selection" between different kinds of talents, stimulating some and starving others. To make this perfectly clear, we will cite at some length Taine's brilliant illustration.

The case chosen for illustration is a very simple one,—that of a state of society in which one of the predominant feelings is melancholy. This is not an arbitrary supposition, for such a time has occurred more than once in human history; in Asia, in the sixth century before Christ, and especially in Europe, from the fourth to the tenth centuries of our era. To produce such a state of feeling, five or six generations of decadence, accompanied with diminution of population, foreign invasions, famines, pestilences, and increasing difficulty in procuring the necessaries of life, are amply sufficient. It then happens that men lose courage and hope, and consider life an evil. Now, admitting that among the artists who live in such a time, there are likely to be the same relative numbers of melancholy, joyous, or indifferent temperaments as at other times, let us see how they will be affected by reigning circumstances.

Let us first remember, says Taine, that the evils which depress the public will also depress the artist. His risks are no less than those of less gifted people. He is liable to suffer from plague or famine, to be ruined by unfair taxation or conscription, or to see his children massacred and his wife led into captivity by barbarians. And if these ills do not reach him personally, he must at least behold those around him affected by them. In this way, if he is joyous by temperament, he must inevitably become less joyous; if he is melancholy, he must become more melancholy.

Secondly, having been reared among melancholy contemporaries, his education will have exerted upon him a corresponding influence. The prevailing religious doctrine, accommodated to the state of affairs, will tell him that the earth is a place of exile, life an evil, gayety a snare, and his most profitable occupation will be to get ready to die. Philosophy, constructing its system of morals in conformity to the existing phenomena of decadence, will tell him that he had better never have been born. Daily conversation will inform him of horrible events, of the devastation of a province, the sack of a town by the Goths, the oppression of the neighbouring peasants by the imperial tax-collectors, or the civil war that has just burst out between half a dozen pretenders to the throne. As he travels about, he beholds signs of mourning and despair, crowds of beggars, people dying of hunger, a broken bridge which no one is mending, an abandoned suburb which is going to ruin, fields choked with weeds, the blackened walls of burned houses. Such sights and impressions, repeated from childhood to old age (and we must remember that this has actually been the state of things in what are now the fairest parts of the globe), cannot fail to deepen whatever elements of melancholy there may be already in the artist's disposition.

The operation of all these causes will be enhanced by that very peculiarity of the artist which constitutes his talent. For, according to the definitions above given, that which makes him an artist is his capacity for seizing upon the essential characteristics and the salient traits of surrounding objects and events. Other men see things in part fragmentarily; he catches the spirit of the ensemble. And in this way he will very likely exaggerate in his works the general average of contemporary feeling.

Lastly, our author reminds us that a man who writes or paints does not remain alone before his easel or his writing-desk. He goes out, looks about him, receives suggestions from friends, from rivals, from books, and works of art whenever accessible, and hears the criticisms of the public upon his own productions and those of his contemporaries. In order to succeed, he must not only satisfy to some extent the popular taste, but he must feel that the public is in sympathy with him. If in this period of social decadence and gloom he endeavours to represent gay, brilliant, or triumphant ideas, he will find himself left to his own resources; and, as Taine rightly says, the power of an isolated man is always insignificant. His work will be likely to be mediocre. If he attempts to write like Rabelais or paint like Rubens, he will get neither assistance nor sympathy from a public which prefers the pictures of Rembrandt, the melodies of Chopin, and the poetry of Heine.

Having thus explained his position by this extreme instance, signified for the sake of clearness, Taine goes on to apply such general considerations to four historic epochs, taken in all their complexity. He discusses the aspect presented by art in ancient Greece, in the feudal and Catholic Middle Ages, in the centralized monarchies of the seventeenth century, and in the scientific, industrial democracy in which we now live. Out of these we shall select, as perhaps the simplest, the case of ancient Greece, still following our author closely, though necessarily omitting many interesting details.

The ancient Greeks, observes Taine, understood life in a new and original manner. Their energies were neither absorbed by a great religious conception, as in the case of the Hindus and Egyptians, nor by a vast social organization, as in the case of the Assyrians and Persians, nor by a purely industrial and commercial regime, as in the case of the Phoenicians and

Carthaginians. Instead of a theocracy or a rigid system of castes, instead of a monarchy with a hierarchy of civil officials, the men of this race invented a peculiar institution, the City, each city giving rise to others like itself, and from colony to colony reproducing itself indefinitely. A single Greek city, for instance, Miletos, produced three hundred other cities, colonizing with them the entire coast of the Black Sea. Each city was substantially self-ruling; and the idea of a coalescence of several cities into a nation was one which the Greek mind rarely conceived, and never was able to put into operation.

In these cities, labour was for the most part carried on by slaves. In Athens there were four or five for each citizen, and in places like Korinth and Aigina the slave population is said to have numbered four or five hundred thousand. Besides, the Greek citizen had little need of personal service. He lived out of doors, and, like most Southern people, was comparatively abstemious in his habits. His dinners were slight, his clothing was simple, his house was scantily furnished, being intended chiefly for a den to sleep in.

Serving neither king nor priest, the citizen was free and sovereign in his own city. He elected his own magistrates, and might himself serve as city-ruler, as juror, or as judge. Representation was unknown. Legislation was carried on by all the citizens assembled in mass. Therefore politics and war were the sole or chief employments of the citizen. War, indeed, came in for no slight share of his attention. For society was not so well protected as in these modern days. Most of these Greek cities, scattered over the coasts of the Aigeian, the Black Sea, and the Mediterranean, were surrounded by tribes of barbarians, Scythians, Gauls Spaniards, and Africans. The citizen must therefore keep on his guard, like the Englishman of to-day in New Zealand, or like the inhabitant of a Massachusetts town in tho seventeenth century. Otherwise Gauls Samnites, or Bithynians, as savage as North American Indians, would be sure to encamp upon the blackened ruins of his town. Moreover, the Greek cities had their quarrels with each other, and their laws of war were very barbarous. A conquered city was liable to be razed to the ground, its male inhabitants put to the sword, its women sold as slaves. Under such circumstances, according to Taine's happy expression, a citizen must be a politician and warrior, on pain of death. And not only fear, but ambition also tended to make him so. For each city strove to subject or to humiliate its neighbours, to acquire tribute, or to exact homage from its rivals. Thus the citizen passed his life in the public square, discussing alliances, treaties, and constitutions, hearing speeches, or speaking himself, and finally going aboard of his ship to fight his neighbour Greeks, or to sail against Egypt or Persia.

War (and politics as subsidiary to it) was then the chief pursuit of life. But as there was no organized industry, so there were no machines of warfare. All fighting was done hand to hand. Therefore, the great thing in preparing for war was not to transform the soldiers into precisely-acting automata, as in a modern army, but to make each separate soldier as vigorous and active as possible. The leading object of Greek education was to make men physically perfect. In this respect, Sparta may be taken as the typical Greek community, for nowhere else was physical development so entirely made the great end of social life. In these matters Sparta was always regarded by the other cities as taking the lead,—as having attained the ideal after which all alike were striving. Now Sparta, situated in the midst of a numerous conquered population of Messenians and Helots, was partly a great gymnasium and partly a perpetual camp. Her citizens were always in training. The entire social constitution of Sparta was shaped with a view to the breeding and bringing up of a strong and beautiful race. Feeble or ill-formed infants were put to death. The age at which citizens might marry was prescribed by law; and the State paired off men and women as the modern breeder pairs off horses, with a sole view to the excellence of the off-spring. A wife was not a helpmate, but a bearer of athletes. Women boxed, wrestled, and raced; a circumstance referred to in the following passage of Aristophanes, as rendered by Mr. Felton:—

LYSISTRATA.
Hail! Lampito, dearest of Lakonian women.
How shines thy beauty, O my sweetest friend!
How fair thy colour, full of life thy frame!
Why, thou couldst choke a bull.

LAMPITO.
Yes, by the Twain;
For I do practice the gymnastic art,
And, leaping, strike my backbone with my heels.
LYSISTRATA.

In sooth, thy bust is lovely to behold. The young men lived together, like soldiers in a camp. They ate out-of-doors, at a public table. Their fare was as simple as that of a modern university boat-crew before a race. They slept in the open air, and spent their waking hours in wrestling, boxing, running races, throwing quoits, and engaging in mock battles. This was the way in which the Spartans lived; and though no other city carried this discipline to such an extent, yet in all a very large portion of the citizen's life was spent in making himself hardy and robust.

The ideal man, in the eyes of a Greek, was, therefore not the contemplative or delicately susceptible thinker but the naked athlete, with firm flesh and swelling muscles. Most of their barbarian neighbours were ashamed to be seen undressed, but the Greeks seem to have felt little embarrassment in appearing naked in public. Their gymnastic habits entirely transformed their sense of shame. Their Olympic and other public games were a triumphant display of naked physical perfection. Young men of the noblest families and from the farthest Greek colonies came to them, and wrestled and ran, undraped, before countless multitudes of admiring spectators. Note, too, as significant, that the Greek era began with the Olympic games, and that time was reckoned by the intervals between them; as well as the fact that the grandest lyric poetry of antiquity was written in celebration of these gymnastic contests. The victor in the foot-race gave his name to the current Olympiad; and on reaching home, was received by his fellow-citizens as if he had been a general returning from a successful campaign. To be the most beautiful man in Greece was in the eyes of a Greek the height of human felicity; and with the Greeks, beauty necessarily included strength. So ardently did this gifted people admire corporeal perfection that they actually worshipped it. According to Herodotos, a young Sicilian was deified on account of his beauty, and after his death altars were raised to him. The vast intellectual power of Plato and Sokrates did not prevent them from sharing this universal enthusiasm. Poets like Sophokles, and statesmen like Alexander, thought it not beneath their dignity to engage publicly in gymnastic sports.

Their conceptions of divinity were framed in accordance with these general habits. Though sometimes, as in the case of Hephaistos, the exigencies of the particular myth required the deity to be physically imperfect, yet ordinarily the Greek god was simply an immortal man, complete in strength and beauty. The deity was not invested with the human form as a mere symbol. They could conceive no loftier way of representing him. The grandest statue, expressing most adequately the calmness of absolutely unfettered strength, might well, in their eyes, be a veritable portrait of divinity. To a Greek, beauty of form was a consecrated thing. More than once a culprit got off with his life because it would have been thought sacrilegious to put an end to such a symmetrical creature. And for a similar reason, the Greeks, though perhaps not more humane than the Europeans of the Middle Ages, rarely allowed the human body to be mutilated or tortured. The condemned criminal must be marred as little as possible; and he was, therefore, quietly poisoned, instead of being hung, beheaded, or broken on the wheel.

Is not the unapproachable excellence of Greek statuary—that art never since equalled, and most likely, from the absence of the needful social stimulus, destined never to be equalled—already sufficiently explained? Consider, says our author, the nature of the Greek sculptor's preparation. These men have observed the human body naked and in movement, in the bath and the gymnasium, in sacred dances and public games. They have noted those forms and attitudes in which are revealed vigour, health, and activity. And during three or four hundred years they have thus modified, corrected and developed their notions of corporeal beauty. There is, therefore, nothing surprising in the fact that Greek sculpture finally arrived at the ideal model, the perfect type, as it was, of the human body. Our highest notions of physical beauty, down to the present day, have been bequeathed to us by the Greeks. The earliest modern sculptors who abandoned the bony, hideous, starveling figures of the monkish Middle Ages, learned their first lessons in better things from Greek bas-reliefs. And if, to-day, forgetting our half-developed bodies, inefficiently nourished, because of our excessive brain-work, and with their muscles weak and flabby from want of strenuous exercise, we wish to contemplate the human form in its grandest perfection, we must go to Hellenic art for our models.

The Greeks were, in the highest sense of the word, an intellectual race; but they never allowed the mind to tyrannize over the body. Spiritual perfection, accompanied by corporeal feebleness, was the invention of asceticism; and the Greeks were never ascetics. Diogenes might scorn superfluous luxuries, but if he ever rolled and tumbled his tub about as Rabelais says he did, it is clear that the victory of spirit over body formed no part of his theory of things. Such an idea would have been incomprehensible to a Greek in Plato's time. Their consciences were not over active. They were not burdened with a sense of sinfulness. Their aspirations were decidedly finite; and they believed in securing the maximum completeness of this terrestrial life. Consequently they never set the physical below the intellectual. To return to our author, they never, in their statues, subordinated symmetry to expression, the body to the head. They were interested not only in the prominence of the brows, the width of the forehead, and the curvature of the lips, but quite as much in the massiveness of the chest, the compactness of the thighs, and the solidity of the arms and legs. Not only the face, but the whole body, had for them its physiognomy. They left picturesqueness to the painter, and dramatic fervour to the poet; and keeping strictly before their eyes the narrow but exalted problem of representing the beauty of symmetry, they filled their sanctuaries and public places with those grand motionless people of brass, gold, ivory, copper, and marble, in whom humanity recognizes its highest artistic types. Statuary was the central art of Greece. No other art was so popular, or so completely expressed the national life. The number of statues was enormous. In later days, when Rome had spoiled the Greek world of its treasures, the Imperial City possessed a population of statues almost equal in number to its population of human beings. And at the present day, after all the destructive accidents of so many intervening centuries, it is estimated that more than sixty thousand statues have been obtained from Rome and its suburbs alone.

In citing this admirable exposition as a specimen of M. Taine's method of dealing with his subject, we have refrained from disturbing the pellucid current of thought by criticisms of our own. We think the foregoing explanation correct enough, so far as it goes, though it deals with the merest rudiments of the subject, and really does nothing toward elucidating the deeper mysteries of artistic production. For this there is needed a profounder psychology than M. Taine's. But whether his theory of art be adequate or not, there can be but one opinion as to the brilliant eloquence with which it is set forth.

June, 1868.

XIV. ATHENIAN AND AMERICAN LIFE.

IN a very interesting essay on British and Foreign Characteristics, published a few years ago, Mr. W. R. Greg quotes the famous letter of the Turkish cadi to Mr. Layard, with the comment that "it contains the germ and element of a wisdom to which our busy and bustling existence is a stranger"; and he uses it as a text for an instructive sermon on the "gospel of leisure." He urges, with justice, that the too eager and restless modern man, absorbed in problems of industrial development, may learn a wholesome lesson from the contemplation of his Oriental brother, who cares not to say, "Behold, this star spinneth round that star, and this other star with a tail cometh and goeth in so many years"; who aspires not after a "double stomach," nor hopes to attain to Paradise by "seeking with his eyes." If any one may be thought to stand in need of some such lesson, it is the American of to-day. Just as far as the Turk carries his apathy to excess, does the American carry to excess his restlessness. But just because the incurious idleness of the Turk is excessive, so as to be detrimental to completeness of living, it is unfit to supply us with the hints we need concerning the causes, character, and effects of our over-activity. A sermon of leisure, if it is to be of practical use to us, must not be a sermon of laziness. The Oriental state of mind is incompatible with progressive improvement of any sort, physical, intellectual, or moral. It is one of the phenomena attendant upon the arrival of a community at a stationary condition before it has acquired a complex civilization. And it appears serviceable rather as a background upon which to exhibit in relief our modern turmoil, than by reason of any lesson which it is itself likely to convey. Let us in preference study one of the most eminently progressive of all the communities that have existed. Let us take an example quite different from any that can be drawn from Oriental life, but almost equally contrasted with any that can be found among ourselves; and let us, with the aid of it, examine the respective effects of leisure and of hurry upon the culture of the community.

What do modern critics mean by the "healthy completeness" of ancient life, which they are so fond of contrasting with the "heated," "discontented," or imperfect and one-sided existence of modern communities? Is this a mere set of phrases, suited to some imaginary want of the literary critic, but answering to nothing real? Are they to be summarily disposed of as resting upon some tacit assumption of that old-grannyism which delights in asseverating that times are not what they used to be? Is the contrast an imaginary one, due to the softened, cheerful light with which we are wont to contemplate classic antiquity through the charmed medium of its incomparable literature? Or is it a real contrast, worthy of the attention and analysis of the historical inquirer? The answer to these queries will lead us far into the discussion of the subject which we have propounded, and we shall best reach it by considering some aspects of the social condition of ancient Greece. The lessons to be learned from that wonderful country are not yet exhausted Each time that we return to that richest of historic mines, and delve faithfully and carefully, we shall be sure to dig up some jewel worth carrying away.

And in considering ancient Greece, we shall do well to confine our attention, for the sake of definiteness of conception, to a single city. Comparatively homogeneous as Greek civilization was, there was nevertheless a great deal of difference between the social circumstances of sundry of its civic communities. What was true of Athens was frequently not true of Sparta or Thebes, and general assertions about ancient Greece are often likely to be collect only in a loose and general way. In speaking, therefore, of Greece, I must be understood in the main as referring to Athens, the eye and light of Greece, the nucleus and centre of Hellenic culture.

Let us note first that Athens was a large city surrounded by pleasant village-suburbs,—the demes of Attika,—very much as Boston is closely girdled by rural places like Brookline, Jamaica Plain, and the rest, village after village rather thickly covering a circuit of from ten to twenty miles' radius. The population of Athens with its suburbs may perhaps have exceeded half a million; but the number of adult freemen bearing arms did not exceed twenty-five thousand.[67] For every one of these freemen there were four or five slaves; not ignorant, degraded labourers, belonging to an inferior type of humanity, and bearing the marks of a lower caste in their very personal formation and in the colour of their skin, like our lately-enslaved negroes; but intelligent, skilled labourers, belonging usually to the Hellenic, and at any rate to the Aryan race, as fair and perhaps as handsome as their masters, and not subjected to especial ignominy or hardship. These slaves, of whom there were at least one hundred thousand adult males, relieved the twenty-five thousand freemen of nearly all the severe drudgery of life; and the result was an amount of leisure perhaps never since known on an equal scale in history.

The relations of master and slave in ancient Athens constituted, of course, a very different phenomenon from anything which the history of our own Southern States has to offer us. Our Southern slaveholders lived in an age of industrial development; they were money-makers: they had their full share of business in managing the operations for which their labourers supplied the crude physical force. It was not so in Athens. The era of civilization founded upon organized industry had not begun; money-making had not come to be, with the Greeks, the one all-important end of life; and mere subsistence, which is now difficult, was then easy. The Athenian lived in a mild, genial, healthy climate, in a country which has always been notable for the activity and longevity of its inhabitants. He was frugal in his habits,—a wine-drinker and an eater of meat, but rarely addicted to gluttony or intemperance. His dress was inexpensive, for the Greek climate made but little protection necessary, and the gymnastic habits of the Greeks led them to esteem more highly the beauty of the body than that of its covering. His house was simple, not being intended

---

[67] See Herod. V. 97; Aristoph. Ekkl. 432; Thukyd. II. 13; Plutarch, Perikl. 37.

for social purposes, while of what we should call home-life the Greeks had none. The house was a shelter at night, a place where the frugal meal might be taken, a place where the wife might stay, and look after the household slaves or attend to the children. And this brings us to another notable feature of Athenian life. The wife having no position in society, being nothing, indeed, but a sort of household utensil, how greatly was life simplified! What a door for expenditure was there, as yet securely closed, and which no one had thought of opening! No milliner's or dressmaker's bills, no evening parties, no Protean fashions, no elegant furniture, no imperious necessity for Kleanthes to outshine Kleon, no coaches, no Chateau Margaux, no journeys to Arkadia in the summer! In such a state of society, as one may easily see, the labour of one man would support half a dozen. It cost the Athenian but a few cents daily to live, and even these few cents might be earned by his slaves. We need not, therefore, be surprised to learn that in ancient Athens there were no paupers or beggars. There might be poverty, but indigence was unknown; and because of the absence of fashion, style, and display, even poverty entailed no uncomfortable loss of social position. The Athenians valued wealth highly, no doubt, as a source of contributions to public festivals and to the necessities of the state. But as far as the circumstances of daily life go, the difference between the rich man and the poor man was immeasurably less than in any modern community, and the incentives to the acquirement of wealth were, as a consequence, comparatively slight.

    I do not mean to say that the Athenians did not engage in business. Their city was a commercial city, and their ships covered the Mediterranean. They had agencies and factories at Marseilles, on the remote coasts of Spain, and along the shores of the Black Sea. They were in many respects the greatest commercial people of antiquity, and doubtless knew, as well as other people, the keen delights of acquisition. But my point is, that with them the acquiring of property had not become the chief or only end of life. Production was carried on almost entirely by slave-labour; interchange of commodities was the business of the masters, and commerce was in those days simple. Banks, insurance companies, brokers' boards,—all these complex instruments of Mammon were as yet unthought of. There was no Wall Street in ancient Athens; there were no great failures, no commercial panics, no over-issues of stock. Commerce, in short, was a quite subordinate matter, and the art of money-making was in its infancy.

    The twenty-five thousand Athenian freemen thus enjoyed, on the whole, more undisturbed leisure, more freedom from petty harassing cares, than any other community known to history. Nowhere else can we find, on careful study, so little of the hurry and anxiety which destroys the even tenour of modern life,—nowhere else so few of the circumstances which tend to make men insane, inebriate, or phthisical, or prematurely old.

    This being granted, it remains only to state and illustrate the obverse fact. It is not only true that Athens has produced and educated a relatively larger number of men of the highest calibre and most complete culture than any other community of like dimensions which has ever existed; but it is also true that there has been no other community, of which the members have, as a general rule, been so highly cultivated, or have attained individually such completeness of life. In proof of the first assertion it will be enough to mention such names as those of Solon, Themistokles, Perikles, and Demosthenes; Isokrates and Lysias; Aristophanes and Menander; Aischylos, Sophokles, and Euripides; Pheidias and Praxiteles; Sokrates and Plato; Thukydides and Xenophon: remembering that these men, distinguished for such different kinds of achievement, but like each other in consummateness of culture, were all produced within one town in the course of three centuries. At no other time and place in human history has there been even an approach to such a fact as this.

My other assertion, about the general culture of the community in which such men were reared, will need a more detailed explanation. When I say that the Athenian public was, on the whole, the most highly cultivated public that has ever existed, I refer of course to something more than what is now known as literary culture. Of this there was relatively little in the days of Athenian greatness; and this was because there was not yet need for it or room for it. Greece did not until a later time begin to produce scholars and savants; for the function of scholarship does not begin until there has been an accumulation of bygone literature to be interpreted for the benefit of those who live in a later time. Grecian greatness was already becoming a thing of the past, when scholarship and literary culture of the modern type began at Rome and Alexandria. The culture of the ancient Athenians was largely derived from direct intercourse with facts of nature and of life, and with the thoughts of rich and powerful minds orally expressed. The value of this must not be underrated. We moderns are accustomed to get so large a portion of our knowledge and of our theories of life out of books, our taste and judgment are so largely educated by intercourse with the printed page, that we are apt to confound culture with book-knowledge; we are apt to forget the innumerable ways in which the highest intellectual faculties may be disciplined without the aid of literature. We must study antiquity to realize how thoroughly this could be done. But even in our day, how much more fruitful is the direct influence of an original mind over us, in the rare cases when it can be enjoyed, than any indirect influence which the same mind may exert through the medium of printed books! What fellow of a college, placed amid the most abundant and efficient implements of study, ever gets such a stimulus to the highest and richest intellectual life as was afforded to Eckermann by his daily intercourse with Goethe? The breadth of culture and the perfection of training exhibited by John Stuart Mill need not surprise us when we recollect that his earlier days were spent in the society of James Mill and Jeremy Bentham. And the remarkable extent of view, the command of facts, and the astonishing productiveness of such modern Frenchmen as Sainte-Beuve and Littre become explicable when we reflect upon the circumstance that so many able and brilliant men are collected in one city, where their minds may continually and directly react upon each other. It is from the lack of such personal stimulus that it is difficult or indeed wellnigh impossible, even for those whose resources are such as to give them an extensive command of books, to keep up to the highest level of contemporary culture while living in a village or provincial town. And it is mainly because of the personal stimulus which it affords to its students, that a great university, as a seat of culture, is immeasurably superior to a small one.

Nevertheless, the small community in any age possesses one signal advantage over the large one, in its greater simplicity of life and its consequent relative leisure. It was the prerogative of ancient Athens that it united the advantages of the large to those of the small community. In relative simplicity of life it was not unlike the modern village, while at the same time it was the metropolis where the foremost minds of the time were enabled to react directly upon one another. In yet another respect these opposite advantages were combined. The twenty-five thousand free inhabitants might perhaps all know something of each other. In this respect Athens was doubtless much like a New England country town, with the all-important difference that the sordid tone due to continual struggle for money was absent. It was like the small town in the chance which it afforded for publicity and community of pursuits among its inhabitants. Continuous and unrestrained social intercourse was accordingly a distinctive feature of Athenian life. And, as already hinted, this intercourse did not consist in evening flirtations, with the eating of indigestible food at unseasonable hours, and the dancing of "the German." It was carried on out-of-doors in the brightest sunlight; it brooked no effeminacy; its amusements were athletic games, or dramatic entertainments, such as have hardly since been equalled. Its arena was a town whose streets were filled with statues and adorned with buildings, merely to behold which was in itself an education. The participators in it were not men with minds so dwarfed by exclusive devotion to special pursuits that after "talking shop" they could find nothing else save wine and cookery to converse about. They were men with minds fresh and open for the discussion of topics which are not for a day only.

A man like Sokrates, living in such a community, did not need to write down his wisdom. He had no such vast public as the modern philosopher has to reach. He could hail any one he happened to pass in the street, begin an argument with him forthwith, and set a whole crowd thinking and inquiring about subjects the mere contemplation of which would raise them for the moment above matters of transient concern. For more than half a century any citizen might have gratis the benefit of oral instruction from such a man as he. And I sometimes think, by the way, that—curtailed as it is to literary proportions in the dialogues of Plato, bereft of all that personal potency which it had when it flowed, instinct with earnestness, from the lips of the teacher—even to this day the wit of man has perhaps devised no better general gymnastics for the understanding than the Sokratic dialectic. I am far from saying that all Athens listened to Sokrates or understood him: had it been so, the caricature of Aristophanes would have been pointless, and the sublime yet mournful trilogy of dialogues which pourtray the closing scenes of the greatest life of antiquity would never have been written. But the mere fact that such a man lived and taught in the way that he did goes far in proof of the deep culture of the Athenian public. Further confirmation is to be found in the fact that such tragedies as the Antigone, the Oidipous, and the Prometheus were written to suit the popular taste of the time; not to be read by literary people, or to be performed before select audiences such as in our day listen to Ristori or Janauschek, but to hold spell-bound that vast concourse of all kinds of people which assembled at the Dionysiac festivals.

Still further proof is furnished by the exquisite literary perfection of Greek writings. One of the common arguments in favour of the study of Greek at the present day is based upon the opinion that in the best works extant in that language the art of literary expression has reached wellnigh absolute perfection. I fully concur in this opinion, so far as to doubt if even the greatest modern writers, even a Pascal or a Voltaire, can fairly sustain a comparison with such Athenians as Plato or Lysias. This excellence of the ancient books is in part immediately due to the fact that they were not written in a hurry, or amid the anxieties of an over-busy existence; but it is in greater part due to the indirect consequences of a leisurely life. These books were written for a public which knew well how to appreciate the finer beauties of expression; and, what is still more to the point, their authors lived in a community where an elegant style was habitual. Before a matchless style can be written, there must be a good style "in the air," as the French say. Probably the most finished talking and writing of modern times has been done in and about the French court in the seventeenth century; and it is accordingly there that we find men like Pascal and Bossuet writing a prose which for precision, purity, and dignity has never since been surpassed. It is thus that the unapproachable literary excellence of ancient Greek books speaks for the genuine culture of the people who were expected to read them, or to hear them read. For one of the surest indices of true culture, whether professedly literary or not, is the power to express one's self in precise, rhythmical, and dignified language. We hardly need a better evidence than this of the superiority of the ancient community in the general elevation of its tastes and perceptions. Recollecting how Herodotos read his history at the Olympic games, let us try to imagine even so picturesque a writer as Mr. Parkman reading a few chapters of his "Jesuits in North America" before the spectators assembled at the Jerome Park races, and we shall the better realize how deep-seated was Hellenic culture.

As yet, however, I have referred to but one side of Athenian life. Though "seekers after wisdom," the cultivated people of Athens did not spend all their valuable leisure in dialectics or in connoisseurship. They were not a set of dilettanti or dreamy philosophers, and they were far from subordinating the material side of life to the intellectual. Also, though they dealt not in money-making after the eager fashion of modern men, they had still concerns of immediate practical interest with which to busy themselves. Each one of these twenty-five thousand free Athenians was not only a free voter, but an office-holder, a legislator, a judge. They did not control the government through a representative body, but they were themselves the government. They were, one and all, in turn liable to be called upon to make laws, and to execute them after they were made, as well as to administer justice in civil and criminal suits. The affairs and interests, not only of their own city, but of a score or two of scattered dependencies, were more or less closely to be looked after by them. It lay with them to declare war, to carry it on after declaring it, and to pay the expenses of it. Actually and not by deputy they administered the government of their own city, both in its local and in its imperial relations. All this implies a more thorough, more constant, and more vital political training than that which is implied by the modern duties of casting a ballot and serving on a jury. The life of the Athenian was emphatically a political life. From early manhood onward, it was part of his duty to hear legal questions argued by powerful advocates, and to utter a decision upon law and fact; or to mix in debate upon questions of public policy, arguing, listening, and pondering. It is customary to compare the political talent of the Greeks unfavourably with that displayed by the Romans, and I have no wish to dispute this estimate. But on a careful study it will appear that the Athenians, at least, in a higher degree than any other community of ancient times, exhibited parliamentary tact, or the ability to sit still while both sides of a question are getting discussed,—that sort of political talent for which the English races are distinguished, and to the lack of which so many of the political failures of the French are egregiously due. One would suppose that a judicature of the whole town would be likely to execute a sorry parody of justice; yet justice was by no means ill-administered at Athens. Even the most unfortunate and disgraceful scenes,—as where the proposed massacre of the Mytilenaians was discussed, and where summary retribution was dealt out to the generals who had neglected their duty at Arginusai,—even these scenes furnish, when thoroughly examined, as by Mr. Grote, only the more convincing proof that the Athenian was usually swayed by sound reason and good sense to an extraordinary degree. All great points in fact, were settled rather by sober appeals to reason than by intrigue or lobbying; and one cannot help thinking that an Athenian of the time of Perikles would have regarded with pitying contempt the trick of the "previous question." And this explains the undoubted pre-eminence of Athenian oratory. This accounts for the fact that we find in the forensic annals of a single city, and within the compass of a single century, such names as Lysias, Isokrates, Andokides, Hypereides, Aischines, and Demosthenes. The art of oratory, like the art of sculpture, shone forth more brilliantly then than ever since, because then the conditions favouring its development were more perfectly combined than they have since been. Now, a condition of society in which the multitude can always be made to stand quietly and listen to a logical discourse is a condition of high culture. Readers of Xenophon's Anabasis will remember the frequency of the speeches in that charming book. Whenever some terrible emergency arose, or some alarming quarrel or disheartening panic occurred, in the course of the retreat of the Ten Thousand, an oration from one of the commanders—not a demagogue's appeal to the lower passions, but a calm exposition of circumstances addressed to the sober judgment—usually sufficed to set all things in order. To my mind this is one of the most impressive historical lessons conveyed in Xenophon's book. And this peculiar kind of self-control, indicative of intellectual sobriety and high moral training, which was more or less characteristic of all Greeks, was especially characteristic of the Athenians.

These illustrations will, I hope, suffice to show that there is nothing extravagant in the high estimate which I have made of Athenian culture. I have barely indicated the causes of this singular perfection of individual training in the social circumstances amid which the Athenians lived. I have alleged it as an instance of what may be accomplished by a well-directed leisure and in the absence or very scanty development of such a complex industrial life as that which surrounds us to-day. But I have not yet quite done with the Athenians. Before leaving this part of the subject, I must mention one further circumstance which tends to make ancient life appear in our eyes more sunny and healthy and less distressed, than the life of modern times. And in this instance, too, though we are not dealing with any immediate or remote effects of leisureliness, we still have to note the peculiar advantage gained by the absence of a great complexity of interests in the ancient community.

With respect to religion, the Athenians were peculiarly situated. They had for the most part outgrown the primitive terrorism of fetishistic belief. Save in cases of public distress, as in the mutilation of the Hermai, or in the refusal of Nikias to retreat from Syracuse because of an eclipse of the moon, they were no longer, like savages, afraid of the dark. Their keen aesthetic sense had prevailed to turn the horrors of a primeval nature-worship into beauties. Their springs and groves were peopled by their fancy with naiads and dryads, not with trolls and grotesque goblins. Their feelings toward the unseen powers at work about them were in the main pleasant; as witness the little story about Pheidippides meeting the god Pan as he was making with hot haste toward Sparta to announce the arrival of the Persians. Now, while this original source of mental discomfort, which afflicts the uncivilized man, had ceased materially to affect the Athenians, they on the other hand lived at a time when the vague sense of sin and self-reproof which was characteristic of the early ages of Christianity, had not yet invaded society. The vast complication of life brought about by the extension of the Roman Empire led to a great development of human sympathies, unknown in earlier times, and called forth unquiet yearnings, desire for amelioration, a sense of short-coming, and a morbid self-consciousness. It is accordingly under Roman sway that we first come across characters approximating to the modern type, like Cicero, Seneca, Epictetus, and Marcus Aurelius. It is then that we find the idea of social progress first clearly expressed, that we discover some glimmerings of a conscious philanthropy, and that we detect the earliest symptoms of that unhealthy tendency to subordinate too entirely the physical to the moral life, which reached its culmination in the Middle Ages. In the palmy days of the Athenians it was different. When we hint that they were not consciously philanthropists, we do not mean that they were not humane; when we accredit them with no idea of progress, we do not forget how much they did to render both the idea and the reality possible; when we say that they had not a distressing sense of spiritual unworthiness, we do not mean that they had no conscience. We mean that their moral and religious life sat easily on them, like their own graceful drapery,—did not gall and worry them, like the hair-cloth garment of the monk. They were free from that dark conception of a devil which lent terror to life in the Middle Ages; and the morbid self-consciousness which led mediaeval women to immure themselves in convents would have been to an Athenian quite inexplicable. They had, in short, an open and childlike conception of religion; and, as such, it was a sunny conception. Any one who will take the trouble to compare an idyl of Theokritos with a modern pastoral, or the poem of Kleanthes with a modern hymn, or the Aphrodite of Melos with a modern Madonna, will realize most effectually what I mean.

And, finally, the religion of the Athenians was in the main symbolized in a fluctuating mythology, and had never been hardened into dogmas. The Athenian was subject to no priest, nor was he obliged to pin his faith to any formulated creed. His hospitable polytheism left little room for theological persecution, and none for any heresy short of virtual atheism. The feverish doubts which rack the modern mind left him undisturbed. Though he might sink to any depth of scepticism in philosophy, yet the eternal welfare of his soul was not supposed to hang upon the issue of his doubts. Accordingly Athenian society was not only characterized in the main by freedom of opinion, in spite of the exceptional cases of Anaxagoras and Sokrates; but there was also none of that Gothic gloom with which the deep-seated Christian sense of infinite responsibility for opinion has saddened modern religious life.

In these reflections I have wandered a little way from my principal theme, in order more fully to show why the old Greek life impresses us as so cheerful. Returning now to the keynote with which we started, let us state succinctly the net result of what has been said about the Athenians. As a people we have seen that they enjoyed an unparalleled amount of leisure, living through life with but little turmoil and clatter. Their life was more spontaneous and unrestrained, less rigorously marked out by uncontrollable circumstances, than the life of moderns. They did not run so much in grooves. And along with this we have seen reason to believe that they were the most profoundly cultivated of all peoples; that a larger proportion of men lived complete, well-rounded, harmonious lives in ancient Athens than in any other known community. Keen, nimble-minded, and self-possessed; audacious speculators, but temperate and averse to extravagance; emotionally healthy, and endowed with an unequalled sense of beauty and propriety; how admirable and wonderful they seem when looked at across the gulf of ages intervening,—and what a priceless possession to humanity, of what noble augury for the distant future, is the fact that such a society has once existed!

The lesson to be drawn from the study of this antique life will impress itself more deeply upon us after we have briefly contemplated the striking contrast to it which is afforded by the phase of civilization amid which we live to-day. Ever since Greek civilization was merged in Roman imperialism, there has been a slowly growing tendency toward complexity of social life,—toward the widening of sympathies, the multiplying of interests, the increase of the number of things to be done. Through the later Middle Ages, after Roman civilization had absorbed and disciplined the incoming barbarism which had threatened to destroy it, there was a steadily increasing complication of society, a multiplication of the wants of life, and a consequent enhancement of the difficulty of self-maintenance. The ultimate causes of this phenomenon lie so far beneath the surface that they could be satisfactorily discussed only in a technical essay on the evolution of society. It will be enough for us here to observe that the great geographical discoveries of the sixteenth century and the somewhat later achievements of physical science have, during the past two hundred years, aided powerfully in determining the entrance of the Western world upon an industrial epoch,—an epoch which has for its final object the complete subjection of the powers of nature to purposes of individual comfort and happiness. We have now to trace some of the effects of this lately-begun industrial development upon social life and individual culture. And as we studied the leisureliness of antiquity where its effects were most conspicuous, in the city of Athens, we shall now do well to study the opposite characteristics of modern society where they are most conspicuously exemplified, in our own country. The attributes of American life which it will be necessary to signalize will be seen to be only the attributes of modern life in their most exaggerated phase.

To begin with, in studying the United States, we are no longer dealing with a single city, or with small groups of cities. The city as a political unit, in the antique sense, has never existed among us, and indeed can hardly be said now to exist anywhere. The modern city is hardly more than a great emporium of trade, or a place where large numbers of people find it convenient to live huddled together; not a sacred fatherland to which its inhabitants owe their highest allegiance, and by the requirements of which their political activity is limited. What strikes us here is that our modern life is diffused or spread out, not concentrated like the ancient civic life. If the Athenian had been the member of an integral community, comprising all peninsular Greece and the mainland of Asia Minor, he could not have taken life so easily as he did.

Now our country is not only a very large one, but compared to its vast territorial extent it contains a very small population. If we go on increasing at the present rate, so that a century hence we number four or five hundred millions, our country will be hardly more crowded than China is to-day. Or if our whole population were now to be brought east of Niagara Falls, and confined on the south by the Potomac, we should still have as much elbow-room as they have in France. Political economists can show the effects of this high ratio of land to inhabitants, in increasing wages, raising the interest of money, and stimulating production. We are thus living amid circumstances which are goading the industrial activity characteristic of the last two centuries, and notably of the English race, into an almost feverish energy. The vast extent of our unwrought territory is constantly draining fresh life from our older districts, to aid in the establishment of new frontier communities of a somewhat lower or less highly organized type. And these younger communities, daily springing up, are constantly striving to take on the higher structure,—to become as highly civilized and to enjoy as many of the prerogatives of civilization as the rest. All this calls forth an enormous quantity of activity, and causes American life to assume the aspect of a life-and-death struggle for mastery over the material forces of that part of the earth's surface upon which it thrives.

It is thus that we are traversing what may properly be called the BARBAROUS epoch of our history,—the epoch at which the predominant intellectual activity is employed in achievements which are mainly of a material character. Military barbarism, or the inability of communities to live together without frequent warfare, has been nearly outgrown by the whole Western world. Private wars, long since made everywhere illegal, have nearly ceased; and public wars, once continual, have become infrequent. But industrial barbarism, by which I mean the inability of a community to direct a portion of its time to purposes of spiritual life, after providing for its physical maintenance,—this kind of barbarism the modern world has by no means outgrown. To-day, the great work of life is to live; while the amount of labour consumed in living has throughout the present century been rapidly increasing. Nearly the whole of this American community toils from youth to old age in merely procuring the means for satisfying the transient wants of life. Our time and energies, our spirit and buoyancy, are quite used up in what is called "getting on."

Another point of difference between the structure of American and of Athenian society must not be left out of the account. The time has gone by in which the energies of a hundred thousand men and women could be employed in ministering to the individual perfection of twenty-five thousand. Slavery, in the antique sense,—an absolute command of brain as well as of muscle, a slave-system of skilled labour,—we have never had. In our day it is for each man to earn his own bread; so that the struggle for existence has become universal. The work of one class does not furnish leisure for another class. The exceptional circumstances which freed the Athenian from industrial barbarism, and enabled him to become the great teacher and model of culture for the human race, have disappeared forever.

Then the general standard of comfortable living, as already hinted, has been greatly raised, and is still rising. What would have satisfied the ancient would seem to us like penury. We have a domestic life of which the Greek knew nothing. We live during a large part of the year in the house. Our social life goes on under the roof. Our houses are not mere places for eating and sleeping, like the houses of the ancients. It therefore costs us a large amount of toil to get what is called shelter for our heads. The sum which a young married man, in "good society," has to pay for his house and the furniture contained in it, would have enabled an Athenian to live in princely leisure from youth to old age. The sum which he has to pay out each year, to meet the complicated expense of living in such a house, would have more than sufficed to bring up an Athenian family. If worthy Strepsiades could have got an Asmodean glimpse of Fifth Avenue, or even of some unpretending street in Cambridge, he might have gone back to his aristocratic wife a sadder but a more contented man.

Wealth—or at least what would until lately have been called wealth—has become essential to comfort; while the opportunities for acquiring it have in recent times been immensely multiplied. To get money is, therefore, the chief end of life in our time and country. "Success in life" has become synonymous with "becoming wealthy." A man who is successful in what he undertakes is a man who makes his employment pay him in money. Our normal type of character is that of the shrewd, circumspect business man; as in the Middle Ages it was that of the hardy warrior. And as in those days when fighting was a constant necessity, and when the only honourable way for a gentleman of high rank to make money was by freebooting, fighting came to be regarded as an end desirable in itself; so in these days the mere effort to accumulate has become a source of enjoyment rather than a means to it. The same truth is to be witnessed in aberrant types of character. The infatuated speculator and the close-fisted millionaire are our substitutes for the mediaeval berserkir,—the man who loved the pell-mell of a contest so well that he would make war on his neighbour, just to keep his hand in. In like manner, while such crimes as murder and violent robbery have diminished in frequency during the past century, on the other hand such crimes as embezzlement, gambling in stocks, adulteration of goods, and using of false weights and measures, have probably increased. If Dick Turpin were now to be brought back to life, he would find the New York Custom-House a more congenial and profitable working-place than the king's highway.

The result of this universal quest for money is that we are always in a hurry. Our lives pass by in a whirl. It is all labour and no fruition. We work till we are weary; we carry our work home with us; it haunts our evenings, and disturbs our sleep as well as our digestion. Our minds are so burdened with it that our conversation, when serious, can dwell upon little else. If we step into a railway-car, or the smoking-room of a hotel, or any other place where a dozen or two of men are gathered together, we shall hear them talking of stocks, of investments, of commercial paper, as if there were really nothing in this universe worth thinking of, save only the interchange of dollars and commodities. So constant and unremitted is our forced application, that our minds are dwarfed for everything except the prosecution of the one universal pursuit.

Are we now prepared for the completing of the contrast? Must we say that, as Athens was the most leisurely and the United States is the most hurried community known in history, so the Americans are, as a consequence of their hurry, lacking in thoroughness of culture? Or, since it is difficult to bring our modern culture directly into contrast with that of an ancient community, let me state the case after a different but equivalent fashion. Since the United States present only an exaggerated type of the modern industrial community, since the turmoil of incessant money-getting, which affects all modern communities in large measure, affects us most seriously of all, shall it be said that we are, on the whole, less highly cultivated than our contemporaries in Western Europe? To a certain extent we must confess that this is the case. In the higher culture—in the culture of the whole man, according to the antique idea—we are undoubtedly behind all other nations with which it would be fair to compare ourselves. It will not do to decide a question like this merely by counting literary celebrities, although even thus we should by no means get a verdict in our favour. Since the beginning of this century, England has produced as many great writers and thinkers as France or Germany; yet the general status of culture in England is said—perhaps with truth—to be lower than it is in these countries. It is said that the average Englishman is less ready than the average German or Frenchman to sympathize with ideas which have no obvious market-value. Yet in England there is an amount of high culture among those not professionally scholars, which it would be vain to seek among ourselves. The purposes of my argument, however, require that the comparison should be made between our own country and Western Europe in general. Compare, then, our best magazines—not solely with regard to their intrinsic excellence, but also with regard to the way in which they are sustained—with the Revue des Deux Mondes or the Journal des Debats. Or compare our leading politicians with men like Gladstone, Disraeli, or Sir G. C. Lewis; or even with such men as Brougham or Thiers. Or compare the slovenly style of our newspaper articles, I will not say with the exquisite prose of the lamented Prevost-Paradol, but with the ordinary prose of the French or English newspaper. But a far better illustration—for it goes down to the root of things—is suggested by the recent work of Matthew Arnold on the schools of the continent of Europe. The country of our time where the general culture is unquestionably the highest is Prussia. Now, in Prussia, they are able to have a Minister of Education, who is a member of the Cabinet. They are sure that this minister will not appoint or remove even an assistant professor for political reasons. Only once, as Arnold tells us, has such a thing been done; and then public opinion expressed itself in such an emphatic tone of disapproval that the displaced teacher was instantly appointed to another position. Nothing of this sort, says Arnold, could have occurred in England; but still less could it occur in America. Had we such an educational system, there would presently be an "Education Ring" to control it. Nor can this difference be ascribed to the less eager political activity of Germany. The Prussian state of things would have been possible in ancient Athens, where political life was as absorbing and nearly as turbulent as in the United States. The difference is due to our lack of faith in culture, a lack of faith in that of which we have not had adequate experience.

We lack culture because we live in a hurry, and because our attention is given up to pursuits which call into activity and develop but one side of us. On the one hand contemplate Sokrates quietly entertaining a crowd in the Athenian market-place, and on the other hand consider Broadway with its eternal clatter, and its throngs of hurrying people elbowing and treading on each other's heels, and you will get a lively notion of the difference between the extreme phases of ancient and modern life. By the time we have thus rushed through our day, we have no strength left to devote to things spiritual. To-day finds us no nearer fruition than yesterday. And if perhaps the time at last arrives when fruition is practicable, our minds have run so long in the ruts that they cannot be twisted out.

As it is impossible for any person living in a given state of society to keep himself exempt from its influences, detrimental as well as beneficial, we find that even those who strive to make a literary occupation subservient to purposes of culture are not, save in rare cases, spared by the general turmoil. Those who have at once the ability, the taste, and the wealth needful for training themselves to the accomplishment of some many-sided and permanent work are of course very few. Nor have our universities yet provided themselves with the means for securing to literary talent the leisure which is essential to complete mental development, or to a high order of productiveness. Although in most industrial enterprises we know how to work together so successfully, in literature we have as yet no co-operation. We have not only no Paris, but we have not even a Tubingen, a Leipsic, or a Jena, or anything corresponding to the fellowships in the English universities. Our literary workers have no choice but to fall into the ranks, and make merchandise of their half-formed ideas. They must work without co-operation, they must write in a hurry, and they must write for those who have no leisure for aught but hasty and superficial reading.

Bursting boilers and custom-house frauds may have at first sight nothing to do with each other or with my subject. It is indisputable, however, that the horrible massacres perpetrated every few weeks or mouths by our common carriers, and the disgraceful peculation in which we allow our public servants to indulge with hardly ever an effective word of protest, are alike to be ascribed to the same causes which interfere with our higher culture. It is by no means a mere accidental coincidence that for every dollar stolen by government officials in Prussia, at least fifty or a hundred are stolen in the United States. This does not show that the Germans are our superiors in average honesty, but it shows that they are our superiors in thoroughness. It is with them an imperative demand that any official whatever shall be qualified for his post; a principle of public economy which in our country is not simply ignored in practice, but often openly laughed at. But in a country where high intelligence and thorough training are imperatively demanded, it follows of necessity that these qualifications must insure for their possessors a permanent career in which the temptations to malfeasance or dishonesty are reduced to the minimum. On the other hand, in a country where intelligence and training have no surety that they are to carry the day against stupidity and inefficiency, the incentives to dishonourable conduct are overpowering. The result in our own political life is that the best men are driven in disgust from politics, and thus one of the noblest fields for the culture of the whole man is given over to be worked by swindlers and charlatans. To an Athenian such a severance of the highest culture from political life would have been utterly inconceivable. Obviously the deepest explanation of all this lies in our lack of belief in the necessity for high and thorough training. We do not value culture enough to keep it in our employ or to pay it for its services; and what is this short-sighted negligence but the outcome of the universal shiftlessness begotten of the habit of doing everything in a hurry? On every hand we may see the fruits of this shiftlessness, from buildings that tumble in, switches that are misplaced, furnaces that are ill-protected, fire-brigades that are without discipline, up to unauthorized meddlings with the currency, and revenue laws which defeat their own purpose.

 I said above that the attributes of American life which we should find it necessary for our purpose to signalize are simply the attributes of modern life in their most exaggerated phase. Is there not a certain sense in which all modern handiwork is hastily and imperfectly done? To begin with common household arts, does not every one know that old things are more durable than new things? Our grandfathers wore better shoes than we wear, because there was leisure enough to cure the leather properly. In old times a chair was made of seasoned wood, and its joints carefully fitted; its maker had leisure to see that it was well put together. Now a thousand are turned off at once by machinery, out of green wood, and, with their backs glued on, are hurried off to their evil fate,—destined to drop in pieces if they happen to stand near the fireplace, and liable to collapse under the weight of a heavy man. Some of us still preserve, as heirlooms, old tables and bedsteads of Cromwellian times: in the twenty-first century what will have become of our machine-made bedsteads and tables?

 Perhaps it may seem odd to talk about tanning and joinery in connection with culture, but indeed there is a subtle bond of union holding together all these things. Any phase of life can be understood only by associating with it some different phase. Sokrates himself has taught us how the homely things illustrate the grand things. If we turn to the art of musical composition and inquire into some of the differences between our recent music and that of

Handel's time, we shall alight upon the very criticism which Mr. Mill somewhere makes in comparing ancient with modern literature: the substance has improved, but the form has in some respects deteriorated. The modern music expresses the results of a richer and more varied emotional experience, and in wealth of harmonic resources, to say nothing of increased skill in orchestration, it is notably superior to the old music. Along with this advance, however, there is a perceptible falling off in symmetry and completeness of design, and in what I would call spontaneousness of composition. I believe that this is because modern composers, as a rule, do not drudge patiently enough upon counterpoint. They do not get that absolute mastery over technical difficulties of figuration which was the great secret of the incredible facility and spontaneity of composition displayed by Handel and Bach. Among recent musicians Mendelssohn is the most thoroughly disciplined in the elements of counterpoint; and it is this perfect mastery of the technique of his art which has enabled him to outrank Schubert and Schumann, neither of whom would one venture to pronounce inferior to him in native wealth of musical ideas. May we not partly attribute to rudimentary deficiency in counterpoint the irregularity of structure which so often disfigures the works of the great Wagner and the lesser Liszt, and which the more ardent admirers of these composers are inclined to regard as a symptom of progress?

  I am told that a similar illustration might be drawn from the modern history of painting; that, however noble the conceptions of the great painters of the present century, there are none who have gained such a complete mastery over the technicalities of drawing and the handling of the brush as was required in the times of Raphael, Titian, and Rubens. But on this point I can only speak from hearsay, and am quite willing to end here my series of illustrations, fearing that I may already have been wrongly set down as a lavulator temporis acti. Not the idle praising of times gone by, but the getting a lesson from them which may be of use to us, has been my object. And I believe enough has been said to show that the great complexity of modern life, with its multiplicity of demands upon our energy, has got us into a state of chronic hurry, the results of which are everywhere to be seen in the shape of less thorough workmanship and less rounded culture.

  For one moment let me stop to note a further source of the relative imperfection of modern culture, which is best illustrated in the case of literature. I allude to the immense, unorganized mass of literature in all departments, representing the accumulated acquisitions of past ages, which must form the basis of our own achievement, but with which our present methods of education seem inadequate to deal properly. Speaking roughly, modern literature may be said to be getting into the state which Roman jurisprudence was in before it was reformed by Justinian. Philosophic criticism has not yet reached the point at which it may serve as a natural codifier. We must read laboriously and expend a disproportionate amount of time and pains in winnowing the chaff from the wheat. This tends to make us "digs" or literary drudges; but I doubt if the "dig" is a thoroughly developed man. Goethe, with all his boundless knowledge, his universal curiosity, and his admirable capacity for work, was not a "dig." But this matter can only be hinted at: it is too large to be well discussed at the fag end of an essay while other points are pressing for consideration.

A state of chronic hurry not only directly hinders the performance of thorough work, but it has an indirect tendency to blunt the enjoyment of life. Let us consider for a moment one of the psychological consequences entailed by the strain of a too complex and rapid activity. Every one must have observed that in going off for a vacation of two or three weeks, or in getting freed in any way from the ruts of every-day life, time slackens its gait somewhat, and the events which occur are apt a few years later to cover a disproportionately large area in our recollections. This is because the human organism is a natural timepiece in which the ticks are conscious sensations. The greater the number of sensations which occupy the foreground of consciousness during the day, the longer the day seems in the retrospect. But the various groups of sensations which accompany our daily work tend to become automatic from continual repetition, and to sink into the background of consciousness; and in a very complex and busied life the number of sensations or states of consciousness which can struggle up to the front and get attended to, is comparatively small It is thus that the days seem so short when we are busy about every-day matters, and that they get blurred together, and as it were individually annihilated in recollection. When we travel, a comparatively large number of fresh sensations occupy attention, there is a maximum of consciousness, and a distinct image is left to loom up in memory. For the same reason the weeks and years are much longer to the child than to the grown man. The life is simpler and less hurried, so that there is time to attend to a great many sensations. Now this fact lies at the bottom of that keen enjoyment of existence which is the prerogative of childhood and early youth. The day is not rushed through by the automatic discharge of certain psychical functions, but each sensation stays long enough to make itself recognized. Now when once we understand the psychology of this matter, it becomes evident that the same contrast that holds between the child and the man must hold also between the ancient and the modern. The number of elements entering into ancient life were so few relatively, that there must have been far more than there is now of that intense realization of life which we can observe in children and remember of our own childhood. Space permitting, it would be easy to show from Greek literature how intense was this realization of life. But my point will already have been sufficiently apprehended. Already we cannot fail to see how difficult it is to get more than a minimum of conscious fruition out of a too complex and rapid activity.

One other point is worth noticing before we close. How is this turmoil of modern existence impressing itself upon the physical constitutions of modern men and women? When an individual man engages in furious productive activity, his friends warn him that he will break down. Does the collective man of our time need some such friendly warning? Let us first get a hint from what foreigners think of us ultra-modernized Americans. Wandering journalists, of an ethnological turn of mind, who visit these shores, profess to be struck with the slenderness, the apparent lack of toughness, the dyspeptic look, of the American physique. And from such observations it has been seriously argued that the stalwart English race is suffering inevitable degeneracy in this foreign climate. I have even seen it doubted whether a race of men can ever become thoroughly naturalized in a locality to which it is not indigenous. To such vagaries it is a sufficient answer that the English are no more indigenous to England than to America. They are indigenous to Central Asia, and as they have survived the first transplantation, they may be safely counted on to survive the second. A more careful survey will teach us that the slow alteration of physique which is going on in this country is only an exaggeration of that which modern civilization is tending to bring about everywhere. It is caused by the premature and excessive strain upon the mental powers requisite to meet the emergencies of our complex life. The progress of events has thrown the work of sustaining life so largely upon the brain that we are beginning to sacrifice the physical to the intellectual. We are growing spirituelle in appearance at the expense of robustness. Compare any typical Greek face, with its firm muscles, its symmetry of feature, and its serenity of expression, to a typical modern portrait, with its more delicate contour, its exaggerated forehead, its thoughtful, perhaps jaded look. Or consider in what respects the grand faces of the Plantagenet monarchs differ from the refined countenances of the leading English statesmen of to-day. Or again, consider the familiar pictures of the Oxford and Harvard crews which rowed a race on the Thames in 1869, and observe how much less youthful are the faces of the Americans. By contrast they almost look careworn. The summing up of countless such facts is that modern civilization is making us nervous. Our most formidable diseases are of nervous origin. We seem to have got rid of the mediaeval plague and many of its typhoid congeners; but instead we have an increased amount of insanity, methomania, consumption, dyspepsia, and paralysis. In this fact it is plainly written that we are suffering physically from the over-work and over-excitement entailed by excessive hurry.

  In view of these various but nearly related points of difference between ancient and modern life as studied in their extreme manifestations, it cannot be denied that while we have gained much, we have also lost a good deal that is valuable, in our progress. We cannot but suspect that we are not in all points more highly favoured than the ancients. And it becomes probable that Athens, at all events, which I have chosen as my example, may have exhibited an adumbration of a state of things which, for the world at large, is still in the future,—still to be remotely hoped for. The rich complexity of modern social achievement is attained at the cost of individual many-sidedness. As Tennyson puts it, "The individual withers and the world is more and more." Yet the individual does not exist for the sake of society, as the positivists would have us believe, but society exists for the sake of the individual. And the test of complete social life is the opportunity which it affords for complete individual life. Tried by this test, our contemporary civilization will appear seriously defective,—excellent only as a preparation for something better.

This is the true light in which to regard it. This incessant turmoil, this rage for accumulation of wealth, this crowding, jostling, and trampling upon one another, cannot be regarded as permanent, or as anything more than the accompaniment of a transitional stage of civilization. There must be a limit to the extent to which the standard of comfortable living can be raised. The industrial organization of society, which is now but beginning, must culminate in a state of things in which the means of expense will exceed the demand for expense, in which the human race will have some surplus capital. The incessant manual labour which the ancients relegated to slaves will in course of time be more and more largely performed by inanimate machinery. Unskilled labour will for the most part disappear. Skilled labour will consist in the guiding of implements contrived with versatile cunning for the relief of human nerve and muscle. Ultimately there will be no unsettled land to fill, no frontier life, no savage races to be assimilated or extirpated, no extensive migration. Thus life will again become comparatively stationary. The chances for making great fortunes quickly will be diminished, while the facilities for acquiring a competence by steady labour will be increased. When every one is able to reach the normal standard of comfortable living, we must suppose that the exaggerated appetite for wealth and display will gradually disappear. We shall be more easily satisfied, and thus enjoy more leisure. It may be that there will ultimately exist, over the civilized world, conditions as favourable to the complete fruition of life as those which formerly existed within the narrow circuit of Attika; save that the part once played by enslaved human brain and muscle will finally be played by the enslaved forces of insentient nature. Society will at last bear the test of providing for the complete development of its individual members.

So, at least, we may hope; such is the probability which the progress of events, when carefully questioned, sketches out for us. "Need we fear," asks Mr. Greg, "that the world would stagnate under such a change? Need we guard ourselves against the misconstruction of being held to recommend a life of complacent and inglorious inaction? We think not. We would only substitute a nobler for a meaner strife,—a rational for an excessive toil,—an enjoyment that springs from serenity, for one that springs from excitement only. . . . . To each time its own preacher, to each excess its own counteraction. In an age of dissipation, languor, and stagnation, we should join with Mr. Carlyle in preaching the 'Evangel of Work,' and say with him, 'Blessed is the man who has found his work,—let him ask no other blessedness.' In an age of strenuous, frenzied, ... and often utterly irrational and objectless exertion, we join Mr. Mill in preaching the milder and more needed 'Evangel of Leisure.' "

Bearing all these things in mind, we may understand the remark of the supremely cultivated Goethe, when asked who were his masters: Die Griechen, die Griechen, und immer die Griechen. We may appreciate the significance of Mr. Mill's argument in favour of the study of antiquity, that it preserves the tradition of an era of individual completeness. There is a disposition growing among us to remodel our methods of education in conformity with the temporary requirements of the age in which we live. In this endeavour there is much that is wise and practical; but in so far as it tends to the neglect of antiquity, I cannot think it well-timed. Our education should not only enhance the value of what we possess; is should also supply the consciousness of what we lack. And while, for generations to come, we pass toilfully through an era of exorbitant industrialism, some fragment of our time will not be misspent in keeping alive the tradition of a state of things which was once briefly enjoyed by a little community, but which, in the distant future, will, as it is hoped, become the permanent possession of all mankind.

January, 1873.

www.ingramcontent.com/pod-product-compliance
Lightning Source LLC
Chambersburg PA
CBHW072131160426
43197CB00012B/2067